Z3
TW

2/51

Understanding
the Scottish Economy

Edited by
Keith P. D. Ingham and James Love

MARTIN ROBERTSON · OXFORD

First published in 1983
by Martin Robertson & Company Ltd.,
108 Cowley Road, Oxford OX4 1JF.

British Library Cataloguing in Publication Data

Understanding the Scottish economy
1. Scotland—Economic conditions—1973
I. Ingham, Keith P.D.   II. Love, James
330.9411'0857   HC257.S4

ISBN 0-85520-676-4
ISBN 0-85520-677-2 Pbk

Typeset by Santype International Ltd., Salisbury
Printed and bound in Great Britain by
Billing and Sons Ltd, Worcester

Contents

Foreword

Scotland is presently entering a period of comparatively rapid economic and social change, and the industrial developments that we are likely to encounter during the next decade will produce a radically different Scotland from that we know today. New industries and technologies, such as electronics, biotechnology, robotics, and advanced engineering are taking root in Scotland and bringing with them the demands of new skills and occupations. Other traditional and well established industries, such as high quality textiles, Scotch whisky, insurance and banking, are also turning their attention to the future, and are poised to expand their products and services into international markets.

The past two decades have been difficult for Scotland and, since the onset of the slower international growth rates following the 1973–74 oil price increases, the industrial restructuring that we have all experienced and endured has been painful, leaving many proud Scots with no obvious outlet for their skills and dedication. One important lesson of the recession has been that Scotland, with an open, export-based economy, can only prosper if it sets its sights firmly on identifying and seizing those industrial and commercial opportunities of the future, where Scotland's traditions, skills and resources give it a clear and enduring comparative advantage over its competitors. This lesson has been heeded, and there is now a wider understanding that economic growth and development depends on accepting and even seeking change, rather than devoting effort and scarce resources to avoiding and ignoring it.

Since the advent of North Sea oil and gas in the early 1970s, the Scottish economy has been subject to considerable study and, as a result, Scotland is now one of the better understood of the European regional economies. However, most of the published studies so far have concentrated on relatively specialized issues and topics. They have been directed at other economists and have not really helped most Scots improve their understanding of the Scottish economy.

This book starts off with two distinct advantages over earlier collections of academic essays on the Scottish economy. First, the contributors have covered a far wider range of subjects than would normally be expected, and thus apart from the analysis of Scotland's employment, output and industrial performance, attention is also given to Adam Smith (the Scot whose 'Wealth of Nations' effectively established economics as a separate discipline); Scotland's links with the Third World; the co-operative movement; and the Scotch whisky industry. Second, the authors have made a conscious attempt to relate economic theory to the real world, and have identified the difficult policy issues which confront us all.

I therefore warmly welcome this book, and feel sure that it will provide a valuable insight on a wide range of economic and industrial issues which continually affect the daily lives of all of us living and working in Scotland.

ROBIN DUTHIE
Chairman
Scottish Development Agency

Note on Contributors

All the contributors are members of the Economics Department of the University of Strathclyde, which includes the Fraser of Allander Institute for Research on the Scottish Economy (FAI), except Neil Fraser who wrote his contribution while a member of staff but who has now entered broadcasting.

Introduction

Teaching of introductory courses in Economics in Scotland has been handicapped by the absence of suitable material concerned with the specifically Scottish dimensions of problems and policies. Statistical data for Scotland are often not widely available and are often presented in a form which is not suitable for teaching purposes. In addition, Economics as a discipline is frequently regarded by students as being abstract in nature and divorced from the 'real world'.

In response to these difficulties the objectives of this book are to make that information which is available on the Scottish economy more widely accessible and to illustrate, using this information, the real-world relevance of the concepts and theoretical constructs taught in introductory courses in schools, colleges and universities. As well as its direct educational value, this book has a more general function of providing a much-needed basis for reasoned and informed discussion of policy issues.

The structure of the book is largely self-explanatory. The first section provides an overview of the structure of the economy, the nature of Scotland's production and the dependence on, and nature of, Scotland's trade. Much of economic activity in Scotland is organized through the market system. Thus, after discussion of Adam Smith's contribution to analysis of markets, the second section is concerned with specific, important markets, with, where appropriate, discussion of different forms of market intervention. Markets, however, do not necessarily produce outcomes, in terms of the provision of goods and services and of income distribution which are socially desirable. Public provision and income distribution are considered in the third section. The government sector, through the impact of policies and public ownership, and external relations, with trading partners and multinational companies, are prominent features of the Scottish economy. These are examined in the fifth and sixth sections respectively. The final section deals with problems arising from the interpretation and use of data relating to Scotland.

This structure is designed to permit coverage of the major aspects of the Scottish economy. Each contribution balances statistical information and theoretical content in an attempt to demonstrate how theory helps us understand the Scottish economy in the 1980s.

The twenty-five contributions in this book have all been written by members and one former member of the Economics Department at the University of Strathclyde which encompasses the Fraser of Allander Institute for Research on the Scottish Economy. We are, of course, grateful to all the authors. In addition to their written contributions, we are indebted to Professors Andrew D. Bain and Anthony Clunies Ross for their support and advice. Jim Walker provided valuable guidance on interpretation of trade data. We have consulted individuals involved in teaching and administration at different levels in the education sector and are particularly grateful for the constructive comments and encouragement received from Gordon MacKenzie at Shawlands Academy, Glasgow, Barry Finlayson and George Frame at Jordanhill College of Education and David Allan at Scotbec. The publishers obtained similarly helpful comments from anonymous readers at three other Scottish universities. Several of the contributions were presented in draft form at an in-service training course arranged in conjunction with Dorothy Stewart, Regional Adviser, at the Dundas Vale Centre, Glasgow in late 1982 and we would like to thank all who participated in that course. One of our biggest debts is to Morag Pryce for her patience and tact in coping with the typing of the manuscript.

KPDI JL

PART I

The Dimensions and Character of the Scottish Economy

I

Structure

IAIN McNICOLL

Each year households and firms in Scotland make many millions of economic decisions. Households decide on the allocation of their expenditures among different goods and services, on the shares of their incomes to be saved and on the proportion of expenditures to be financed by borrowing. Firms take decisions on what final and intermediate products to produce, the quantities to be produced, the amounts of capital and labour to be employed, the shares of their output to be exported and the methods of financing their investment and production activities. The *microeconomic* decisions made by households and firms in Scotland determine the *macroeconomic* dimensions of the Scottish economy which is itself part of the total economic activity in the UK monetary and economic union.

MARKET AND GOVERNMENT

Broadly, the market mechanism ensures the supply of the wide range of products demanded in an advanced industrial society. However, the aggregate outcome of individual decisions in UK markets does not necessarily ensure: (a) the adequate provision of certain items such as health, defence and education services (see Chapters 10, 11, 13); (b) a desirable distribution of income (see Chapter 14), and (c) satisfactory performance of *macroeconomic* variables such as the growth of income and employment, the stability of the price level and the balance of international payments.

These problems lead governments to intervene. Within the UK, monetary and fiscal policies are designed for the needs of the whole union and do not have a separate Scottish dimension, although in their regional policies successive governments have recognized problems affecting Scotland particularly strongly (see Chapter 16).

Centralized decision-making for the union does not require separate 'national' income accounts for the Scottish region and the very nature of the union, with, for example, no restrictions on factor and product markets, makes the preparation of separate accounts extremely difficult. To develop an understanding of the Scottish economy requires, ideally, a record of all transactions involving Scottish residents. If information were available on the transactions between firms and final consumers the Scottish economy might then be analysed in terms of the conventional macroeconomic *circular flow of income* approach (see Fig. 1.1).

Using this approach, Scottish *Gross Regional Product* (GRP), which measures the addition to Scottish wealth produced during a particular year, may be estimated as the sum of:

(1) *Expenditures* on Scottish goods and services by households, firms and the government (Fig. 1.1, Block A).
(2) *Factor incomes* generated in production in Scotland (Fig. 1.1, Block B).

The circular flow approach does not cover, however, certain aspects which would add considerably to our understanding of the Scottish economy. Measuring the *value* of expenditures and incomes tells us nothing about the industrial composition of the goods and services produced. In addition, the circular flow

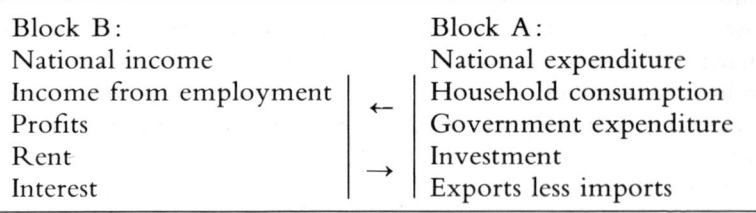

Block B:		Block A:
National income		National expenditure
Income from employment	←	Household consumption
Profits		Government expenditure
Rent	→	Investment
Interest		Exports less imports

Fig. 1.1   The circular flow system

approach concentrates on the purchases by households, firms and the government for *final* consumption but ignores purchases among firms of components and *semi-finished* goods, known as *intermediate* products, as inputs to their own activities.

These problems may be overcome by examining the economy using *input – output analysis* which directly examines how expenditures are transformed into incomes through the industrial sector (see Box 1.1). This is done by adding analysis of industry transactions to the elements of the circular flow approach (see Fig. 1.2).

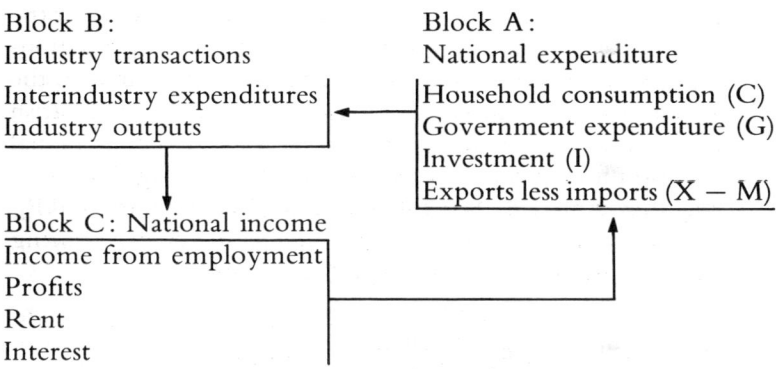

Block B:
Industry transactions

Interindustry expenditures
Industry outputs

Block A:
National expenditure

Household consumption (C)
Government expenditure (G)
Investment (I)
Exports less imports (X − M)

Block C: National income
Income from employment
Profits
Rent
Interest

Fig. 1.2   The input–output system

BOX 1.1   *The Scottish input–output table*

An input–output table records the value of *inputs* of various goods and services which are used to produce the *output* of each industry. More generally, the input–output table shows what different industries buy from, and sell to, each other. The table also records the value of inputs from non-industrial sectors, primarily land, labour and capital, and the value of sales to non-industrial users and government. In the Scottish economy where external trade is important export sales and import purchases are recorded.

The Scottish table was constructed for 1973 and has seventy-eight separate industrial sectors. It also has 5 non-industrial sellers and seven non-industrial buyers.

Scottish input–output table 1973 (£ million)

	Primary	Manufac-turing	Services	Final demand	Total output
Primary	79.9	301.9	82.7	260.0	724.5
Manufacturing	103.1	646.7	304.6	4163.9	5218.3
Services	122.1	495.1	765.4	3294.2	4676.9
Imports	82.4	1701.8	524.7	1887.1	4196.0
Value added	337.0	2072.8	2999.5	968.1	6377.3
Total input	724.5	5218.3	4676.9	10573.3	21193.0

The table here shows a small summary of this larger matrix. Looking along each *row* of the table tells us what the industry on the left *sold* to the industry on the top. For example, the primary sector sold £301.9 million to manufacturing, i.e. whisky, vehicles and other manufactures. Looking down each *column* tells us what the industry at the top *purchased* from the industry on the left. For example, service industries bought £82.7 million from the primary sector. The full-size table contains many more entries but is interpreted in exactly the same way.

As with all statistics, the input–output table must be interpreted carefully. Collecting information on every transaction carried out by every individual is clearly impossible and the collection of data for the Scottish input–output table involved some aggregation over individuals, e.g. firms producing a similar product were grouped into a single industry. Moreover, certain of the data were estimated using sampling techniques or were derived from other sources. Finally, not all of the definitions used in constructing the table would be agreed on by all analysts.

The construction of an input–output table requires many man-hours of effort and the collection of a great deal of information. For these reasons this type of exercise is undertaken very infrequently. An input–output table has been constructed for Scotland for 1973 at the Fraser of Allander Institute of the University of Strathclyde. By providing information on the sales and purchases made by different industrial sectors this table permits: (a) examination of the structure of Scottish industry; (b) examination of the interdependencies among Scottish industries; as well as (c) measurement of Scotland's GRP for 1973 from either the incomes side (Fig. 1.2, Block C) or the expenditure side (Fig. 1.2, Block A), as in the circular-flow approach.

The Structure of Scottish Industry

The real value of an input–output table lies in allowing examination of the industrial structure of the economy. It permits measurement of the *size* of individual industries in a number of ways based on, for example, industry outputs and incomes paid by industries. An interesting measure is the proportion of the value of final demand met by each industry (see Table 1.1).

Table 1.1 involves a more disaggregated industry classification than is employed in the version of the input–output table given in Box 1.1. The service industries are included in both, however, and may be used to illustrate how we estimate an industry's share in final markets. We first estimate final demand as the sum of exports plus other final demand for each of the five sectors identified in Table 1.1. Summing these five estimates we obtain a figure of £7718 million. The estimate for an individual sector is then expressed as a share of this figure. The value of services, i.e. Transport and communications, Distribution, Finance and Other services, amounts to £3294.3 million, which is 42.6 per cent of £7718 million.

Similarly, manufacturing can be shown to contribute 34 per cent while the primary sector (agriculture, forestry and fishing) contributed only 5 per cent.

Comparing Scotland with the UK as a whole, it seems that the primary and manufacturing sectors are relatively more important in Scotland (see Table 1.2). On the other hand, services are more important in the UK. Generally, however, the structures of the Scottish and UK economies are very similar, although within particular sectors some significant differences still exist; in manufacturing, for example, food processing is much more important in Scotland than in the UK, while the reverse is true for vehicle manufacture.

Industry Interdependence

Certain Scottish industries are closely linked with one another through the exchange of goods and services. Sometimes the link

TABLE 1.1 Scottish input–output tables, 1973

(current prices, £ million)

Purchases from	Sales to					Final demand		Total output
	Primary	Whisky	Vehicles	Other Manufacture	Services	Exports	Other Final demand	
Primary	79.9	9.0	0.2	292.7	82.7	125.5	134.5	724.5
Whisky	0.0	8.6	0.0	13.1	0.1	274.7	49.4	345.8
Vehicles	0.3	0.1	0.0	4.4	8.0	218.0	18.8	249.6
Other								
Manufacture	102.8	22.8	22.5	575.2	295.5	2882.0	721.1	4622.9
Services	122.1	81.4	10.4	403.3	765.4	250.5	3043.8	4676.9
Imports	82.4	61.1	132.8	1507.9	524.7	0.0	1887.1	4196.0
Value added	337.0	162.8	83.7	1826.3	2999.5	0.0	968.0	6377.3
Total input	724.5	345.8	249.6	4622.9	4676.9	3750.7	6948.2	21193.0

Notes: (1) Exports include exports to the rest of the UK. (2) Other final demand comprises households, tourists, government and investment. (3) Value added comprises wages, profit, interest and rent.

TABLE 1.2   *Industry contributions to GRP, 1973*

| | Percentage of total | |
Industry	Scotland	UK
Agriculture, forestry and fishing	5.0	3.1
Mining and quarrying	1.4	1.4
Manufacturing	34.1	31.1
Construction	8.7	7.0
Gas, electricity and water	3.0	2.8
Transport and communications	6.6	8.1
Distribution	10.2	10.6
Finance	6.0	8.6
Other services	19.6	21.3
Public administration and defence	5.4	5.9

Source : Scottish input–output tables and *National Income Blue Book*

is obvious, as with steel and motor vehicles. Sometimes, however, it is less obvious: for example, employees of an electronics firm may spend part of their incomes in local shops, creating an indirect link between the shops and the firm. If industries are interrelated, then a change in circumstances in one industry will have effects on the others. For example, if the demand for cars falls, the motor vehicle industry will buy less steel. The steel industry in turn will buy less iron ore. The iron-ore industry may have to pay off workers and this would have adverse effects on local shops and restaurants and so on. It can be seen that the initial effect on the steel industry is *multiplied* as it causes chain-reaction effects throughout the economy (see Box 1.2). Appropriately, the total of these chain-reaction effects are measured by a '*multiplier*' (see Chapter 15).

The input–output table allows us to measure all these linkages, obvious and less obvious, among Scottish industries. Multiplier values for a number of Scottish industries are given in Table 1.3. Each multiplier is interpreted as follows: for a one unit change in demand for the products of the industry cited, the multiplier value gives the total change in demand for all Scottish products. We can now be much more precise about the overall effects of a decline in the demand for motor vehicles. Given a multiplier

BOX 1.2   *Ravenscraig*

The threatened closure in late 1982 by the British Steel Corporation of the Ravenscraig steel works, a major employer in Scotland, highlighted the importance of linkage and multiplier effects.

Steel is produced at Ravenscraig from iron ore, which is imported through the terminal at Hunterston, and from both local and imported coking coal. Specialized equipment and machinery for steel production are supplied by Fullwood Foundry near Motherwell, R. D. Tennent at Coatbridge and Craigneuk. Part of the bulk steel output is processed at Ravenscraig and part at the Clydesbridge, Dalzell, Gartcosh and Glengarnock plants.

Closure of Ravenscraig would have meant almost certain closure of Hunterston, would probably have led quickly to closures at Dalzell, Fullwood, Gartcosh and Glengarnock and would have placed others such as Clydebridge under even greater difficulties than they already face. The likely number of jobs which would have been lost in these plants would have amounted to over 7000.

Likely job losses

Ravenscraig	4400	NCB	1750
Gartcosh	600	BR	200
Hunterston	100	SSEB	200
Clydebridge	750	British Gas	200
Dalzel	800	CPA	50
Fullwood	130	Other	1000
Glengarnock	240		
Others	100		
Total	7120		3400

In addition to companies within the steel industry, many other suppliers of goods and services would have been seriously affected by closure at Ravenscraig. The entire production of Polkemmet mine at Whitburn goes to Ravenscraig. Loss of sales to Ravenscraig might have led to Polkemmet's high-quality coal displacing that of already struggling pits, such as Cardowan in

Glasgow and Killoch in Ayrshire, in other markets. British Gas would also have found themselves losing an important customer. Ravenscraig accounts for about one-third of all BR's freight revenue in Scotland, for about 3 per cent of total SSEB sales and for about 4 per cent of total Scottish gas sales. Other suppliers who would have been affected include the Clyde Port Authority, Shell/BP, road-hauliers, British Oxygen and companies providing servi s such as catering, cleaning, crane hire and security. Job losses for these suppliers in Scotland would probably have amounted to 3400.

The reduction in income associated with job losses of 10 500 will also have produced multiplier effects. Assuming a multiplier value of 1.25 over 2600 further jobs would have been lost.

In total, therefore, something like 13 000 jobs would have disappeared if Ravenscraig had been closed.

---

value for vehicles of 1.83 (see Table 1.3), a reduction in demand for vehicles of £1000 will lead to a decrease in the total demand for Scottish products of £1830 (= 1000 × 1.83). Of this £1830, £1000 is the immediate fall in vehicle demand and £830 is the additional fall in demand caused by the chain-reaction effect.

TABLE 1.3 *Selected Scottish industry output multipliers*

Industry	Multiplier value
Agriculture	2.59
Whisky	2.17
Oil and chemicals	1.54
Vehicles	1.83
Construction	2.72
Education	3.09

The values of the multiplier differ considerably among industries. In general, an industry which is highly integrated with the rest of the economy will have a higher multiplier than one which has few linkages and in many cases the secondary effects are more substantial than the initial effect. Whisky blending with a multiplier of 2.17 has greater links with other Scottish industries than oil and chemical production with a multiplier of 1.54. Significantly, oil and chemicals which have grown rapidly in recent years have the lowest multiplier value of those recorded.

By looking closely at the linkages for all industries, it is possible to identify certain industries which both buy and sell more than average within Scotland. Such industries can be regarded as 'key' sectors, in that they create significant chain-reaction effects in other industries *and* they themselves are very sensitive to chain-reaction effects. The input–output table identifies certain industries as being 'key sectors' in Scotland in 1973 (see Table 1.4).

TABLE 1.4   *Key sectors in Scotland, 1973*

Agriculture
Meat and fish products
Grain and other food
Iron, steel and aluminium
Timber products
Construction
Electricity
Miscellaneous business services

This is useful from a regional policy point of view, for it identifies industries which, if developed, would have relatively high multiplier effects throughout the Scottish economy. Significantly, some of the largest Scottish industries in terms of output or employment, such as whisky blending or shipbuilding, do not appear on the list. On the other hand, industries which are currently quite small in Scotland, such as timber products or miscellaneous business services do appear to be potentially 'key' sectors.

Scottish Income

Scotland's GRP may be estimated by classifying expenditures on final demand as in Fig. 1.2, Block A, or by identifying incomes as in Fig. 1.2, Block C. Estimating income from the expenditure side, for example, involves summing *C, G, I* and

$(X - M)$. In 1973 these categories of expenditures at market prices were valued at £6677 million (see Table 1.4). Market prices differ from prices at factor cost by the amount of *net taxes*, i.e. taxes — subsidies. Adjusting for net taxes in 1973 of £1043 million, we arrive at an estimate of GRP at factor cost of £5634 million.

Income may also be estimated by summing the *value-added* in economic activities. At market prices the value-added in satisfying final demand for goods and services in Scotland was £6377 million (see Table 1.1). Adjusting to factor cost, we obtain an estimate of £5334 million. However, some goods produced were not sold in the market but were instead added to stocks. The value added in producing these stocks was £300 million. Thus, total value-added was £5634 million.

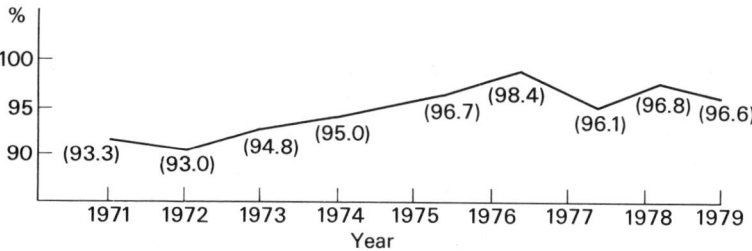

Fig. 1.3   Scottish GRP per head as percentage of UK GNP

At £5.6 billion Scotland's GRP represented 8.8 per cent of total UK Gross Domestic Product in 1973. Scotland's GRP per head was £1083. This compares with a UK figure of £1166, i.e. Scotland's GRP per head was only 92.9 per cent of the UK average (see Fig. 1.3). This result indicates Scotland's position as a relatively poor region of the UK. Later evidence suggests that Scotland's relative performance improved after 1973, with GRP per head rising to 98.4 per cent of the UK figure in 1976.

This improvement was, of course, largely due to the emergence of the North Sea Oil industry, which is concentrated in Scotland. In the late seventies, however, Scotland's position worsened again with GRP per head falling to 96.6 per cent of UK average by 1979.

The largest component of GRP on the income side is income from employment, while on the expenditure side household

TABLE 1.5   *Scotland's GRP, 1973 (£ million)*

Income		Expenditure	
Income from employment	3646	Consumer expenditure	3856
Other factor income			
(profit, rent, interest)	2288	Government	1179
Less stock appreciation	300	Investment	1895
		exports — imports	−253
		Gross domestic expenditure	
		at market prices	6677
		Adjustment to factor	
		cost	−1043
GRP at factor cost	5634		5634

expenditure is predominant (see Table 1.5). This shows the importance of household activities in the Scottish economy. It will also be noted that household spending was greater than employment income, because, of course, other factor incomes were paid to households as dividends, interest, rent or net government transfers. In fact, Inland Revenue Statistics suggest that household income in Scotland was approximately £4 billion in 1973.

In 1973 Scotland had a deficit on trade in goods and services of £253 million. Total exports were £3944 million and imports were £4197 million. Exports and imports represented 70 per cent and 74 per cent respectively of 1973 Scottish GRP, demonstrating conclusively the importance of external trade to the Scottish economy.

2

'Made in Scotland' (Production)

JOHN SCOULLER

The well-being of the Scottish nation in terms of income, wealth and employment depends crucially on the performance of our productive sectors. In attempting to understand the Scottish economy, we must, therefore, answer important questions about the goods and services we produce in Scotland. *How much* does Scotland produce? *What* is the nature of the industrial economy in Scotland? *Why* does Scotland produce a particular pattern of goods and services? *How well* does Scottish industry perform compared with other countries? *How Scottish* is Scottish production?

HOW MUCH?

In 1979 the Scottish economy produced goods and services worth £14 300 million (see Table 2.1). This is about 9 per cent of total UK output and output per person in Scotland is just slightly below that in the UK as a whole (97 per cent).

This output, which includes all measurable items of the national and regional product, is a very comprehensive measure. It includes such, perhaps unexpected, items as the imputed rents from house ownership even though such owners may not rent out their houses; distribution services such as the activities of shops; financial services provided by, for example, banks and building societies (see Chapter 5); public services like defence, law and order, education and health (see Chapters 11, 13, 14); and public administration.

A narrower measure is industrial production which includes only manufacturing, construction, gas, electricity, water and

TABLE 2.1   *What Scotland Produces: Scottish gross domestic product in 1979*

Source	Output (£ million)	Percentage of total
Agriculture, forestry, fishing	510	3.6
Mining and quarrying	312	2.2
Manufacturing	3950	27.6
Construction	1202	8.4
Gas, electricity and water	451	3.2
Transport and communications	1231	8.6
Distributive trades	1414	9.9
Insurance, banking and finance	976	6.8
Ownership of dwellings	601	4.2
Professional and scientific services ⎱ Miscellaneous services ⎰	3125	21.9
Public administration and defence	1052	7.4
Adjustment for financial services	−525	(3.7)
Total	14 300	100.0

mining and quarrying. These sectors created just over 40 per cent of Scottish output in 1979 and are clearly vitally important to the economy. However, they may be becoming less crucial. In common with other developed industrial countries, Scotland may be said to have entered a *post-industrial* condition, which some suggest, is a newly emerging third phase in a cycle of economic development. Post-industrial states are those in which the service sector – distribution, financial services, public services and administration, transport and tourism (see Chapter 8) – account for most output and employment. In Scotland in 1979 these sectors produced 58.8 per cent of output (see Table 2.1).

Pre-industrial states, characteristic of developing countries, produce mainly agricultural output, with small manufacturing and service sectors. *Industrial* states are dominated by industrial production, in particular the manufacturing and utility sectors. It is clear that Scotland has entered the third phase – though it can be suggested that in some respects this country suffers problems associated with all three phases (see Chapter 16) – and this may not be entirely welcome because the transition has been marked

by a serious absolute decline in the manufacturing sector as well
as by a growth in the tertiary sector.

Manufacturing

The Scottish manufacturing sector accounts for 28 per cent of
total output and 67 per cent of industrial production. Arguably,
manufacturing activities are the most important for the overall
vitality of the modern economy: they comprise the so-called
'engine of growth'. This is not simply because of size (as we have
seen, the service sector is larger) but because success as a trading
nation in the competitive world economy depends largely on
success in manufacturing. The Japanese, with a dynamic manufacturing sector, have the most successful economy in the world.
Other sectors of their economy, such as agriculture and retailing,
are far less efficient and dynamic. It may be, therefore, that Scotland's, and Britain's, economic problems, particularly unemployment, derive largely from relative stagnation in the
manufacturing sector.

In terms of output the major Scottish industries are food, drink
and tobacco (23 per cent of total output), mechanical engineering
(13 per cent), chemicals (10 per cent), and shipbuilding (9 per
cent), whilst in terms of employment the major industries are
food, drink and tobacco (16.5 per cent), mechanical engineering
(14 per cent), shipbuilding (11 per cent), textiles (9.5 per cent) and
electrical engineering (8 per cent).

Compared with the UK as a whole, Scotland is more dependent for employment on food, drink and tobacco, textiles, instrument engineering, and mechanical engineering, and it is less
dependent on chemicals, electrical engineering, and metal goods
(see Table 2.2).

The Nature of Scottish Industry

Scotland is, like most other Western countries, a mixed economy;
that is one in which there are elements of capitalist private enterprise and socialist public enterprise (see Chapter 18). The industrial sector in Scotland, again as in other Western economies, is
dominated by a few very large corporations, both public and
private, and in the latter case many will be wholly-owned subsidiaries of giant foreign corporations such as IBM.

TABLE 2.2   *Employment in Scottish manufacturing as a proportion of UK manufacturing employment, 1977*

	Percentage
Food, drink and tobacco	13.3
Instrument engineering	11.8
Textiles	11.7
Mechanical engineering	9.3
Timber, Furniture, etc.	8.5
Average*	8.5
Clothing and footwear	8.3
Paper, printing and publishing	8.2
Metal manufacture	8.1
Chemicals and allied industries	7.5
Shipbuilding, marine engineering and vehicles	7.3
Coal and petroleum products	7.0
Electrical engineering	6.8
Bricks, pottery, glass, cement	6.6
Leather and fur goods	6.5
Other manufacturing	5.2
Metal goods	5.1

* Total Scottish employment in manufacturing as a proportion of total UK manufacturing employment.

The textbook picture of the competitive firm is based on nineteenth century conditions when firms were relatively small, single product and entrepreneurial, and operated in competitive markets at the national level. The modern corporation, in contrast, is very large in terms of sales and employment; produces a wide range of products often totally unrelated to one another, like bricks, beds, and books as in the case of Thomas Tilling Ltd; operates in a number of different countries, as many as eighty in the case of IBM; and operates in competitive markets at the international level.

Associated with the growth of large corporations has been the increasing separation between the *ownership* and *control* of firms. In larger corporations the owners do not manage the enterprise and the people who run the enterprise, the managers, do not own it. This is in contrast with the traditional enterprise, the entrepreneurial firm, where ownership and management were connected (see Box. 2.1).

BOX 2.1   *Ownership, control and the theory of the firm*

The theory of the firm is a central part of traditional micro-economic theory. This theory is based on the convenient, but reasonably realistic, assumption that firms are run by their owners who are interested in making as much money as possible (i.e. maximizing their profits). With this assumption traditional economic theory is able to offer a powerful analysis of the competitive market economy.

This theory has been challenged on the grounds that it no longer represents the reality of modern industry. The 'managerialist' school argues that ownership and control have become separated in the modern giant corporation. The owners no longer control, and the controllers no longer own. The interests of the owners can no longer be assumed to be paramount in the running of the firm.

The separation occurs because, as firms grow, they sell shares to raise capital. Ownership thus becomes diffused among many shareholders who will increasingly find difficulty in organizing collectively to influence and guide their company. Major shareholders may, in fact, be disinclined to exercise control. Pension funds, insurance companies and other financial institutions, which are the largest holders of shares in British and Scottish industry, are concerned with the value and return on shares and thus with the performance of a company. Usually if a company performs badly, such an institutional owner will sell the shares and buy others which are doing better rather than involve itself in the management and control of the firm.

Managerial motives are thus likely to become more important and ownership motives less important. Several new theories of the firm have been suggested to take account of this change. Some have argued that managers will pursue a policy of *revenue maximization* which would lead firms to produce more, advertise more, and charge a lower price than in traditional theory. Others suggest that managers will pursue policies to achieve *faster growth* and so would earn lower profits and create lower stock market values than traditional profit-maximizing firms.

The separation of ownership from control has gone less far in Scotland than in the UK as a whole. Many large Scottish firms still have significant connections between owners and management, at least in the sense that the directors as a group own a sizeable proportion of the companies' shares – for example, the Weir Group Ltd, Collins Publishers Ltd. The foreign firms in Scotland are generally wholly-owned subsidiaries and so owned and controlled by the same organization, though, of course, the parent company is itself likely to exhibit the separation of management and ownership. Nevertheless, many of the best known companies in Scotland do conform to the national pattern of increasing separation between ownership and control.

Because of their size, modern corporations may be able to dominate the industries in which they operate. This may have serious implications since economic theory suggests that the intensity of competition is a major determinant of efficiency. The theory of perfect competition holds that firms can survive only if they produce at the lowest possible cost. If, however, there is a lack of competition in an industry, and particularly when an industry is monopolized, it is argued that:

(1) Firms will tend to produce less and charge higher prices giving rise to allocative inefficiency.
(2) Firms' inputs of labour, capital and other inputs may be badly managed, giving rise to organizational inefficiency.

Most Scottish industries are dominated by a few large producers. But this does not necessarily mean that there are high levels of inefficiency in these industries because Scotland is not an isolated market. To appreciate the level of competition in Scottish industry it is necessary to consider that:

(1) Scottish firms sell a large proportion of their output outside Scotland and thus compete with, for example, Japanese and American producers.
(2) Scottish firms selling in Scotland must compete with non-Scottish producers of the same or similar products.

There is one industry which is distinctly Scottish: Scotch whisky (see Chapter 25). This industry is very highly concentrated with one dominant producer, Distillers Co. Ltd, and a few smaller firms such as Arthur Bell & Sons Ltd, Wm Teachers &

Sons Ltd and Seagram Distillers Ltd, making up the industry. Even so, we are unable to draw easy conclusions about the intensity of competition. There is no totally separate market for whisky as such; there is a market for alcoholic spirits of which whisky is one.

WHY?

THE PATTERN OF PRODUCTION

The success of the Scotch whisky industry and its relative importance in Scottish industry is a reflection of its ability to compete in the national and international economy. Similarly, the overall pattern of what Scotland produces depends on the ability of products and firms to compete in the Scottish market with potential imports and in foreign markets with goods made in other countries.

In the context of international competition, Scotland will produce the goods and services which she can make relatively efficiently. This may derive from *comparative advantage* based on differences in factor endowments or production functions, or the *availability of resources,* or the exploitation of *technical knowledge or innovations,* all of which may enable Scottish firms to produce goods relatively cheaply. They may also cater for *special consumer preferences* (see Chapter 3).

Thus Scotland has the necessary labour skills to produce and export engineering products; deposits of oil and coal; and the technical knowledge, mainly in foreign firms, to produce sophisticated electronic equipment. It is also uniquely placed to supply the world taste for Scotch whisky.

However, trading advantages change. Those countries with whom Scotland trades will develop and international patterns of demand will alter. In the early twentieth century, Scotland was a profitable place to build ships and turbines. However, as the demand for passenger ships and naval craft declined whilst the demand for large oil tankers increased Scotland lost its comparative advantage in shipbuilding. Scottish shipyards were badly located, i.e. too far up river, to build large tankers and the Scottish workforce proved resistant to change in work practices and the acquisition of new skills and required what, in an international context, were relatively high wages. Scotland is now only a very minor shipbuilder in world terms, and without government subsidies would be even smaller.

Fortunately, Scotland has proved to have advantages in other areas of production, in food and drink, electronics and light engineering. However, Scotland's adjustment has not been sufficient to prevent major social disruptions in the form of high unemployment and low incomes, particularly in those areas dominated by the declining heavy industries.

HOW WELL? HOW EFFICIENT?

How well does Scotland's industry perform today compared with others? Productivity – average output per head – in Scottish manufacturing is just about the same as for the UK as a whole; it is 99 per cent of the UK level. Scotland does better in food, drink and tobacco and in chemicals, but less well in metal production and shipbuilding. However, by international standards the performance of both British and Scottish industry is poor. Britain has the lowest growth rate in manufacturing output and productivity of all the developed industrial economies (see Table 2.3).

Scottish industry, after growing relatively successfully in the 1960s, has stagnated in the 1970s. In the 1970s industrial output increased by only 6 per cent whilst in the 1960s it increased by 50

TABLE 2.3 *Growth in manufacturing output and productivity, 1955–77*

	Output per annum (percentage)	Productivity per annum (percentage)
Japan	10.0	7.9
Netherlands	5.3	5.6
France	5.5	5.4
Italy	6.3	5.3
West Germany	5.4	5.1
Belgium	4.8	4.8
USA	3.3	3.7
UK	2.2	2.9
Scotland	2.6	3.7

per cent. In the 1970s only the public utilities sector (gas, electricity and water) has grown rapidly whilst the manufacturing sector has hardly grown at all with the exception of two industries: food, drink, and tobacco, and chemicals. Production in several manufacturing industries declined considerably in the 1970s – particularly in metal manufacturing and engineering.

Scotland's industrial decline in the 1970s has mirrored the decline of British industry as a whole. The decline of the car, steel, shipbuilding, and textile industries are national, indeed European, phenomena from which Scotland has suffered to much the same extent as other parts of Britain and Europe. However, being a relatively small economy, with a well-defined national identity, major plant closures such as the Talbot car assembly plant at Linwood and the British Aluminium Company smelting plant at Invergordon, are more significant and feel more painful in Scotland.

There are two main reasons for the decline of Scottish industry in the 1970s.

(1) The world economy slowed down dramatically in the 1970s caused in part by the OPEC oil price increases. This led to increasingly intensive international competition in industries like steel and cars as all the industrial countries tried to maintain their share of slowly growing markets.

(2) The sterling exchange rate rose dramatically as North Sea Oil came into production. Scottish and British exports became more expensive and imports, particularly of consumer durables – cars, videos, refrigerators – became much cheaper (see Chapter 20).

Under these conditions many Scottish firms, particularly those in international industries, such as steel and engineering, some of whom were already finding continued existence difficult, were put out of business (see Table 2.4).

The fundamental reasons for closure of firms and so the decline of British industry are commonly held to be; (a) too low a level of investment in new plant and equipment, and in human skills, (b) inefficiency, particularly in the use of labour (overmanning) because of mismanagement and restrictive union practices, (c) a failure to adapt quickly enough to changing world circumstances.

TABLE 2.4 *Large-scale redundancies and closures in Scottish firms, 1980–81 (over 400 jobs lost)*

Date	Company	Location	Product	Closure/ Redundancy	Jobs Lost
February 1980	SCM Ltd	Queenslie	Typewriters	Redundancy	500
May 1980	Talbot Scotland Ltd	Linwood	Cars	Redundancy	1300
	Coats Paton Ltd	Glasgow	Textiles	Partial closure	463
June 1980	The Weir Group Ltd	Cathcart	Pumps	Redundancy	590
	Scottish Stamping & Eng. Co. Ltd	Ayr	Engineering products	Redundancy	400
	BSR Ltd	East Kilbride	Record players	Closure	1700
October 1980	ICI Ltd	Ayrshire	Chemicals	Closure	750
January 1981	Rolls-Royce (UK) Ltd	Hillington/ East Kilbride	Aero engines	Redundancy	400
February 1981	Talbot Scotland Ltd	Linwood	Cars	Closure	4800
March 1981	Hoover Ltd	Cambuslang	Electrical goods	Redundancy	400
May 1981	Glacier Metal Co. Ltd	Kilmarnock	Metal products	Redundancy	400
June 1981	Glacier Metal Co. Ltd	Kilmarnock	Metal products	Redundancy	400
September 1981	Rolls-Royce (UK) Ltd	Hillington	Aero engines	Redundancy	500
	Dunlop Tyres Ltd	Renfrew	Tyres	Closure	500
October 1981	Caterpillar Tractor Co. Ltd	Uddingston	Tractors	Redundancy	800

In 1980 and 1981 115 instances of major redundancies were reported with a totel of 30 069 jobs lost (*Glasgow Herald*, 16 February 1982)

The Scottish dimension to these problems is that our firms may experience these weaknesses more severely and that there are extra difficulties which are specific to Scotland:

(1) Some plants may be too small to achieve lower costs through scale economies.

(2) Some may bear high transport costs compared with other European producers because Scotland is relatively remote from the major European markets.

(3) Many plants are branches belonging to and controlled by companies outside Scotland – in England and US particularly (see Chapter 19). Remote control may reduce the effectiveness of management, though this is not usually held to be true of US-owned firms. Branch plants may be marginal to activities of the group of companies. In times of recession one whole plant such as this may be closed completely rather than inefficiently reducing production in all company subsidiaries. Scotland, with a high proportion of branch plants, is more vulnerable.

The Public Sector

On the other hand, Scotland is a *mixed economy* with a major part of output produced by enterprises in the public or *nationalized* sector, which tend to be less exposed to possible closure during recession. Almost all of mining and quarrying is in the public sector (the National Coal Board) as is all of gas, electricity and water (the South of Scotland Electricity Board and the North of Scotland Hydro-Electric Board, the British Gas Corporation and local authority Water Boards). Major parts of manufacturing are publicly-owned; the British Steel Corporation at Ravenscraig and Craigneuk, British Shipbuilders on Upper and Lower Clyde and Aberdeen, Rolls-Royce in Glasgow and British Leyland in Bathgate (see Chapter 18). However, the fact that these firms are publicly owned does not imply that their output is not produced under competitive market conditions. This is particularly true of the manufacturing firms, which although, by definition, monopolies in Scotland (and in the UK), have to compete internationally.

The Ravenscraig steel mill at Motherwell is, along with the rest of the British steel industry, suffering badly in competition with steel produced more cheaply in many countries throughout

TABLE 2.5 Non-Scottish activities of large Scottish companies estimated percentage of UK employment in Scotland, 1979/80

Name	Location of main office	Product	UK employ-ment	Estimated percentage employed in Scotland
Walter Alexander Ltd	Glasgow	Coachbuilders	1752	50
William Baird Ltd	Glasgow	Textiles	10886	8
Arthur Bell & Sons Ltd	Perth	Whisky and spirits	1965	20
Black and Edington Ltd	Port Glasgow	Camping, canvas and leisurewear	3068	12
Coats Paton Ltd	Glasgow	Textiles	20337	22
Distillers Co Ltd	Edinburgh	Whisky and spirits	20240	35
J. W. Galloway Ltd	Glasgow	Sausages	665	23
Grampian Holdings	Glasgow	Conglomerate including light engineering and publishing	2886	12
Christian Salvesen Ltd	Edinburgh	Conglomerate including seafood processing	6086	15
Scottish & Newcastle Breweries Ltd	Edinburgh	Beer	27830	5
Scottish, English & European Textiles Ltd	Edinburgh	Clothes and furniture fabrics	583	26

Notes: These companies are those among the fifty largest Scottish firms with the lowest proportion of total employees in Scotland. The total UK employment is not only those employed in manufacturing. Some firms will have a greater concentration of manufacturing in Scotland than implied here because, for example, sales and marketing activities are concentrated in England and Wales. On the other hand, some of these companies, notably Coats Patons Ltd, employ very large numbers of people abroad.

the world. Ravenscraig is unprofitable as currently operated and if it was in the private sector would probably have to be closed. However, because it is publicly-owned, and the implications of closure have important political consequences it has so far been kept open. It has been estimated that 13 000 jobs would be lost: at Ravenscraig itself, in other Scottish steel plants, coal mining, the railways, electricity generation, engineering and service industries (see Chapter 1). The nationalized parts of Scottish production may, therefore, be less vulnerable.

HOW SCOTTISH IS SCOTTISH PRODUCTION?

Many firms and factories in Scotland are not, in terms of ownership and control, Scottish. If we require that a Scottish firm must be registered for legal purposes in Scotland and also have its head office in Scotland, then it has been estimated that, for 1973, about 41 per cent of Scottish manufacturing employment was in 'Scottish' firms, nearly 40 per cent was in 'English' firms and 19 per cent in foreign-owned firms.

The industries in which Scottish ownership is lowest (in employment terms) are electrical engineering, vehicles, chemicals, instrument engineering and metals. Scottish ownership is highest in timber, leather goods, textiles and printing and publishing. Relatively few important 'Scottish' companies operate in the modern dynamic science-based sectors of industry. Scotland's position in these industries, which is reasonably strong, depends on investment by foreign-owned firms, which fortunately find Scotland an attractive place for investment.

However, many 'Scottish' firms have most of their activities, and so their employment, outside Scotland (see Table 2.5). This is not necessarily a criticism of these firms. It is more an indication that Scottish industry is truly international. Much production is controlled from outside the country; major Scottish companies operate largely outside Scotland; much Scottish capital is employed outside Scotland, directed there by Scottish financial institutions, whilst the country attracts inflows of capital from elsewhere to maintain and develop its industrial base. Whether Scotland can continue to attract this capital, in competition with many other countries, is a key question for Scotland's industrial future.

3

Scottish Trade

JAMES LOVE and WILLIAM J. STEWART

In 1973 Scotland had a *deficit* on *visible trade* of £290 million. This meant that households, firms and the public sector in Scotland consumed more than was being produced domestically. By 1978 the balance of trade had moved into a *surplus* of £1537 million. Scottish production then exceeded domestic demand. International trade allows the pattern of *consumption* to differ from that of domestic *production* and, like other trading nations, Scotland may enjoy *gains from trade* by specializing in the production and export of products which can be produced relatively efficiently at home and importing goods produced more cheaply abroad. Which products does Scotland export and import? What determines the structure of Scotland's trade? Is the imbalance in Scotland's trade important?

SCOTTISH EXPORTS AND IMPORTS

Scotland is closely integrated into the UK economy. Visible trade with the rest of the UK (RUK) was much greater than with the rest of the world (ROW) in 1973 and the deficit of £290 million resulted from the deficit with RUK (see Table 3.1). The data for 1978 do not distinguish between transactions with RUK and ROW but excluding exports of oil and gas there was an overall surplus on visible trade of £746 million. Production of oil and gas in the North Sea was well in progress by 1978 and inclusion of exports of these items, which in the official UK accounting framework are not attributed to Scotland but to a fictitious 'Continental Shelf' region would raise the surplus to the £1537 million mentioned above.

TABLE 3.1*   *Scottish Balance on visible trade, 1973 and 1978 at current prices (£ million)*

	1973			1978	
	RUK	*ROW*	*Total (excluding oil and gas)*	*Total (excluding oil and gas)*	*Total*
Exports	2286	1216	3502	2914	3945
Imports	2648	1144	3792	2168	2408
Balance	− 362	72	− 290	746	1537

Note: In using the various tables presented here it should be recognized that difficulties of estimation and differences in definition and statistical methods create inconsistencies in estimates of trade statistics from different sources.

Exports

Whisky dominates the commodity group 'Whisky and other spirits' which was the single most valuable source of export revenues from ROW in 1973, and earned more than twice as much as the second largest group, 'Computers and electronics' (see Table 3.2). Among the firms producing computers and electronics are Burroughs in Cumbernauld and Glenrothes, Ferranti in Edinburgh, Marconi in Hillend (Fife) and Philips in Dunfermline and Hamilton. The traditional dependence of Scottish exports on heavy-engineering products is also evident. Apart from shipbuilding, engineering products accounted collectively for a large share of exports to ROW. Shipbuilding was the most important exporter to ROW among the engineering industries, although within this category by 1973 the actual building of ships had been largely replaced by the construction of rigs and floating platforms for the offshore oil industry.

For manufactured goods, the pattern of Scottish exports to ROW in 1978–80 is similar to that for 1973 (see Table 3.3). Again whisky is included here in the most important industrial group, 'Food, drink and tobacco'. Engineering exports are again important. The widespread recession in economic activity during the 1970s induced a deep depression in world shipping and the nominal *value* of Scottish ROW exports from the shipbuilding and marine-engineering group fell by approximately 10 per cent

TABLE 3.2   *Scottish exports to ROW, 1973 at current prices*
(£ million)

	Current prices (£ million)
Whisky and other spirits	234.57
Electrical machinery	34.66
Computers and electronics	107.73
Construction equipment	47.87
Office equipment	17.91
Shipbuilding/Marine engineering	96.86
Man-made fibres	8.03
Industrial engines	28.62
Spinning and weaving	25.93
Aerospace equipment	28.01
Agricultural machinery	6.14
Paint and other chemicals	54.27
Instrument engineering	25.45
Rubber products	17.07
Machine tools	8.13
Hosiery and knitted goods	18.92
Sea transport and ports	19.37
Wire products	8.39

TABLE 3.3   *Scottish manufactured exports, 1978–80 at current prices*
(£ million)

Industry Group	1978	1979	1980
Food, drink and tobacco	723	770	812
Chemicals and petroleum products	380	363	374
Metal manufacturing and metals, n.e.s.	402	366	366
Mechanical engineering	564	747	703
Instrument and electrical engineering	302	355	443
Shipbuilding and marine engineering	82	75	108
Vehicle	261	248	290
Textiles, leather, clothing and footwear	255	242	273
Other manufacturing	246	244	394
Total	3216	3410	3762

TABLE 3.4   *Scottish imports from ROW, 1973*

	£ million
Oil and gas exploration	120.74
Metallic ores, etc.	32.77
Sea transport and ports	30.87
Office equipment	19.26
Paper and board	57.65
Timber products	66.40
Construction equipment	34.83
Instrument engineering	27.18
Sugar and confectionary	18.00
Coal mining	21.85
Industrial plant and equipment	62.93
Electrical machinery	7.95
Agriculture	120.11
Spinning and weaving	21.74

from £97 million in 1973 to £88 million on average over 1978–80.. However, the Scottish economy, like most other industrial economies, experienced substantial price inflation over the period 1973–80, often at annual rates in excess of 15 per cent, and thus in *real* terms Scottish exports from this group must have fallen by considerably more than this 10 per cent over the period.

Imports

Scottish imports from ROW differ considerably in composition from exports. The most important import groups are 'Oil and gas exploration' and 'Agriculture' (see Table 3.4) and certain groups, for example 'Oil and gas exploration' and 'Metallic ores', appear on the import list but are not included among exports. In addition, there are important differences between the composition of imports and that of exports within similar commodity groups.

DETERMINANTS OF TRADE SPECIALIZATION

Several factors determine the pattern of Scottish exports and imports including the following.

International specialization according to comparative advantage. The theory of comparative advantage is one of the oldest and most enduring theories in Economics and holds that countries specialize in the products they can produce relatively efficiently. The source of comparative advantage is identified in terms of differences in *production functions* or in *factor endowments*. Thus, Scotland produces and exports some products and imports others within the same broad commodity groups, for example, in the 'Construction equipment' and 'Electrical' groups. Scotland does appear to have a comparative advantage in producing certain engineering products. John Brown in Clydebank, for example, are successful in exporting gas turbines. In contrast, the closure of the Fort William pulp-mill and the Invergordon smelter indicate a comparative disadvantage in the production of paper and aluminium respectively.

The relative efficiency with which a country produces goods may, of course, change over time. For example, with higher labour costs relative to non-European competitors such as South Korea and Taiwan, Scotland has lost her comparative advantage in shipbuilding. On the other hand, the experience gained from the North Sea may enable Scotland to acquire a comparative advantage in the provision of offshore equipment.

The availability of resources. This explanation may be applied to Scottish oil exports. Oil is produced and exported because it is available in the North Sea while other countries with high demands for energy do not have their own supplies. Scotland imports iron ore, hardwood, cane sugar and hard wheat within the groups 'Metallic ores', 'Timber products', 'Sugar and confectionery' and 'Agriculture' respectively. These products are not produced domestically either because the resource is absent or because the product cannot be grown under Scottish climatic conditions.

Special consumer preferences. Exports of Scotch whisky, like Swiss exports of watches, appear to result largely from foreign consumers' attachment to a particular country's export, due perhaps to past excellence or persuasive advertising.

Technological knowledge and innovation. During the 1950s and 1960s the many US companies investing in Scotland, for example, Honeywell at Newhouse and IBM at Greenock, brought with them new technologies, which, along with the availability of skilled labour, gave these companies an advantage in the production of electronic equipment. Scotland then became a production base for exports to other European markets (see Chapters 19, 22). Most of Scottish imports in 1973 within the group 'Oil and Gas Exploration' were of capital equipment which required specialist knowledge and techniques that had been developed abroad and were not then available domestically.

Monetary and fiscal policies affecting aggregate demand. The macroeconomic policies pursued by central government may affect both imports and exports. Generally, expansionary policies may be expected to increase the demand for imports and to reduce the supplies of exportables while deflationary policies do the opposite. Under the fixed exchange-rate regime of the 1950s and 1960s UK economic performance was characterized by the phenomenon of 'stop–go'. Typically, attempts to reflate the domestic economy were ended as increased domestic demand 'sucked in' greater imports without any corresponding increase in exports. The resulting trade deficit required deflationary measures.

Exchange-rate policy. As a member of a full monetary union Scotland has the same *sterling* exchange rate as England, Wales and Northern Ireland. In the early 1970s the UK, along with other leading industrial nations, abandoned the fixed-exchange-rate system in favour of a system that is more responsive to market forces. Exchange-rate appreciation raises the prices of exports in foreign currency and reduces import prices in domestic currency while depreciation does the reverse. The monetary authorities can intervene in foreign exchange markets by buying and selling sterling to affect the sterling exchange rate, and consequently, the prices of our exports in foreign markets and the prices we pay for imported goods. Another factor of particular significance for the UK is short-term capital flows. Given London's importance as a financial centre much short-term capital is held there. But changes in interest rates abroad, for example in New York, may produce swift and large capital flows with resulting pressures on the *sterling* exchange rate, and may require action in the UK to influence UK interest rates and/or the sterling exchange rate.

Export subsidies and import restrictions. Exports represent foreign demand for Scottish output, and therefore, *inject* income and employment into Scotland. In contrast, imports involve the purchase of the output of other nations and are a form of *leakage* from Scottish income. Concern with the effects of trade on income and employment frequently leads to government intervention. Scotch whisky exports are subject to a great many restrictions abroad, most of which are directed at the most processed form of whisky rather than whisky in bulk form. Discrimination against finished products is a common feature of trade restrictions since final processing is less likely to be tied to one country for reasons of natural resources and is also often the stage at which most jobs are created. Importing countries wish to encourage imports of bulk-blended and bulk-malt whisky and to establish their own facilities for processing and bottling.

Both abroad and in Britain, governments subsidize shipbuilding activities. By the 1970s declining relative productivity, reinforced by subsidies to foreign shipyards, had led to closures, mergers and rationalization of Scottish yards which were often accompanied by large-scale redundancies. One of the best examples of the UK government's support for shipbuilding was the subsidies given to an order from Poland signed in 1977 for twenty-two bulk carriers and two floating cranes. Nineteen of the bulk carriers were built at Govan, with some work on one of these being done at Robb-Caledon in Dundee, and the two floating cranes were built at Leith.

Common trade policies adopted by blocks of countries. The UK government's freedom to discriminate in trade is limited by membership of the EEC which has in effect become the deciding body on trade policy with non-EEC members. No overt discrimination is allowed against imports from other EEC members, and the UK must adopt a common tariff policy against non-EEC countries. These arrangements have affected the pattern of Scottish trade (see Chapter 22).

THE IMPLICATIONS OF IMBALANCE IN SCOTLAND'S
TRADING POSITION

Scotland's membership of a full monetary and economic union means not only that there is a common exchange rate with RUK but also that there are no restrictions on internal movements of goods, capital and labour and no comprehensive record is kept of such transactions among members of the union. The preparation of separate Scottish estimates, such as those presented earlier on visible trade, is, therefore, complex, costly and subject to error.

Visible trade represents only part of Scotland's transaction with RUK and ROW. Trade in *invisibles* is the other component of the *current account* of a country's *balance of payments*. However, problems arise in identifying Scottish trade in invisibles. First, as for other elements in the balance of payments, there is the difficulty of defining what is meant by a Scottish resident. Some tricky problems arise. Armed forces operating overseas, for example, are usually regarded as residents of the country whose government they represent, so that American servicemen who may do a tour of duty lasting several years at the Holy Loch are treated as residents of the USA. Transactions between them and local residents must be regarded as foreign transactions. Residents of Scotland would include the branches and subsidiaries of foreign-owned companies but not overseas branches and subsidiaries of Scottish companies and they would include the Scottish components of UK organizations such as central government departments and large corporations.

A second problem is that of identifying Scottish residents' payments and receipts for invisible transactions. Insurance premiums are paid to the Perth-based company, General Accident, for example, by both Scottish and non-Scottish residents, and the company pays out to claimants both resident and non-resident without distinguishing between them. Interest, profits and dividends present similar problems. Central government expenditure and revenues relating to Scotland are not always separated from those for RUK (see Chapter 15).

Similar problems arise with capital transactions, so that, while Edinburgh has a thriving capital market (see Chapter 5), many

TABLE 3.5 Scotland's balance on current account, 1973, at current prices (£ million)

| | RUK | | | ROW | | | Balance with |
	Exports	Imports	Balance	Exports	Imports	Balance	RUK and ROW
Services	338	335	3	104	70	34	37
Tourism	122	52		71	26		
Visible trade							−290
Balance on current account							−253

capital transactions involving Scottish residents take place through London.

Scottish earnings from invisibles are dominated by tourism, and in 1973 there were surpluses on services with both RUK and ROW (see Table 3.5). These surpluses were not sufficient, however, to offset the deficit on the balance of visible trade.

A deficit on current account involves reducing a country's net claims on ROW. A country suffering excessive falls in its international reserves can take policy measures aimed at eliminating a deficit on current account. As part of a full union Scotland cannot independently pursue the necessary policies on money supply, interest rates, the exchange rate, government expenditures, taxation and transfers. These are determined centrally to reflect the needs of the union as a whole and do not have a particular Scottish dimension. However, the usual concerns surrounding balance of payments disequilibrium do not apply within a full economic and monetary union. There is no possibility that Scotland, which uses UK currency for all its internal transactions, will run short of UK money for its ordinary purchases from RUK. However, if Scottish trade with RUK showed an increasing deficit this would reduce Scottish output and employment. This may increase emigration from Scotland, movements of capital or, more likely, government transfer payments such as regional aid to industry, unemployment benefits and social security payments (see Chapter 16).

PART II

Markets

4

Adam Smith's *Wealth of Nations*: the Legacy of a Great Scottish Economist

ROY H. GRIEVE

A LANDMARK IN SOCIAL SCIENCE

Adam Smith – born in Kirkcaldy, professor at Glasgow, government official in Edinburgh – was one of the outstanding figures of the 'Scottish Enlightenment' which in the eighteenth and early nineteenth centuries made a brilliant contribution to the world's intellectual and artistic heritage. The publication in 1776 of his classic work *An Inquiry into the Nature and Causes of the Wealth of Nations* marks the coming of age of economics as an intellectual discipline. The *Wealth of Nations* presented a penetrating analysis of the capitalist industrial economy which was then taking shape. The book was an immediate success. It powerfully influenced public opinion, offered statesmen a programme of action and provided a body of ideas which formed the basis of development of economic theory for the next hundred years. It has worn well: the continuing relevance of Smith's essential principles is remarkable.

BOX 4.1   *Adam Smith, philosopher*

Adam Smith was born in 1723 in the 'little seaport town' of Kirkcaldy, posthumous child of the Comptroller of Customs. He was educated at the parish school and, 1737–40, at the University of Glasgow (the old College in the High Street) where 'his favourite studies were mathematics and natural philosphy, and the political history of mankind'. Proceeded on the Snell scholarship to Balliol College, Oxford, where he remained six years.

His academic career began with public lectures in Edinburgh, 1748. Elected Professor of Logic at Glasgow, 1751, he transferred to the Chair of Moral Philosophy the next year. 'His reputation filled his classrooms; those branches of science taught by him became fashionable, and his opinions were discussed in the clubs and literary societies of Glasgow.' He resigned his Chair in 1764, to become tutor to the young Duke of Buccleuch, with whom he travelled on the Continent (making a stay at Versailles), 1764–66. On his return he retired to private life in Kirkcaldy and London in order to write and, after nearly ten years, published the *Wealth of Nations*. He was appointed a Commissioner of Customs at Edinburgh in 1778.'

While the *Wealth of Nations* occupies a pre-eminent place in the history of economic thought, Adam Smith was much more than an economist. The *Wealth of Nations* was intended as but one chapter of a wide-ranging study of man in society. As a philosopher Smith sought to reveal the conditions of human progress, moral and intellectual, as well as material. His great project embraced, along with economics, ethics and psychology, law and politics. Of the four major works he planned, only two were given to the world. Prior to the *Wealth of Nations* the *Theory of Moral Sentiments* (1759) presented Smith's system of ethics. (The lines by Robert Burns, a great admirer of Smith's books,

> O wad some Pow'r the giftie gie us
> to see oursels as others see us

can in all probability be taken as the poet's rendering of the theme of the *Theory of Moral Sentiments*). The manuscripts of treatises on law and on the progress of the arts and sciences, still 'on the anvil' at the time of his death, Smith caused to be destroyed.

Adam Smith was of a kindly and sociable disposition. While stories are told of his absent-mindedness, he was known also as a capable administrator. He remained (though not unsusceptible) a bachelor. The only certain likeness we have of him, apart from a little cartoon sketch, is the Tassie medallion portrait of 1787 – hold a current Royal Bank £1 note to the light.

He died in Edinburgh, 1790.

'WEALTH' AND THE MEANS OF ECONOMIC PROGRESS

What, in the first place, does Smith mean by 'the wealth of nations'? The 'wealth of every nation' is defined, not as a hoard of gold and silver, but as an abundance of 'all the necessaries and conveniences of life which (the nation) annually consumes'. But we should not suppose that Smith equates the possession of material wealth with the *well-being* of society. The definition must be read in context: economic development is the subject of the *Inquiry*. Smith's purpose was twofold: (a) to identify the sources of economic progress – of increase in the wealth of nations; and, (b) on the basis of that understanding, to determine the proper role of the state in relation to the economic order.

On what does this wealth, and its increase, depend? With a given population, the quantity of 'necessaries and conveniences' which can annually be supplied to consumers must depend, as Smith indicates, on the number (directly or indirectly) engaged in the production of these goods and on the *productivity of their labour* (output per man). The latter is the key factor: if standards of living are to rise, the productivity of labour must increase.

There are two means, says Smith, of raising productivity; (a) *by division of labour* – splitting up complete operations of production into separate, specialist employments, and (b) *by application of 'machines and instruments'* which 'facilitate and abridge labour' and 'enable one man to do the work of many'.

To supply labour with more and better equipment and to build up the *infrastructure* of the economy (facilities such as roads, bridges and harbours) means that *capital accumulation* has to be achieved. For that to be possible the economy must produce, over a period of time (say, a year), more output than required to replace the materials, equipment and subsistence of the workforce used up in the course of production in that period. The economy, that is to say, must be able to produce a *surplus* of output over what is necessary merely to maintain the existing level of production. Accumulation takes place when this surplus capacity is used to produce a net addition to the community's stock of capital goods – when part at least of the surplus is 'ploughed back' in the form of *investment* rather than used up in current consumption.

Smith puts great stress on the virtue of saving. He hammers home the point that the growth potential of the economy will not be realized if its surplus production capacity is squandered on profligate consumption or wasted in maintaining an *excessive* number of 'unproductive labourers'. Of all the classes within society it is the capitalists especially whom Smith expects to live with frugality and to save.

Smith supposes that all resources made available by saving will automatically be required for investment. He sees no problem with regard to entrepreneurs' willingness to invest. Growth is envisaged as a self-sustaining process − production capacity and demand for output expanding together as costs fall, real incomes and purchasing power increase and markets widen. Widening markets in turn induce further improvements in productivity.

THE 'INVISIBLE HAND' AND THE SYSTEM OF NATURAL LIBERTY

Smith's picture of economic growth is of a continuing process of increasing division of labour and investment, giving rise to progressively higher productivity and output. His vital insight is that this expansion is achieved not by means of any conscious overall plan, but is, as it were, the accidental by-product of individual actions motivated by *individual self-interest*. The dynamic of the system is 'the uniform, constant, and uninterrupted effort of every man to better his condition', which he generally seeks to do by 'the acquisition of a fortune'. It is the desire for 'betterment' − to 'get on' − that prompts saving rather than consumption. It is the striving of the individual entrepreneur, in his own particular sphere of operations, to exploit all possible opportunities of profit by improvement of productivity and extension of production capacity, that drives the economy forward on the path of growth.

> (It) is only for the sake of profit that any man employs a capital in the support of industry. . . . As every individual, therefore, endeavours as much as he can to direct that industry that its produce may be of the greatest value, every individual necessarily labours to render the annual revenue of the society as great as he can. He generally, indeed,

neither intends to promote the public interest, nor knows how much he is promoting it. . . . (By) directing that industry in such a manner that its produce may be of the greatest value, he intends only his own gain, and he is in this, as in many other cases, led by an invisible hand to promote an end which was no part of his intention (Book IV, Chapter II).

The striking and famous metaphor of the '*invisible hand*' vividly expresses the idea of a spontaneous, 'natural', tendency to order and harmony in economic affairs.

The 'invisible hand', operating through the pursuit of private profit, promotes the general expansion of the economy. It ensures also, at the level of particular markets and products, that the composition of output is consistent with the pattern of demand. Entrepreneurs will increase capacity and supply to markets where the relation of demand to supply is such that the going price offers an abnormally high profit. Conversely, they will abandon sectors where price is too low to yield an acceptable return on capital. Thus as entrepreneurs, *concerned only with their own profits,* respond to price signals, individual investment and production decisions are co-ordinated with each other and with final demand.

From his analysis of the economic mechanism Smith draws a conclusion of the first importance. His proposition is this: the most effective means of promoting economic progress is to establish

the simple system of natural liberty (whereby) every man, so long as he does not violate the laws of justice, is left perfectly free to pursue his own interest in his own way, and to bring both his industry and capital into competition with those of any other man (Book IV, Chapter IX).

The great merit of the system of natural liberty is that, in allowing the expression of natural forces, it harnesses independent initiative and effort, individual knowledge and experience, to the public interest.

For this self-acting economic machine to function effectively, the free movement of capital and labour should not be obstructed

BOX 4.2 *Mercantilism*

'Mercantilism' (or, in Smith's language, 'the Mercantile System') denotes the long-established system of national economic management practised by the states of Europe, Britain included, in Smith's time. Governments sought through extensive and detailed intervention – in the form of tariffs and subsidies, monopoly charters and other specific regulations – to shape the pattern of national trade and industry. For each country the object was (incompatibly) the same – to maximize exports and minimize imports of manufactures so as to achieve a surplus on the balance of trade and therefore an inflow of the precious metals.

Smith regarded the Mercantilist programme as misconceived in both object and method. He saw it as indicative of failure to appreciate the possibility of mutual gains from international division of labour, specialization and trade, and of want of understanding of the operation of the 'invisible hand'. The effects of the system, he believed, were to favour sectional interests at the expense of the community in general and, by standing in the way of individual enterprise, to retard economic progress.

or diverted by restrictions and privileges such as comprised the *Mercantilist* system (see Box 4.2) of Smith's day. If the individual businessman best knows where his own particular interest lies, it is folly, Smith argues, for the statesman 'to load himself with a most unnecessary attention' by attempting 'to direct private people in what manner they ought to employ their capitals'. Again, free competition in the product markets is essential to protect the public interest. The state should not grant perpetual monopoly privileges (as then enjoyed by the East India and other great trading companies). Monopoly means restricted supplies and high prices, 'the highest that can be squeezed out of the buyers.' Smith has no illusions about the readiness of the capitalist to exploit the public if in a position to do so. The 'mean rapacity' of merchants and manufacturers must be kept in check by the pressure of competition, which serves also as a spur to efficiency and progress.

WAGES AND PROFITS

In Smith's account of the distribution of national output amongst the members of society, capitalists, landlords and workers confront each other as rival claimants to shares of the national cake. What each class gets (in profits, rent or wages) depends on its bargaining strength. The propertied classes have the advantage over the workers.

> What are the common wages of labour depends everywhere upon the contract made between two parties, whose interests are by no means the same. . . . It is not, however, difficult to foresee which of the two parties must, upon all ordinary occasions, have the advantage in the dispute, and force the other into compliance with their terms. . . . A landlord, a farmer, a master manufacturer, or a merchant, though they did not employ a single workman, could generally live a year or two upon the stocks which they have already acquired. Many workmen could not subsist a week . . . and scarce any a year without employment. In the long-run the workman may be as necessary to his master as his master is to him; but the necessity is not so immediate.

Smith makes no bones about it – distribution depends on 'muscle' – on the ability of each class to shoulder aside competitors for a share of national income. Although things have changed since Smith's time – the balance of power in the labour market being tilted to the other side – Smith's treatment of distribution in terms of social relations and market power remains valid today.

Despite the conflict between labour and capital over the division of current output, a coincidence of interests, paradoxical as it may seem, *does* exist in the capitalist economy. Profits on capital are as necessary to the workers as to the capitalists themselves. Profit provides both incentive and means to the capitalist to undertake investment. Investment creates employment and is essential for economic growth, which in time raises the living standards of all members of the community.

THE DUTIES OF THE STATE

In advocating the system of natural liberty and mounting his 'very violent attack' on the Mercantilist system of state regulation, Smith is arguing with great force that the state should not seek to do what would be better done by private enterprise. It must, however, be emphasized that Smith at the same time requires a positive contribution from the state. He regards that contribution as of vital importance for economic progress and social welfare. The primary function of the state is to ensure security of person and property (without which, incidentally, enterprise could not flourish). But that is not all: certain economic and social obligations, complementary to the system of natural liberty, are laid by Smith upon the state. These fall into two broad categories.

Intervention to foster economic development. Intervention is recommended to create conditions under which the driving force of *individual* self-interest may most effectively advance the *general* interest.

It is the duty of the state

> [to erect and maintain] certain public works and certain public institutions, which it can never be for the interest of any individual, or small number of individuals, to erect and maintain, because the profit could never repay the expenditure to any individual or small number of individuals, though it may frequently do much more than repay it to a great society (Book IV, Chapter IX).

As instances of essential works which may require public provision, roads, bridges, harbours, canals and street lighting are mentioned. The quoted passage neatly expresses the notion of *market failure* on account of *externalities*: social and private interest fail to coincide because the reward of the private agent does not fully reflect the benefit (or cost) of his action (or inaction) to the community as a whole. The maintenance of roads is a case in point: Smith argues that responsibility cannot safely be left in private hands as remuneration (from tolls) would be independent of efficient performance. Smith observes also that administrative means must be devised to make sure that public agencies such as road authorities, not subject to effective discipline through the market, perform in accordance with the community's interest.

Smith does not draw a rigid line between spheres of public and private activity. Take the case of canals. Although he allows that these may be made and maintained by private enterprise, they are nevertheless listed as possible state undertakings. Or notice his comments on the postal service: he is quite happy, simply because the business is evidently well conducted, that it should be in public hands. It is the adequate provision and efficient operation of necessary facilities, rather than the matter of ownership in itself, that are important to Smith.

Certain actions by the state which may, within the framework of natural liberty, promote progress are approved. Special privileges may be awarded, but temporarily, to companies opening up particularly risky markets; likewise patent rights may be granted to encourage innovation. Some mention is made of tax measures to influence individual decisions. Most unexpected perhaps is that Smith approves the imposition of a maximum rate of interest. (This rather drastic intervention in the market is said to favour productive borrowers against spendthrifts, thereby promoting investment.)

Intervention to prevent injustice and suffering. State intervention is required also to prevent the injustice and suffering to which the system of natural liberty could give rise.

Smith affirms that the state is obliged to restrain and protect when the unfettered pursuit of individual self-interest threatens the safety or rights of others. A specific instance of state regulation (prohibition of the issue of banknotes of small denomination) gives occasion to an emphatic statement of principle.

> Such regulations may, no doubt, be considered as in some respects a violation of natural liberty. But these exertions of the natural liberty of a few individuals, which might endanger the security of the whole society, are, and ought to be, restrained by the laws of all governments. . . . The obligation of building party walls, in order to prevent the communication of fire, is a violation of natural liberty,

exactly of the same kind with the regulations of the banking trade which are here proposed (Book II, Chapter II).

State activity of a welfare character is required by Smith. He demands state action to prevent the undesirable social effects he fears will otherwise be associated with economic progress. He is greatly concerned that increasing division of labour and specialization will do serious damage, intellectual, spiritual and physical, to working people.

> The man whose whole life is spent in performing a few simple operations . . . generally becomes as stupid and ignorant as it is possible for a human creature to become. . . . The uniformity of his stationary life naturally corrupts the courage of his mind . . . It corrupts even the activity of his body. . . . His dexterity at his own particular trade seems in this manner to be acquired at the expense of his intellectual, social, and martial virtues. But in every improved and civilized society this is the state into which the labouring poor, that is, the great body of the people must necessarily fall, unless government takes some pains to prevent it (Book IV, Chapter I, part III).

For the common people a system of compulsory, subsidized parish schools (on the Scottish model) must be set up throughout the country. For the good of body and spirit the government should 'take proper pains' to support the practise of military exercises. To counter extreme and gloomy doctrines, the state should encourage the study of science and philosophy and the provision of public entertainments and exhibitions, thus to 'amuse and divert', inspiring 'gaiety and good humour'.

It may be noted that Smith, while recognizing that the state itself would derive benefit from such welfare policies, is explicit that, even were that not so, social problems would 'deserve the most serious attention of government'.

ACTIVITIES OF THE STATE IN THE PRESENT DAY

In the two centuries that have passed since publication of the *Wealth of Nations* circumstances have changed – economic conditions are very different and social attitudes have altered. In

Britain today the state plays a much larger part than envisaged by Smith at the dawn of the industrial era.

Smith was very conscious of the damage that monopoly could inflict on the public interest. He seems, however, to have taken the view that, were Mercantilist privileges eliminated, the problem of monopoly would disappear. He believed (mistakenly, as is now evident) that large joint-stock companies would not, except in special circumstances, survive in competition with smaller and, he thought, more efficient owner-managed enterprises. But developments of technology and organization have led in many industries to concentration of market power and the need for measures to constrain monopolistic behaviour in the private sector. Public ownership of 'natural monopolies' has been favoured. Utilities (gas, electricity, railways, etc.) and other key industries (coal, steel) have been nationalized partly for practical, partly for doctrinaire reasons. (Nationalization, incidentally, brings a problem perceived by Smith – that of ensuring the satisfactory performance of a *public* monopoly.) State acquisition of 'lame ducks' to ensure their survival has further extended the nationalized sector.

In Smith's time trade unions were prohibited by law. Today labour monopolies in key sectors possess great economic and political power. Wage-push inflation and the 'external' social costs of strike action constitute problems unknown in the eighteenth century. Intervention in collective bargaining by means of incomes policy and through arbitration may be defended as necessary to protect the general interest.

Many instances of conflict between the interest of society and the private pursuit of profit have become apparent. Smith's principle of protective regulation has found widespread application – in respect of product standards, conditions of work, public health and the environment.

Smith certainly took a positive view of state intervention and public spending for welfare purposes. The provision of state-subsidized education which he so urgently recommended is, however, no more than a first step in the direction of a general welfare programme. On the subject of poverty and the possibility of its relief by *transfer payments*, the *Welfare of Nations* is surprisingly silent. The explanation may be that Smith accepted great disparities in conditions of life as inevitable and looked to economic growth rather than transfers as affording the better prospect of improvement to the poorest members of society. The post-war Welfare State is the product of a different distribution of political power and of different perception of what should, and could, be done. Today welfare outlays – in the form both of direct public provision of services (health, education) and of transfer payments (to the elderly, the sick, families, the unemployed) form a substantial portion of public spending (see Table 4.1).

Smith did not specify the maintenance of full employment as one of the duties of the state. He simply did not envisage a problem of general unemployment. Purchases for investment

TABLE 4.1 *Two centuries of public spending in Britain* *Public spending, 1770 (as percentage of national income)*

Debt charges	3.7
Defence	3.0
Civil List	0.7
Other civil government	0.7
Poor relief (estimate)	1.0
County expenditures (jails, vagrants, constables, bridges, etc.)	0.1
Total public spending	9.2
Total (excluding defence and interest)	2.5

The growth of public spending (by central and local government, excluding public corporations; as percentage of GNP)

	1890	1910	1938	1955	1974
Social services (including transfers)	2	4	11	16	25
(Transfers)	(1)	(1)	(7)	(7)	(15)
Other civil and defence	7	9	19	21	19
Total public spending	9	13	30	37	44
Total (excluding defence and interest)	5	8	17	23	35

would, he supposed, automatically take up all the surplus of output the economy could produce over its consumption needs. The possibility that total demand for output might be insufficient to induce employers to take on all available labour was not recognized. While, to the modern reader with the benefit of hindsight, it is a weakness of the *Wealth of Nations* that aggregate demand is too readily assumed to 'look after itself', Smith could hardly be expected to have foreseen that instability of production and employment would become a most serious social and economic problem: the pattern of major cyclical fluctuations in the British economy dates from the 1780s or 1790s. Only in 1936 did J. M. (later Lord) Keynes's epoch-making *General Theory* establish that there is no sound basis for faith that the economy naturally tends to a state of full employment. The practical implication is that the government is obliged to manage, by use of fiscal and monetary instruments, the level of aggregate demand in the interest of full employment.

Finally, a fundamental question presents itself. Two hundred years ago Britain was on the way to becoming the world's leading industrial power. Does the present British problem of competitive weakness and 'de-industrialization' suggest that a broad industrial strategy, as operated in France and Japan, could usefully supplement the 'invisible hand' by shaping the context in which investment decisions are made? (We ask 'supplement' not 'supplant': the problems experienced with systems of command planning in Eastern Europe and the Soviet Union demonstrate the dangers of attempting to dispense altogether with the services of the 'invisible hand'.)

TWO LESSONS FOR TODAY

The *Wealth of Nations* propounds a forceful case for economic freedom − for liberation of enterprise from the constraints of 'the Mercantile system'. But Smith's advocacy of the system of natural liberty should not be understood as dogmatic prescription of *laissez-faire*, of a 'hands off' stance of government in relation to economic and social affairs. It is as a *means* of achieving society's objectives that non-intervention may be judged proper, not as an end or virtue in itself.

Smith is alert to the possibility that the 'invisible hand' may on occasion fail the public interest. He is open-minded in allowing that when such failure occurs, judicious government intervention may achieve a better outcome for the community. He lays particular responsibilities on the state in answer to particular economic and social problems he has identified; he is practical rather than doctrinaire. Commonsense and compassion characterize his discussion. To Smith, social suffering is not something to be tolerated helplessly as the immutable result of natural forces.

An ideal economic system, as envisaged by Smith, would yield society the benefits of individual initiative and effort while at the same time involve the state in correcting the deficiencies of private action and in safeguarding the interests of the community in general. To decry government intervention and public spending as inherently 'bad' (or to assert with equal dogmatism that public ownership and central planning are necessarily 'good') would be quite contrary to the spirit of the *Wealth of Nations*. *A balance of individual and collective responsibilities is required.* We may note that Smithian lesson.

Smith's ideal is, in principle, as relevant in the twentieth as in the eighteenth century. The practical question that concerns us today is this: what 'division of labour' between the state and the natural economic mechanism will, *in circumstances as they exist,* best serve the community's interest? It is the *manner* in which Smith tackled the question of the role of the state, rather than the specific answer he gave in 1776, that is of direct present relevance. (The particular duties he recommended of the state do not go as far as required by present conditions.) Smith, as we have seen, judged the appropriate functions of the state in the light of the problems that were apparent to him. It is evident that no detailed specification of its duties, which would be universally applicable, can be formulated. *Smith's handling of the issue of intervention implies that, in any particular circumstances, what is required of the state must be a matter of judgement — by an informed, compassionate and open mind — and not of dogma.* That again is a lesson we may take from the *Wealth of Nations*.

5

Markets for Finance

ANDREW D. BAIN

The two most obviously Scottish characteristics of our financial system are Scottish banks and Scottish bank notes. Indeed, it is the Bank of Scotland, the Royal Bank of Scotland and the Clydesdale Bank – the three Scottish clearing banks – who issue the notes.

But this does not mean that Scotland has its own separate financial system. It is closely integrated with that of the rest of Britain. All three clearing banks – the most important financial institutions in Scotland – are Scottish-registered companies with their Head offices in Edinburgh or Glasgow, but none is totally Scottish-owned. The Clydesdale is a wholly-owned subsidiary of the Midland Bank; 35 per cent of the shares in the Bank of Scotland are held by Barclays Bank; and the Royal Bank of Scotland is, along with Williams and Glyns in England, one of the two principal operating companies in the Royal Bank of Scotland Group, in which Lloyds Bank holds a 16 per cent share.

More importantly, the major Scottish financial institutions win much of their business in the rest of the UK and other countries and institutions based elsewhere are increasingly penetrating the Scottish market. There are about forty offices and branches of English and overseas banks in major centres in Scotland.

COMPETITIVE MARKETS

It is the role of every country's financial system to provide the payments and credits without which specialized production and exchange cannot take place. And it is the financial system which provides savers with the facilities they need and channels their savings to investors and other borrowers.

Financial institutions in Britain operate within the context of the market; they compete for the saver's money and they compete for the borrower's business. Competition operates through; (a) the provision of services (e.g. convenient branches), (b) the terms on which they take or provide funds (e.g. the security required for loans), and (c) the prices (or rates of interest) they pay or charge.

Some parts of the market are organized, e.g. the Stock Exchange where long-term securities are bought and sold, but more commonly there are no formal arrangements, as in the 'markets' for personal deposits and loans.

In Scotland in the last ten years, competition has generated change and development. The Scottish clearing banks have been challenged in the domination of commercial banking by incomers from England and overseas. The Trustee Savings Banks have amalgamated into larger groups and now form part of a national system. Building societies from England have made substantial inroads into the Scottish deposit and mortgage markets. The Scottish Stock Exchanges have joined with London to form part of the UK Stock Exchange.

For the Scottish-based financial institutions to seek business elsewhere is no novelty. But in the last decade banks have increased their business in England and abroad, and some of the investment management groups have successfully offered their services to the world at large. The trend has been towards greater integration, and it has been a two-way process.

DEPOSIT–TAKING INSTITUTIONS

The clearing banks attract about half the deposits of savings in Scottish institutions. The Trustees Savings Banks (TSBs) – Aberdeen, South of Scotland, Tayside and Central Scotland, and West of Scotland – now combined into a single bank, take about one-quarter, and the building societies (e.g. Halifax, Nationwide, Abbey National) about three-quarters, of the balance (Table 5.1). In addition there are several merchant banks, branches of English and foreign banks and other organizations such as the National Savings Bank which take deposits.

TABLE 5.1   *The deposit market in Scotland, 1980*

	£ million	Percentage
Scottish clearing banks	4200	51
Trustee Savings Banks	1000	12
Building societies	3000	37
Total	8200	100

Practically all these institutions operate through a network of High Street branches. They are all also important employers. The clearing banks account for nearly 70 per cent of the branches and over 80 per cent of employees (Table 5.2). National Savings Bank facilities are provided at about 2250 post offices throughout the country.

The Three Clearing Banks

The size of the three clearing banks reveals their supremacy: total liabilities at the end of 1980 amounted to nearly £8000 million, including £500 million of notes, nearly £5000 million of sterling deposits and nearly £1500 million of deposits in foreign currencies (Fig. 5.1). Sterling deposits are employed mainly in sterling liquid assets and loans, and foreign currency deposits are similarly employed in foreign currency assets of varying type and maturity. These banks provide a very high proportion of the money transmission, payments and retail banking services in Scotland, and they are responsible for most of bank lending to industry and commerce as well as to private individuals.

The clearing banks make considerable use of the London financial markets, both as an important source of deposits (perhaps 15 per cent of their sterling deposits and a much larger proportion of

TABLE 5.2   *Branches and employment of major deposit-taking institutions in Scotland, 1980*

	Branches	Employment
Clearing banks	1460	23000
Trustee Savings Banks	280	2700
Building societies	380	1800

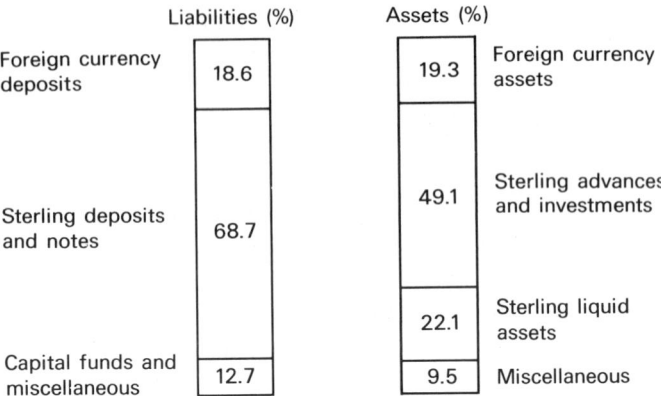

Fig. 5.1 Scottish clearing banks' balance sheets, December 1980. Figures for the banks refer to sterling deposits from the non-bank private sector and the public sector. They are probably a slight over-estimate of the sterling deposits garnered through Scottish offices of the banks

their foreign currency deposits) and as a place where they can hold the more liquid parts of their assets. It is this arrangement which is the principal determinant of the general level of interest rates in Scotland because the interest cost of deposits in London represents the short-run marginal cost of funds to the banks.

The Scottish clearing banks have faced increasing competition in the following.

(1) Their dealings with industrial and commercial companies. English clearing banks and overseas banks have set up branches, as have independent Scottish-based merchant banks. These competitors have sometimes been able to provide more sophisticated corporate financial services, larger loan facilities or wider international connections. The Scottish banks have responded by improving and extending the range of their own services. Developments include the creation of a highly successful merchant bank (the British Linen Bank) by the Bank of Scotland, the opening of a limited number of foreign branches and representative offices, and the formation of international divisions in all

the banks. Nevertheless, the incoming banks are highly competitive and are well-placed to provide services for customers with whom they deal elsewhere, business which might otherwise have been undertaken by one of the Scottish banks.

(2) The High Street retail deposit market. Since amalgamating into four regional groups in the mid-1970s the TSBs have begun to offer a full range of retail banking services to their customers – primarily individuals and small traders – and they are gradually extending their retail lending activities. Building societies have won a major increase in their share of the deposit market, with total deposits rising from under £400 million in 1970 to nearly £3000 million ten years later. For comparison, clearing-bank deposits rose from about £1000 million to a little over £4000 million in the same period. The interest rates paid by building societies have compared favourably with those on bank deposits in recent years, which has helped building societies to attract funds. In addition there has been a very rapid programme of branch expansion, from 107 branches in 1970 to 375 in 1980. Almost 90 per cent of the building society branches in Scotland belong to English societies and they take well over 90 per cent of the deposits.

Building Societies

There are now only twelve Scottish *building societies,* of which ten have only a single office. The largest is the Dunfermline Building Society with thirty-six branches including three in England.

The predominance of English building societies has led to the allegation that the building societies draw money away from Scotland. This charge does not stand up to examination: in the last five years building-society shares and deposits with Scottish branches rose by £1770 million, while their mortgage lending increased by £1700 million. Since about 20 per cent of building-society shares and deposits are normally held as liquid assets this means that Scottish branches contributed only £70 million to liquidity, compared with the £350 million which might have been expected.

OTHER INSTITUTIONS

There are nine *life assurance* companies with head offices in Scotland, whose total world-wide assets exceed £7,000 million. The largest are Standard Life (£2900 million in 1980), Scottish Widows (£1600 million) and Scottish Amicable (£900 million). All obtain a high proportion (over 80 per cent on average) of their UK business from outside Scotland, and some, such as Standard Life, have important overseas activities. Only one general insurance company, General Accident, is located in Scotland, but with total assets exceeding £2000 million it is one of the world's largest. About half its business is transacted in the UK.

With over £3000 million of investment and unit trust funds under management, together with substantial funds held for pension schemes and other purposes, *investment management* is another activity well represented in Scotland. There are about a dozen groups managing funds in excess of £100 million. The funds under management are attracted from all over the UK and abroad, and some 40 per cent of the assets are held overseas.

The importance of these institutions for Scotland lies principally in the employment opportunities they offer, in terms of both the number of jobs – around 6000 in insurance head offices and fund management groups – and the scope and range of senior posts involved. Head offices also have important local multiplier effects. They make demands on many other business services provided locally – accounting, legal and printing, for example – which are not required by the branch offices of other organizations. On the financing side, while the managers of investment funds do not give preference to Scottish enterprises, they are on the look out for favourable investment opportunities. Scottish companies with good prospects are, therefore, in a position to turn to these funds for risk capital.

Industrial financing in Scotland can also be arranged through the *merchant banks,* four of which are Scottish – British Linen, James Finlay Corporation, McNeill Pearson, Noble Grossart – or with the assistance of the Industrial and Commercial Finance Corporation (ICFC) and the Scottish Development Agency (SDA). The ICFC specializes in providing loan and risk capital to smaller companies. Support from the SDA may be obtained by enterprises which have a good chance of viability in the long run but which experience difficulty in obtaining sufficient private finance.

Early in 1982, Lovable, a Scottish bra manufacturer in Cumbernauld employing 300 people was saved by the coordinated efforts of these public institutions and the private sector. The ICFC and the SDA each provided £200 000 of equity capital and the Royal Bank of Scotland offered a £450 000 overdraft facility.

Scotland is well-provided with *hire-purchase* and other *instalment financing* facilities, though only one major company, Lloyds and Scottish is actually based in Scotland. At present Lloyds Bank own 60 per cent of its shares, the balance belonging to the Royal Bank of Scotland. Lloyds and Scottish is now amalgamating with Bowmaker, as English-based finance house.

Glasgow still retains a trading floor of the *Stock Exchange*, and there are sixteen firms of stockbrokers in Scotland to serve the needs of Scottish clients. However, most of the purchases and sales of shares by institutional investors pass through the Stock Exchange in London.

SCOTLAND AS A FINANCIAL CENTRE

The commercial banking system in Scotland has retained a strong regional flavour. Scottish bank notes are the most visible sign. The right to issue their own notes is valuable to the banks, because by issuing their own notes to customers who require cash the banks avoid having to tie up a significant part of their assets (perhaps 5 per cent) in a form which earns no interest – Bank of England notes – as a 'float' for the tills in their branches. They can therefore invest practically all their deposits in earning assets – one respect in which they have an advantage over their counterparts in England.

Much more important, however, is the presence of the banks' Head Offices in Edinburgh or Glasgow. This means that lines of communication are short, with the advantage that decisions about loans and investments can be taken speedily and with the benefit of local knowledge. Moreover, the primary commitment of all the Scottish banks, regardless of their ownership or their efforts to spread their wings abroad, has to be to their customers in Scotland.

This emphasis on Scotland does not mean that financial conditions in Scotland can differ significantly from the rest of the UK. Interest rates and other credit terms move in parallel throughout the UK. Large deposits are very mobile, and if the interest rates paid by the Scottish banks differed from those elsewhere they would quickly gain or lose considerable sums. Moreover, financial institutions in Scotland are bound by the same systems of monetary and prudential control as their counterparts in England.

But it is not only, or even mainly, the banks which make Edinburgh much the most important financial centre in Britain, outside of London. Financial institutions located in Edinburgh are able to benefit from substantial *external economies of scale*. The presence of a significant number of institutions of different types provides a wide range of facilities and services on which both old-established institutions and newcomers can draw. No doubt this is one reason why so many banks have chosen to open offices in Edinburgh in recent years and why the new indigenous merchant banks have been able to thrive. These advantages spill over to some extent to the rest of Scotland.

How far Edinburgh's pre-eminence depends on the retention of ultimate control of these financial institutions in Scotland is a moot point. In recommending against the proposed merger between the Royal Bank of Scotland Group and the Standard Chartered Bank the Monopolies and Mergers Commission found that the loss of ultimate control for Edinburgh would be damaging to Scottish interests and concluded that as a result the merger would be contrary to the public interest. Nevertheless, while the presence of senior management, with the power to decide on all domestic lending applications, is clearly essential for the banks, the need for strategic decision-taking on matters such as international development to remain in Edinburgh is less evident. For the other major financial institutions – the insurance companies and investment management groups – whose business is widely spread, ultimate control and the geographic location of their head office functions are more closely connected. Experience suggests that if control were to be removed, the employment opportunities and associated services would be likely to follow later.

BOX 5.1   *Glossary*

Clearing banks: The 4 English (Midland, Barclays, National Westminster and Lloyds) and the 3 Scottish clearers are the largest of the 350 UK commercial banks. They are incorporated companies and offer a wide range of services including deposit (or saving) and chequing accounts, investment advice, mortgage and loan facilities, and money transmission. They are so called because payments due between them are aggregated and only the net balance is transferred.

Trustees Savings Banks: These are incorporated societies offering a range of services similar to the clearing banks. Grouped in regional organizations their central body, the Central TSB provides the network with its own clearing mechanism.

National Savings Bank: Part of the Government Department of National Savings, it operates nationwide through 20 000 post offices, providing simple savings facilities aimed mainly at the small saver.

Building Societies: These are mutual organizations. Most of the money invested in them, 97 per cent, is in the form of share accounts, which are equivalent, for practical purposes, to savings deposits with the banks. They make mortgage advances for house purchase at variable rates of interest normally for 20–50 years.

In 1978 Insurance companies, pension funds, investment and unit trusts owned 46 per cent of UK Government securities and 47 per cent of ordinary shares.

Insurance Companies: These engage in two main types of business: general insurance, in which people are insured against loss from, for example, fire or accidents in return for a premium payment; and life assurance which often involves the payment of a capital sum at death or on survival to the end of a fixed period, in return for a regular annual payment. Life assurance is an important form of contractual saving, and the accumulated savings held by life assurance funds have an important influence on the capital market.

Pension funds: Accumulated through contractual contributions of employees and employers during the person's working life, the money being invested. At retirement the employee often receives a capital sum plus a regular payment, or pension.

Investment Trust: These are joint-stock companies often managed by investment management companies in which the investor (saver) buys a share of the company with the prospect of a regular income from its investments.

Unit Trust: Funds in which the investor receives units in proportion to his contribution and gets a share in the assets of the trust and the income earned.

Merchant Banks: Offer a range of financial services, including help in the sale of new securities, management of various funds, investment advice, provision of risk-capital, and some banking services. They do not engage in retail deposit-taking and lending, or money transmission.

Stock Exchange: Long-term securities of companies and the public sector (shares and bonds) are issued and traded in securities markets. The Stock Exchange is the main market for raising new long-term capital and for trading existing securities. There are two major participants: jobbers, who fulfil the market-making function by dealing in securities as principals for their own profit and loss, and stockbrokers who act as intermediaries bringing buyers and sellers to the jobbers.

Industrial and Commercial Finance Corporation (ICFC): Owned by Finance for Industry, itself 15 per cent owned by the Bank of England and the rest by clearing banks. The ICFC provides share and loan capital, financial advice and other services to small and medium-sized companies.

Scottish Development Agency (SDA): Set up in 1975 it is government funded and supervized, its purpose being to further economic activity, including helping small companies, safeguarding employment, promoting industry and furthering environmental improvement in Scotland.

6

The Labour Market
in Scotland

DAVID BELL

In September 1982, more than 350 000 were registered as unemployed in Scotland. Of these more than 27 000 were school-leavers who had recently joined the labour market. Job Centres, however, only had about 14 000 unfilled vacancies. Though nearly all of us will spend a large proportion of our life either working or looking for work, most people do not think of this as a market activity.

THE LABOUR MARKET

The labour market, like the market for butter or beer, has buyers and sellers who bargain for the purchase or sale of a particular commodity (normally called labour) at a particular price (normally called the wage rate). The purchasers of labour do not buy it for its own sake: two man-hours of labour are unlikely to be of *direct* value to an employer. Its use lies in what can be produced in those two hours. The employer will expect to sell whatever has been produced in order to make a profit. The demand for labour is thus a *derived* demand: unless the entrepreneur can find a market for his finished products, he will see no necessity to hire labour.

This is an important characteristic which distances the labour market from other types of market. Yet it is by no means the only one. Consider what happens when the wage rate rises. Other things being equal, the demand for labour should fall. Employers will try to substitute other factors of production, buying more plant and equipment, for example, in order to reduce their labour requirements. On the other side of the market, by contrast, it is by no means certain that the supply of labour will increase. Some workers may feel that instead of taking home a higher income, they would prefer to maintain their income around its old level and reduce the amount of time spent working. Less work means more time to enjoy leisure activities. Thus it is possible that an increase in price (wages) *could* lead to a reduction in supply, a reaction which is almost unique to the labour market.

Another crucial distinguishing feature of most labour markets in industrialized countries is that they do not *clear*. It is obvious to the most casual observer that the usual position of the labour market is one where supply exceeds demand. When the number of persons seeking work exceeds the number of available vacancies, unemployment results. Elementary economics texts invariably portray the type of market where demand and supply are equal. At the going price, there are no goods left unwanted on the shelves and no buyers frustrated by their inability to purchase the good. Yet in the labour market, particularly at present, there are many workers who cannot find a buyer for their labour.

Unemployed workers find it difficult to break back into the labour market for a number of reasons, many of which are connected with the market's idiosyncratic nature. For example, workers are not constantly hired and rehired, say, every Monday morning. Employers explicitly or implicitly make agreements with their employees that they should work for a usually fairly long period of time. These arrangements effectively remove a large number of jobs from the active labour market. Though it is normally in the interests of employers and employees to set such contracts, the result is that the unemployed are barred from competing across the full range of employment available.

Another problem facing the unemployed worker seeking employment is that the labour market is not a homogeneous unit. In fact there are many labour markets. These are mainly distinguished by occupation and geographical position. The degree of overlap between markets is dependent on the mobility, both occupational and geographical, of the workforce: such mobility is usually limited. It is difficult to imagine much movement between, for example, the market for fishermen in the Western Isles and that for brain surgeons in Edinburgh.

THE SCOTTISH LABOUR MARKET

The Scottish labour market, which is an amalgam of many smaller labour markets, may be examined in terms of its main characteristics.

Size. Around 2.3 million out of Scotland's population of 5.1 million are actively involved in the labour market. The remainder are either too young, too old, or have some other reason for not participating. The most common other reason is that they are housewives who do not have sufficient time to take on a job as well as look after a family. There is another significant and growing group, however, who are not participating in the labour market because they are disillusioned with it. Many of the long-term unemployed, believing that their situation is hopeless, stop actively searching for work. Trying to rebuild the confidence of these individuals is one of the biggest problems currently facing the government's labour-market agencies.

Composition. Of those who do participate in the labour market, the majority (1.9 million) are employees. There are about 130 000 persons who work for themselves: these are mostly farmers, tradesmen and small retailers. The remaining 350 000 or so are unemployed. The unemployed (or more precisely those who receive unemployment benefit) are classed as labour-market participants because they are thought to be actively seeking work.

Sex distribution. In 1981 950 000 of the working population in Scotland were female and 1.41 million male. One of the most crucial post-war changes in the structure of the Scottish labour market has been the increase in the number of working women. Changing attitudes, smaller families, more labour-saving household gadgets and increasing numbers of suitable jobs, particularly in services, have contributed to this sudden increase in female participation. The distribution in 1981 contrasts, for example, with that for 1961 when only 800 000 were female and 1.53 million were male.

Unemployment. A worrying feature of the Scottish labour market which has been apparent for some time is rising unemployment

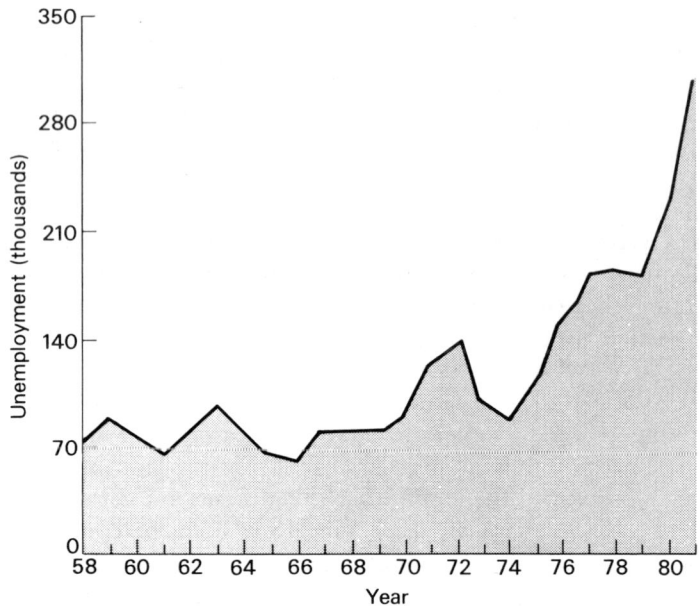

Fig. 6.1   Total unemployment in Scotland 1958–81

(see Fig. 6.1). In 1961, unemployment in Scotland averaged 68 400: in 1981 it averaged 307 200, a 349 per cent increase!

COSTS OF UNEMPLOYMENT

The costs of unemployment are massive: each additional person made unemployed will cost the government between £4500 and £5000 each year. The government loses revenue, mostly income tax, due to unemployment and has to make various payments, mainly unemployment and supplementary benefits, to maintain the unemployed person. These are the main costs to the exchequer: they do not, of course, include the direct costs, both material and psychological, to the individual.

Unemployment does not affect all sections of the working population equally. Some labour markets are particularly vulnerable. Some parts of the country have had a long history of high unemployment. The Highlands and Islands, Dumfries and Galloway and Strathclyde Region all tend to have unemployment rates above the Scottish average. In very small areas extremely high levels of unemployment can be recorded, particularly if there has recently been a large plant closure in the locality.

The unemployment experience of different occupational groups also varies widely. Professional people rarely experience unemployment: amongst unskilled labourers it is a fairly common occurrence. It is also true that some industries are more prone to cycles in activity, thus causing corresponding cycles in unemployment. To understand this more fully, we need to look closely at the way in which Scotland's 1.9 million employees are distributed between industries.

EMPLOYMENT BY SECTOR

Changes in the overall level of employment and its composition reflect gradual changes in the pattern of demand for goods and services and in levels of productivity. With these changes have come corresponding movements in the 'derived' demand for labour.

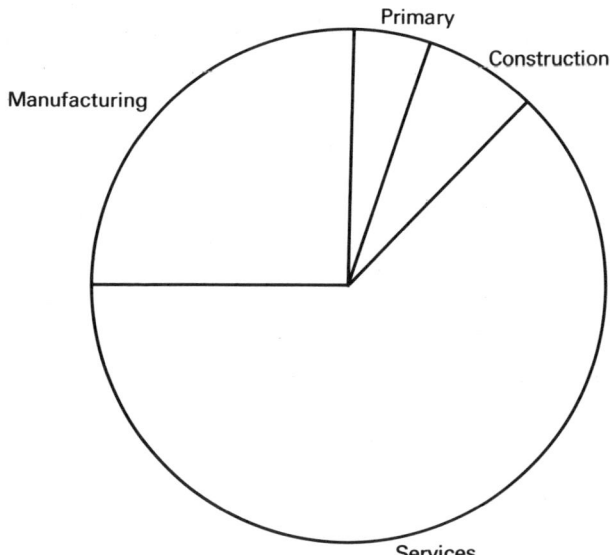

Fig. 6.2   Distribution of employment in Scotland, June 1981

The decline in the manufacturing sector has had a profound effect on the Scottish economy in the last twenty years. In 1961 Scotland had about 728 000 manufacturing employees: by 1981 this figure had been reduced to 489 000. This decline is due partly to improvements in productivity and partly to Britain's gradual loss of its once pre-eminent position in world trade. Less than one Scottish worker in four is now employed in producing manufactured goods (see Fig. 6.2).

Until recently, the decline in manufacturing was offset by a compensating rise in service employment. Professional, educational and legal services have expanded rapidly. There has also been a well-publicized increase in the numbers employed in public administration from 131 000 in 1971 to 149 000 in 1981.

The oil industry has had a significant, but not massive, effect on the Scottish labour market. In 1978, 50 000 Scottish workers owed their employment directly to North Sea oil. The effect of oil on the government's finances (oil revenues in 1981/82 amounted to £6.4 billion!) has been much more important than its direct effects on the Scottish labour market (see Chapter 20).

WAGES AND BARGAINING

Employment is not the only important economic variable determined within the labour market. Wage levels are of critical importance in any economy. They play an important part in determining consumption, profits and the rate of price inflation. In turn, wage levels themselves depend on the relative bargaining strengths of employers and employees and on the institutional structure of wage negotiation. In manufacturing industry, trade unions often negotiate a nationwide agreement on minimum rates of pay. Bargaining to secure a wage rate above this minimum is normally conducted at the local level. In services there is a wider spread of methods of pay bargaining. Some occupations use nationwide scales from which no deviation is permitted while many small service-sector employers strike a bargain with their employees with little or no regard for conditions and remuneration elsewhere.

Since they developed at a time when very few females actually worked, the trade unions have traditionally been dominated by males. With their roots in the male-dominated manufacturing sector, the union movement has only gradually adapted to the increasing importance of services. The traditional type of craft union has gradually been superseded by larger, conglomerate unions which cover a whole range of occupations and skills and by unions from sectors where employment has actually been rising. Recessions have an adverse effect on trade unions, particularly those in the manufacturing sector. As unemployment rises, membership dwindles, leaving many unions in difficult financial circumstances. Unemployment also weakens unions' bargaining positions: employers are aware that they have greater opportunities to replace existing staff when unemployment is high. As might then be expected, the number of working days lost through strikes tends to fall as unemployment rises (see Fig. 6.3). There is a tendency for unemployment and working days lost through strikes in Scotland to move in opposite directions.

Trade unions comprise one group of institutions out of a number which are closely involved in the labour market. The government, through the Department of Employment and Manpower Services Commission, also has a heavy institutional

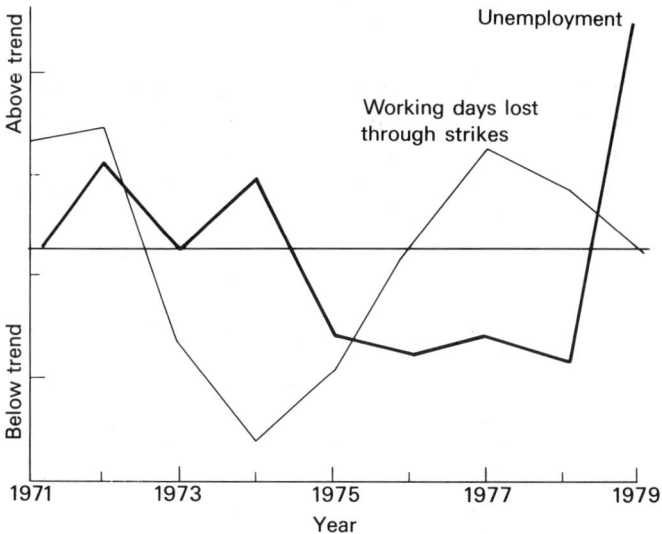

Fig. 6.3 Cycles in unemployment and working days lost through strikes

involvement. These agencies basically try to make the labour market work more effectively and also attempt to alleviate some of the problems which already exist. The Manpower Services Commission, for example, operates the Special Employment Programmes which have been principally aimed at smoothing the transition for young people from school to working life. Making the labour market work more effectively is of prime concern to policymakers. Overall economic efficiency cannot be attained if the labour market is functioning inefficiently. Yet because such a high proportion of the population have a stake in the labour market and because it is intimately linked with many aspects of human welfare, there are inevitably a great number of conflicting interests concerned with its behaviour. While this makes the labour market an intriguing area of study for economists, many politicians despair at the difficulties confronting any proposal aimed at changing its behaviour.

Earnings and hours of work vary considerably among different types of workers (see Table 6.1). Equal pay legislation has not meant that the sexes receive equal rates of pay. Women are far

TABLE 6.1   *Earnings and hours, Scotland and Great Britain, April 1981*

		Average weekly earnings (£)	Of which overtime (£)	Average weekly (hours)	Of which overtime (hours)
Scotland					
Males:	Manual	124.8	17.0	44.9	5.0
	non-manual	161.8	5.6	38.8	1.6
Females:	Manual	73.3	2.6	39.8	1.0
	non-manual	92.5	1.1	36.4	0.4
	part-time	33.8		20.9	
Great Britain					
Males:	Manual	121.9	14.8	44.2	4.5
	non-manual	163.1	4.6	38.4	1.3
Females:	manual	74.5	2.4	39.4	1.0
	non-manual	96.7	1.1	36.5	0.4
	part-time	33.0		19.6	

Workers are full-time unless otherwise stated.

more concentrated in poorly paid types of work. Whether these types of work are poorly paid *because* the workers are mainly female is difficult to demonstrate with certainty. Part-time female workers, a growing proportion of the workforce, are poorly paid even relative to other females. In 1981 their average hourly earnings were £1.62 compared with £1.84 for manual females, the next most poorly paid group.

Non-manual workers tend to receive more than manuals and also enjoy significantly shorter hours. This is true both for Scotland and for Great Britain as a whole. One noticeable difference between Scotland and Great Britain, however, is that male manual workers are, on average, better paid in Scotland whereas all other categories of full-time worker receive lower average weekly earnings. This advantage which Scottish male manual workers enjoy can mostly be explained by their higher overtime earnings. Their standard hourly rates of pay are actually marginally less than those in Great Britain as a whole.

Hours of work also vary considerably among groups. Although lip service is often paid to the desirability of achieving a shorter working week, there has been little movement in that direction in the last years. The tendency is for normal hours to fall but these are made up by additional overtime working. Females are more reluctant to work overtime because of family commitments. Also, there are legal restrictions on the hours which children and females work.

7

Farming Today

LYLE MOAR

Agriculture contributes about 2 per cent of Scotland's gross national product and uses approximately 86 per cent of Scotland's land area. Spending on food in Scotland accounts for about 25 per cent of the household budget. With an inelastic demand for food, households would face severe financial pressures and uncertainties if retail food prices were permitted to fluctuate widely.

Whilst much of the spirit of free trading remains in agricultural markets the industry was in fact one of the first to receive direct government aid. Indeed the role of government has been the single most important factor determining trends in agricultural markets since the 1930s. Although it has taken many forms over the past fifty years intervention has always attempted to promote price stability. Efficient and steady markets ensure that supplies will be maintained and protect consumers from wide fluctuations in the prices of their essential food purchases.

EMPLOYMENT AND FARM SIZE

Scottish farming is essentially an industry of small, family controlled businesses: 45 per cent of farms use *only* family labour, whilst 90 per cent have family participation, most of which is in a management role. Just under 60 per cent of farms are operated by the owner. Compared with other forms of industrial activity even the largest units are relatively small – the average is just over forty employees per unit.

Between 1970 and 1980 employment on farms fell (Fig. 7.1). This was mainly among full-time employees, with a small increase in part-time, casual and seasonal employment.

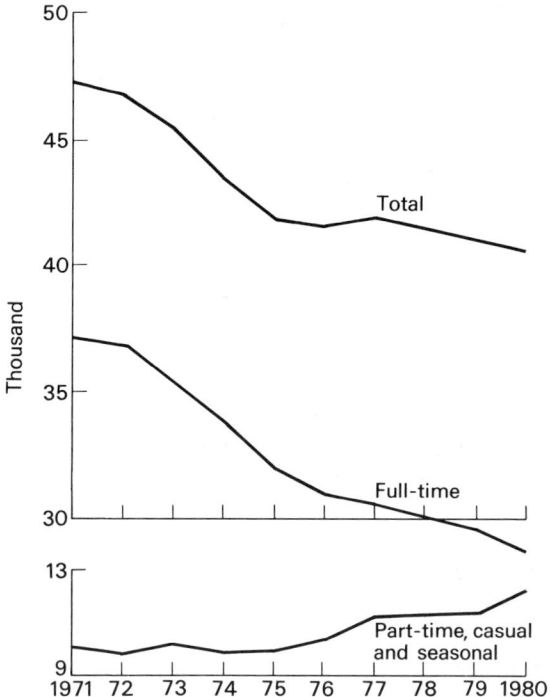

Fig. 7.1   Scottish employment in agriculture

Perhaps the most visible change on Scotland's landscape has been the increase in forestry. Recently about 20 000 hectares of agriculture land has been lost each year to forestry, housing, roads, recreation facilities or hydroelectric schemes, with forestry regularly absorbing 95 per cent of these hectares.

Within Scotland there are regional variations in farm size. For example, just over 50 per cent of the smallest units are concentrated in the north-west of Scotland where crofting is a dominant activity (see Box. 7.1). At the opposite end of the size spectrum over 60 per cent of the largest units are located in the Highlands.

BOX 7.1   *Crofting*

Crofting is unique to Scotland and is concentrated in the counties of Argyll, Caithness, Inverness, Orkney, Ross and Cromarty, Sutherland, and Shetland. Crofting is a type of farm tenure. As a result of the security and protection of tenancy provided by Parliament in 1886 most crofts have generally been worked by succeeding generations of one family. However, economic and social changes have highlighted the rigidities of the 1886 Act. Crofters were tied to an outmoded landlord–tenant relationship which effectively curtailed incentives to develop the crofts.

Since the 1976 Crofting Reform Act crofters have the right to own and employ the assets and improvements which they and their forebears have created, frequently from their own funds. One consequence has been that crofters can now offer these assets as security to the banks in order to generate capital for further improvement work.

The number of crofts has fallen steadily over the past decade, but since 1976 there has been an increasing number of crofters purchasing their croft units.

Number of crofts

Year	No. of crofts	No. of owner-occupiers
1973	18 196	
1974	18 149	
1975	18 111	
1976	18 070	868
1977	18 050	964
1978	18 032	1081
1979	17 997	1290
1980	17 894	1507

Typically crofting land is poor, and this, combined with a harsh climate and distance from major agricultural markets, restricts the range of farming options open to crofters. Most crofts are unable to provide a full income for the family. Less than 5 per cent of crofters depend on agriculture for their whole livelihood. Generally, most crofts are only worked part-time, and traditionally the crofter has combined either fishing, forestry or weaving with farm work. This pattern is beginning to change as crofters are increasingly becoming long distance commuters (to work offshore for the oil industry or in cities and on lowland farms). The size of croft is measured in terms of the labour input required rather than by land area. Approximately 70 per cent of crofts are worked for less than 40 man days per year whilst a further 26 per cent only require between 40 and 250 man days labour.

Although crofting generates only a small proportion of Scottish agriculture's share of the economy it plays an important role in maintaining rural employment in some of the most remote areas of the UK. A number of specific aid schemes are available to crofters to help to improve their crofts. These include The Crofting Counties Agricultural Grants Scheme and the Crofters Building Grants and Loans Scheme.

OUTPUT AND PRICES

The total value of agricultural output has grown only slowly over the past decade (see Fig. 7.2) but within this total there has been a continual change in the structure of agricultural production. Up to 1975 both crops and livestock expanded rapidly. Since then both have experienced wide fluctuations in terms of both the volume and the value of output of the various product categories.

Price and quantity fluctuations are to be expected in a market system. Most industries facing this problem organize their operations to cope with any sudden reversals. Manufacturing firms, for example, make a wide range of goods so they are less reliant on the market for a single product. The opportunity of farmers to diversify is limited to a large extent by the small size of most farms. This is especially true in Scotland where a high proportion of the land is *marginal* and is suitable for only certain agricultural activities. Thus, agriculture suffers more severe fluctuations than other sectors.

The prevailing market prices act as signals to farmers to help them to plan their future operations. Information on prices is published in local and national newspapers as well as the specialist agricultural press. Since this information is available to all farmers it should be no surprise, therefore, that many reach broadly similar conclusions. Consequently, when potato prices are high in one year this will encourage more farmers to plant potatoes for the following year. This occurred in the mid 1970s when the

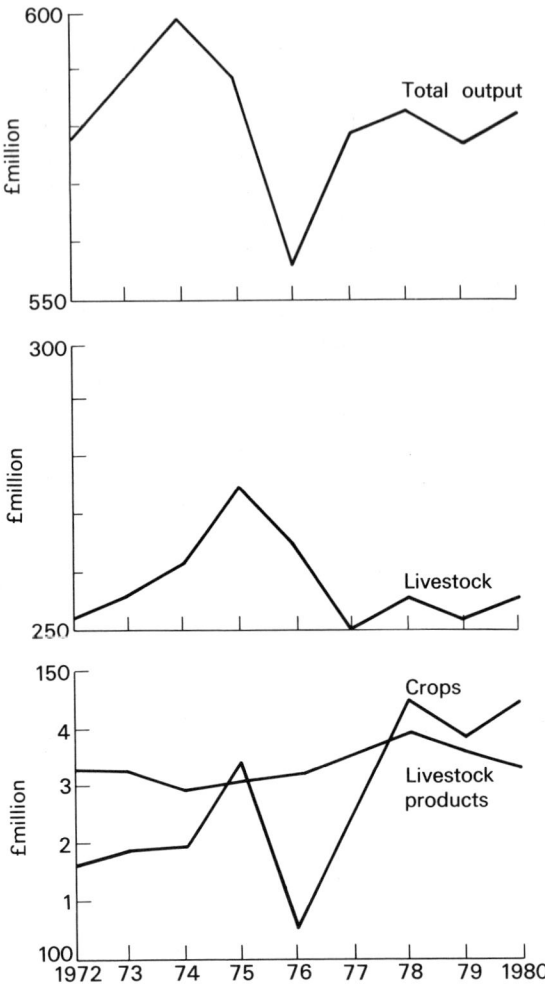

Fig. 7.2   Scottish output of agricultural products (1975 prices)

poor harvest in 1975 reduced supplies in the following year. Potato prices rose. Farmers then planted more potatoes and supplies increased in subsequent years, forcing prices down. Economists have developed the 'cobweb model' as an explanation of the wide price and quantity fluctuations in agricultural markets which result from reactions to price changes (see Box 7.2).

BOX 7.2   *The cobweb model*

The cobweb model was originally developed (in the USA before the Second World War) to analyse the tendency for the price of hogs to rise to a peak, fall to a trough then rise again. Since then it has frequently been applied to other agricultural markets where prices vary cyclically. It is a dynamic model which examines price and output responses over a number of seasons or years. In particular, the model shows whether prices and quantities are moving towards or away from an equilibrium.

The supply curve indicates the amount farmers intend to produce *next* season given a price *this* season. Once these plans are made they cannot be changed and farmers must sell their harvest next season at whatever price the market dictates. The inelasticity of *current* supply means that excess demand results in price rises. Given the perishable nature of much agricultural produce, excess supplies often cannot be stored and market prices are depressed.

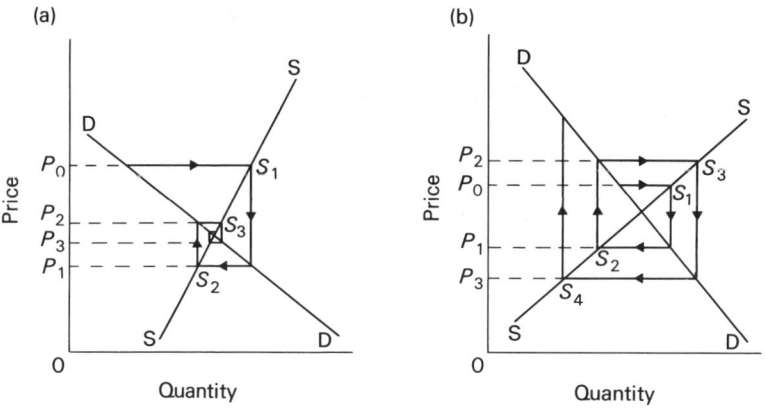

Box 7.2   The Cobweb Model

In Fig. (a) with a current market price of P_0 the farmers prepare to produce S_1 in the next season. But to clear in season 1 they must accept a price P_1. Thus, in season 1 the farmers will only plant S_2 for season 2, but will find that he will actually obtain price P_2. Following this procedure, the market gradually moves nearer a stable equilibrium. Such convergence occurs when *planned* supply is relatively price inelastic and demand is relatively price elastic. The market could, however, be unstable and unable to move towards an equilibrium (as in Fig. (b)). This situation arises when supply is relatively price elastic and demand is relatively price inelastic.

There are two separate processes of adjustment involved in the cobweb model; (a) given a price, farmers adjust supplies for the coming season, and (b) for a given supply, price adjusts to clear the market. The model has not been popular with farmers because it implies that they never learn from their experience of market trading!

Developments in farm technology are widely disseminated by agricultural societies, machinery suppliers, television and radio programmes for farming, a number of farming magazines (many of which are produced specifically for Scottish farming interests) as well as informally among farmers themselves. Farming communities are noted for a high degree of cooperation and work sharing.

Some of these features correspond to the economists' model of perfect competition where a large number of small firms are price takers in the market and where technological information is available to all. Although there are broad similarities between farming units and the firm in the model of perfect competition, there are important features of agricultural markets which suggest that this model may not be entirely appropriate as the basis for predicting the farmers' responses to price/quantity fluctuations.

Under perfect competition a farmer will be required to minimize long-run costs and to use the least-cost method of production. Failure to do so would force some farmers out of the industry in the long run. Yet despite evidence that small units in farming have hardly ever been viable, the rate of failure of farm businesses is very low. Indeed, many of those leaving the industry do so for tax or retirement reasons rather than as a direct response to the economic pressures which may make farms unprofitable. In short, some characteristics of the rational profit-maximizing firm depicted in perfect competition are exhibited by Scottish farmers hardly at all, although it is true that over the long run the number of farms has gradually declined. How do we explain this paradox? There are two reasons.

Increased bank borrowing. Over the past few years farm incomes have been falling. The growth in output (see Fig. 7.2) has not been enough to overcome the sharp rises in the costs of farm inputs. In 1980, for example, average prices for inputs rose by 14 per cent whilst output prices increased by only 6 per cent. Farmers, in their attempts to reduce costs, have tended to replace labour with capital equipment. This has been achieved by many farmers greatly increasing their borrowing from the banks. Advances from Scottish banks to farmers have increased by over 200 per cent in the four-year period from 1977 to 1981. Meanwhile the cost of borrowing, the rate of interest the farmers have to pay, has risen as a result of central government pressures and national economic policies.

The willingness of banks to lend these sums is partially related to the sharp increase in land values over the same period. Land, it must be emphasized, is the farmer's most important asset. However, it is also a difficult asset to convert into cash without destroying the farm itself, and this most farmers are reluctant to do. Nevertheless the banks have been prepared to accept it as collateral for loans. But farmers are not putting all these funds into new capital equipment. Rather, a high proportion has been used for current spending: salary costs, overheads, materials and other current expenditures. Thus it is likely that in the near future some farmers may no longer be able to meet their increased bank commitments since without the new equipment there is unlikely to be a significant increase in output.

Indeed, it is surprising that the banks, aware that loans are largely to meet current expenditures, have lent so generously, irrespective of the rise in land values. A cardinal rule in banking has always been never to lend money to firms to cover outstanding debts. This is exactly what the banks have been doing when lending to farmers. The banks, of course, may regard agriculture as a special case because of the nature of agricultural production which has always received preferential treatment from government and other funding agencies. Farmers deal closely with the rural banks and the bank managers recognize the important economic role farmers have in the rural areas. In many ways the farmers are the lynchpin of the rural economy. Despite the long-run decline, farming remains the most important source of rural employment. Farmers have strong linkages with local industries, sustaining numerous jobs in local agricultural suppliers, machinery distribution and servicing, and veterinary services as well as village shops and other non-farming businesses in the villages. Similarly, the farmers' output provides a major input of raw material to the food processing industries in Scotland, which themselves represent approximately 5 per cent of Scottish gross national product. In technical terms the income and employment multipliers of farming investments are relatively high throughout the rural economy. In addition, they help to ensure that a high proportion of the value added associated with various stages of food production is retained in Scotland.

Government support. Clearly the performance of the agricultural sector can have serious consequences for major sectors of the Scottish economy, and especially those located in the rural areas. Governments recognize that the survival of the rural economy justifies special assistance and that there are welfare and strategic reasons to maintain a constant domestic (British) supply of foods, to protect the population from wide price variation and to provide incentives to maintain and increase farm production.

GOVERNMENT POLICIES FOR AGRICULTURE

Over the past fifty years a wide range of agricultural policies have been introduced in order to; (a) raise farm incomes, (b) reduce the wide fluctuations in prices paid to farmers for agricultural products, (c) protect consumers, (d) improve efficiency on farms. The main types of assistance to farmers favoured by UK governments have been; (a) price guarantees, (b) production grants and subsidies, (c) grants for capital improvements, (d) grants and loans for other improvements, (e) support for agriculture in special areas (such as in the Highlands and Islands of Scotland), (f) assistance for specific purposes – these include drainage schemes, Beef Premium Scheme, building grants, Brucellosis Incentive Scheme, calf subsidies.

Before Britain joined the EEC in 1973 these policies relied on a system of deficiency payments which operated by allowing consumers to purchase food at prevailing world prices (which are generally lower than in the UK), whilst farm incomes were raised by payments from the exchequer.

Thus the distortion of the market is minimized. The world market price is paid by the customer and determines the volume of domestic production. If the market price is less than the production cost the 'deficiency' is paid as a subsidy to the farmer and domestic supply is maintained. This allows farmers to continue producing certain agricultural products, albeit more expensively than in other countries, and ensures availability of supplies as well as reducing the UK's dependence on imports.

In the UK, where exchequer payments are used to subsidize food prices and tax revenues are raised through a progressive system of personal taxation, food subsidies represent an important form of income redistribution.

Common Agricultural Policy

In 1973 the UK joined the EEC and had to alter agricultural policy to conform with the Common Agricultural Policy (CAP). The UK was allowed a five-year transition period in which to adjust food prices to full EEC levels. Although the objectives of the CAP are broadly similar to previous UK agricultural policy consumer protection from high food prices is less important.

The CAP relies primarily on price guarantees and protection for agricultural markets. There are two approaches: first, the CAP relies on threshold prices and/or export restrictions to protect the markets from *both* high and low prices; secondly, intervention prices and/or direct payments to producers guarantee a minimum price for a range of basic agricultural products. The CAP policies concentrate on influencing the supply side of agricultural markets; this is generally done by restricting the available supplies. As a consequence prices to consumers are raised and farm incomes are protected.

The CAP sets 'intervention prices' at which the national agencies are compelled to purchase all relevant commodities offered to them. Intervention prices are generally required just after harvest time when supplies are at their highest and market prices are at their lowest. Where possible the authorities release stocks back on to the market when prices start to rise. If prices remain at a low level (intervention stocks are generally only a small proportion of total supplies) then the authorities are unable to return stocks to the market because prices would be forced even lower. The resulting stockpiling of certain food products, notably butter, milk, wine and beef, has proved a sensitive issue to consumers throughout the EEC, especially when they have been sold to non-EEC countries at reduced prices.

Apart from the price guarantees and subsidies the CAP has a number of special programmes which it sponsors in conjunction with each member state. These include modernization aid to help low income farms attain incomes comparable with local non-farming incomes, help for giving up farming (this is paid mainly to farmers nearing retiring age), farming in difficult areas (this is for areas prone to depopulation and where agricultural production is constrained by climate or terrain).

The CAP budget dominates EEC expenditure. However, there is mounting pressure to expand non-agricultural schemes, which will reduce the CAP's share of EEC funds (see Chapter 22).

With floating exchange rates between member states international trade in agricultural produce becomes complicated. The CAP has, therefore, imposed 'Green Rates' which are essentially a form of fixed exchange rates used only for agricultural produce. Otherwise, the support prices would change on a daily basis.

To compensate for the difference between the 'Green' and actual exchange rates a system of subsidies and levies is adopted. These are called monetary compensatory amounts (MCA). When the actual exchange rate is above the green rate then exports from the UK receive a subsidy, whilst imports are taxed, but if it is below the green rate then exporters must pay a levy and importers receive a subsidy. The MCAs are required to offset currency effects, ensuring that EEC members trade on equal terms, and are financed from the EEC budget (see Fig. 7.3).

Scotland is more dependent on farming than the rest of the UK and, therefore, when CAP policies swing in favour of the UK it is likely that Scotland will be one of the main beneficiaries. The early concern about joining the CAP arose from the unfamiliar methods of providing aid to farming. These initial fears are now largely overcome, although there are many problems remaining. Farmers are actively involved in lobbying for changes to the CAP which will protect the long-term interests of Scottish farming. It is likely that the long-run decline in agricultural

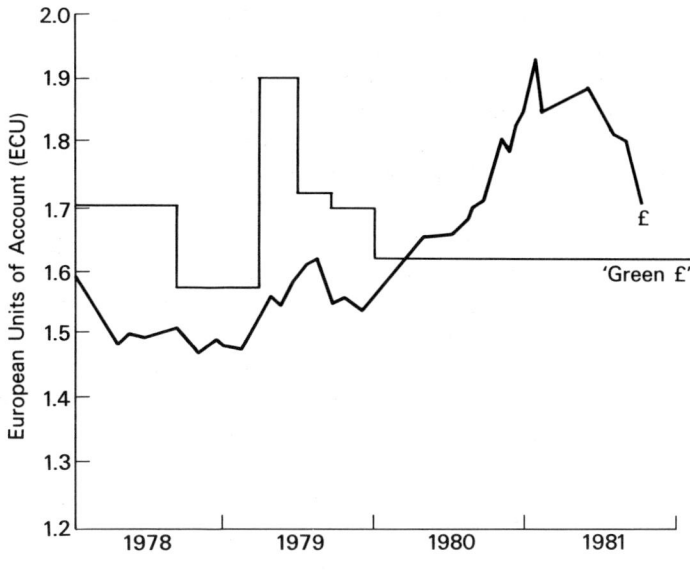

Fig. 7.3   Changes in Sterling and Green £

employment has now levelled out in Scotland; thus the industry should be able to concentrate on implementing new techniques to ensure a stable and even prosperous future for Scottish agriculture.

The Drawbacks of Intervention

The preoccupation with the need to intervene in agriculture often obscures the drawbacks of support and aid.

(1) Stabilizing farm prices may perpetuate production patterns which are not conducive to the efficient allocation of resources. By being insulated by the CAP against the rigours of the market small and inefficient French farmers, for example, continue to operate.

(2) Stabilizing prices at levels higher than those that might prevail *on average* in an unrestricted market results in excess supplies, for example, the 'wine lakes' and 'butter mountains' of the EEC.

(3) Artificially high prices to producers involve a welfare loss to consumers.

(4) Price supports for a particular product are usually non-discriminatory and subsidies are, therefore, provided not only to poor farmers but also to the relatively rich.

8

Tourism

MARK BROWNRIGG

Tourism is a major industry in the Scottish economy. Its activities cover not only holiday accommodation provision but also a wide range of other industries via tourists' expenditure on other items such as food, souvenirs, entertainments and travel. While the total number of tourists in Scotland has been between 12 and 13 million each year over the period 1973–80, there are some signs of a recent decline in the industry's output. First, the total of tourists from Great Britain has fallen from 12.5 million to 11.7 million, against a smaller increase in the number of overseas tourists from 800 000 to 1.2 million. Secondly, there has been a major switch by British tourists from long-stay to short-stay holidays, so that total bednights have fallen from 70 million to 55 million – again out-weighing the minor increase by overseas tourists from 9.8 million to 11.1 million bednights. Consequently spending, in 1980 prices, after rising to a peak of £829 million in 1977 has fallen steadily to £650 million in 1980.

The Scottish industry has performed less well than its UK counterpart over the period. Tourist spending in the UK market increased in real terms by 74 per cent from 1973 to a 1977 level of £4.8 billion, £2.6 billion by UK residents and £2.2 billion by overseas visitors. This revenue accounts for 6 per cent of all consumer spending.

Over the period 1970–80, foreign tourists' spending in the UK rose from £518 million to £3488 million in current prices, or from £977 million to £1655 million in constant 1975 prices (with a peak of £1999 million in 1977). Against this, there has been a marked switch of UK tourist demand from domestic to foreign holidays, so that UK consumer expenditure abroad rose from £420 million to £2585 million in current prices, or £867 million to £1676 million in constant 1975 prices. Nevertheless, export receipts from tourism have exceeded import payments by a substantial margin in each year.

The contribution of the tourist industry to the Scottish labour market is a little difficult to assess. Jobs are spread over many important service industries, though mostly in hotels and catering, distribution (shops, etc.) and transport (see Table 8.1). Also, many jobs are of a part-time and seasonal nature. A part-time seasonal job in, say, a guest house is scarcely comparable in its economic impact with a full-time, full-year job in, say, a new manufacturing project.

TABLE 8.1   *Scottish employment in tourism, 1976*

	(%)
Hotels and catering	52
Distribution, transport and other services	32
Manufacturing (crafts, souvenirs, food processing, etc.)	12
Primary (agriculture, market gardens, fisheries)	2
Construction	1

The tourist industry in Scotland in 1980 supported the equivalent of about 24 800 full-time jobs (FTEs) directly (i.e. in establishments where tourists actually spend their money) and a further 25 300 FTEs indirectly in other industries servicing these establishments and the people working in them. Over the period 1973–80, the total of FTE employment in the tourist industry declined from 56 000 to 50 000 jobs, with the biggest loss component (about 4500 FTEs) affecting the 'direct' employment sector.

DEMAND AND SUPPLY

Two trends emerge from this analysis. First, for the UK as a whole, tourism has made a major economic contribution over the 1970s, but its rate of development has faltered since 1977.

Secondly, the Scottish tourism industry has declined more than in proportion to that of the UK as a whole.

Demand

The main influences on *demand* in the holiday market are: (a) the capacity of the customer to spend on holiday, determined by the level of *disposable income*, and (b) the *purchasing power* of this disposable income, determined by the relative movement of tourism prices and, for tourists from abroad, the exchange valuation of sterling.

If the national market is split into, first, its growth phase up until 1977, and then the subsequent years, we can see that up to 1977:

(1) Real disposal income increased fairly steadily over the first period in all of our main 'customer' nations, i.e. America, Germany, France, Scandinavia, Australia/New Zealand and Japan. Over the same period, devaluation and then floating exchange rates tended to increase the purchasing power of these nations. These two factors combined to create a very substantial growth in export sales of tourism over the period and, while London has always benefited most from international tourism, all UK regions, including Scotland, derived a clear benefit.

(2) Trends in the domestic demand for tourism in the UK moved in the opposite direction. United Kingdom real disposable income began to decline and tourism prices were rising faster than consumer prices in general. Thus demand from UK residents for holidays in the UK as a whole fell from 83 million to 75 million trips over the period 1972–76 alone. For Scotland there was a decline from 10 million to 7 million holiday trips over the same period.

The years from 1977 to the present have merely confirmed these early signs of erosion within the market for tourism. Overseas demand for UK holidays has reflected three distinct sets of problems.

(1) The world recession has slowed down, or even reduced, the growth in real disposable income among our 'customer' nations.

(2)   The heavy weighting of wages in the labour-intensive
       tourism industry, when taken with our relatively higher
       rate of price inflation, has distorted the relative competi-
       tiveness of UK tourism.

(3)   Relatively high interest rates and North Sea oil have com-
       bined to increase the UK exchange rate; over 1977–80 the
       effective exchange rate of sterling against all currencies rose
       by about 21 per cent. Given the demand determinants iden-
       tified above, it is not surprising that UK international
       tourism receipts declined over the period.

At the same time, domestic demand for UK tourism has also
been influenced by these factors. Despite the rising levels of
unemployment within the UK – ironically, tourism has been one
of the main beneficiaries from spending of redundancy payments
– the higher purchasing power of sterling up till early 1981, taken
with lower international levels of inflation, has combined to
create a major diversion of demand from UK to overseas holidays.

Reflecting these forces, between 1977 and 1980 visits abroad
by UK residents grew by 52 per cent, while the number of
overseas visitors to the UK rose by only 1 per cent. Obviously
the Scottish tourism market has reflected these broad national
trends. But there have also been some unique features which have
left Scotland relatively worse off within the UK market for
tourism. In Scotland 75 per cent of domestic tourists come from
Scotland itself, or the north and north-west of England. But these
regions have suffered particularly from the UK recession, with
unemployment levels rising by about 41 per cent over 1976–80,
compared to the 30 per cent increase for Great Britain as a whole.
Secondly, the Scottish tourism industry has traded heavily in the
past on its remoteness, as well as its scenery; about 75 per cent of
all holiday trips in Scotland are made by car. While travel is still a
relatively minor *complementary good* in the overall holiday
package, there is some evidence that holiday and recreational car
trips are highly *price elastic*. These factors have combined to
reduce the volume of demand for Scottish tourism and, simultaneously, to change its geographical pattern towards a greater
concentration on the more central routes and areas.

Supply

Analysis of the supply-side characteristics of Scottish tourism would ideally examine features such as the numbers and size of productive units within the industry, and identify trends for profitability, growth and decline. It is here that the absence of a satisfactory series of data is particularly frustrating, and limits the scope of the analysis.

The largest sector of the tourist industry is concerned with the provision of accommodation. Table 8.2 gives some idea of the varied size and nature of production units within this sector, viewed through their 'output' for 1980.

TABLE 8.2 *Accommodation used by British tourists in Scotland, 1980*

	(%)
Licensed hotel	11
Small hotel/Guest house	9
Bed and breakfast	2
Rented	9
Static caravan	10
Touring caravan	7
Camping	4
Friends and relatives	43
Other	7
Total	100

Two figures underline the difficulties of making a systematic analysis of the industry. First, the large single category of accommodation used (43 per cent) was that provided by friends and relatives. Secondly, there must be some element of doubt over the figure of 2 per cent attributed to the bed and breakfast group. So great is the incidence of tax and social security evasion in the latter, that several studies have found it difficult to find reliable data. It is probable that the informal bed and breakfast trade has the same relationship to official tourism as the 'black economy' has to official statistics in the national context.

In any industry, supply will tend to adjust to reflect the changing pattern of consumer preference and demand. Given the ease of *entry to and exit from the industry* enjoyed by many sectors, this must be particularly true of tourism. In fact, accompanying the *income* effects of the declining demand there has been a pronounced swing of demand from hotels and guest houses towards self catering, reflecting, in part, the loss of traditional clients to overseas holidays, and, in part, an additional *substitution* towards the cheaper form of accommodation. Between 1974–80 accommodation usage of hotels and guest houses in Scotland fell from 24 per cent to 20 per cent, against the increase for self catering cottages and static caravans of 14 per cent to 29 per cent.

It could be expected that *investment flows* would mirror this swing. Indeed, for hotels the combination of lower overall tourist traffic and the switch within this to cheaper accommodation has reduced the occupancy rate for even the peak months of July and August, from 61 per cent and 69 per cent respectively in 1978 to 43 per cent and 52 per cent in 1981. Added to this low level of capacity utilization there has developed widespread competitive discounting in hotel tariff prices, which must carry some implications for profit, or return on investment. While there are no comprehensive data on hotel investment levels, there are signs in the Scottish Tourist Board's (STB) application approvals for assistance under the Development of Tourism Act of 1969, of a fall in real and monetary terms over 1979–81. At the same time, there has been a steady growth of self-catering capacity, supported by both the STB and the Highlands and Islands Development Board. This sector could have reached a situation of over-supply in simple physical terms. Indeed, there is evidence that, reflecting this, there are signs of a downturn in recent application approvals for the STB.

It seems, then, that the smaller and less formal sectors of accommodation have grown more quickly in recent years. It is also likely that peripheral areas have suffered particularly from rationalization forces within the industry. If so, this could have serious repercussions; the locational disadvantages of these remote areas for manufacturing industry has placed an undue responsibility for economic regeneration on tourism and its linked service industries. If tourism demand has declined there, it will not simply have reduced an important but supplementary source of income; it could cast doubts on the viability of the local economic base and undo many years of policy support and reconstruction.

Whatever the current problems for tourism in Scotland, or indeed the UK as a whole, there can be little argument that the industry provides a major source of economic activity and a major contribution towards external trade. It has not, however, been able to isolate itself from the influence of world and UK recession. It is both *income* and *price elastic*. Thus the slow down of growth in real disposable incomes both abroad and domestically has checked the growth in demand for tourism – although there is some evidence of asymmetry in income elasticity, in the sense that people are reluctant to cut down or forego holiday expenditure. Rising labour and fuel costs have affected adversely the relative price of the UK holiday package, and exchange-rate movements over 1977–80 have tended to exaggerate rather than damp down this loss of competitive edge. The result has been to slow down markedly the growth of high spending international tourism in the UK, and to accelerate the substitution by UK residents of foreign for domestic long-stay holidays, for long the staple of the UK industry.

With some degree of economic recovery both externally and domestically, there should be some return to the more buoyant growth in demand of the 1960s and 1970s. The extent to which the UK and the Scottish tourism industry can hold or increase their share of this market growth will depend upon the relative price of tourism in these countries.

9

Producers' Cooperatives

FRANK H. STEPHEN

Over the past ten years, cooperative organizations have attracted increasing attention. Among the most widely publicized co-operatives have been the *Scottish Daily News,* Kirby Manufacturing and Triumph–Meriden. But cooperative enterprises are not a recent development. Cooperation has long been practised through local cooperative societies, which in most Scottish towns have supplied groceries, footwear, hardware and drapery and paid members 'dividends' in relation to the value of purchases. Within the familiar cooperative societies, which are now increasingly controlled by the national Cooperative Wholesale Society, the aim was to reduce costs through bulk buying for their members as customers. During the past ten years, often promoted by the interests of the Highland and Islands Development Board in some of the remoter areas of Scotland, cooperatives have been encouraged also to serve members as suppliers; for example, farmers' and fishermens' cooperatives are also involved in bulk selling of members' output. This enables members to retain those profits which were previously paid to wholesalers (see Box. 9.1). Recent emphasis has been placed, however, on the importance of members as both owners and workers in individual, production ventures.

A producers' cooperative is essentially an enterprise owned and controlled by those working in it. Interest in workers' ownership and control may be traced to several inter-related factors.

(1) Cooperatives may be a means of safeguarding employment, especially when, as in recent years, there are few other employment opportunities. It has become commonplace when a firm

ceases trading or closes a plant for workers to propose the formation of a cooperative as an alternative to closure. Recently,
several cooperatives, Randolph Leisurewear in Buckhaven,
Grange Carpets in Monifieth, Craigton Bakery in Glasgow and
Inchinnan Engineering, have been formed after closures of firms
by previous owners.

(2) Cooperatives are often regarded as a means of achieving a
more democratic and equitable system of work and of moving
away from the familiar confrontations between workers and
managers. This is often associated with a political aversion to the
capitalist system.

(3) Extensive publicity has been given to the success of cooperatives abroad. The Mondragon cooperatives in the Basque region
of Spain, a group of over 80 separate enterprises, provide
employment for more than 15 000 people. Most significantly it is
highly successful in such fields as machine tool and domestic
electrical appliance manufacture. In other European countries,
particularly France and Italy, there are also thriving cooperative
sectors. Even the USA which tends to be identified as a highly
individualistic economy has a growing number of cooperatives
including some of the most successful manufacturers of plywood.

Cooperatives in Scotland tend to be relatively small and to
operate in unspectacular sectors. It is difficult to provide any
accurate estimate of the number of Scottish cooperatives, their
employment and the value of their output. This is because the
statistics collected and published by the government do not
separate out firms according to the form of ownership. Furthermore, not all cooperatives register themselves as such. Some are
registered companies limited by guarantee, some are partner-
ships, some are ordinary joint-stock companies and others are
registered with the Registrar of Friendly Societies. In January
1982 the Scottish Cooperatives Development Committee indicated that the number of recognized cooperatives in Scotland had
grown from 4 in 1977 to more than 30 with estimated employment of 300 and turnover of £3 million. Clearly this represents a
very small proportion of economic activity in Scotland. The
largest number of cooperatives comes under the industrial

BOX 9.1   *Co-Chomunn – community cooperatives*

There is a long tradition of cooperation in the Scottish Islands among farmers, crofters, fishermen, knitters and craftworkers, informally in the management of local township common grazing and more formally in purchasing and marketing co-operatives.

Encouraged by the Highlands and Islands Development Board (HIDB), twelve new community cooperatives – in gaelic, *Co-Chomunn* – have been set up in the Western Isles since 1977 with others proposed, some in the Highlands and the Northern Isles (see map, Fig. 9.1).

These are not strictly only producer cooperatives as modelled in this chapter, but are 'multi-functional' businesses. Typically they operate a variety of rural enterprises mainly in agriculture, fishing, building and manufacturing, and community services. They are directly owned and controlled by the community. Members buy shares and elect and control the management committee on the basis of one person, one vote.

For example, on Harris the members paid £25 per share to create *Co-Chomunn Na Hearadh* in 1979. The total capital raised was £12 000 which was supplemented pound for pound by the HIDB, who also provided a management grant plus their normal assistance for specific projects. The cooperative now has a more than £200 000 annual turnover on ten projects, including coal delivery, management of the Harris Craft Guild, craftshop and exhibition centre, ship chandlery and an expanding market-gardening operation. Importantly, it offers community services, including catering, a meeting hall and a mini-bus. It has created jobs for fourteen people, including part-time seasonal work.

Overall, the community cooperatives, many of which are very new and all of which are still expanding, have by May 1982, created 120 new jobs: 22 full-time, 80 part-time and the rest seasonal. Perhaps even more crucially, these are enterprises which though large and important in community terms are mostly unprofitable and too small for commercial enterprises. It is hoped they will help fight the continuing problems of emigration and community decline by developing, through self-help, community identity and self-confidence.

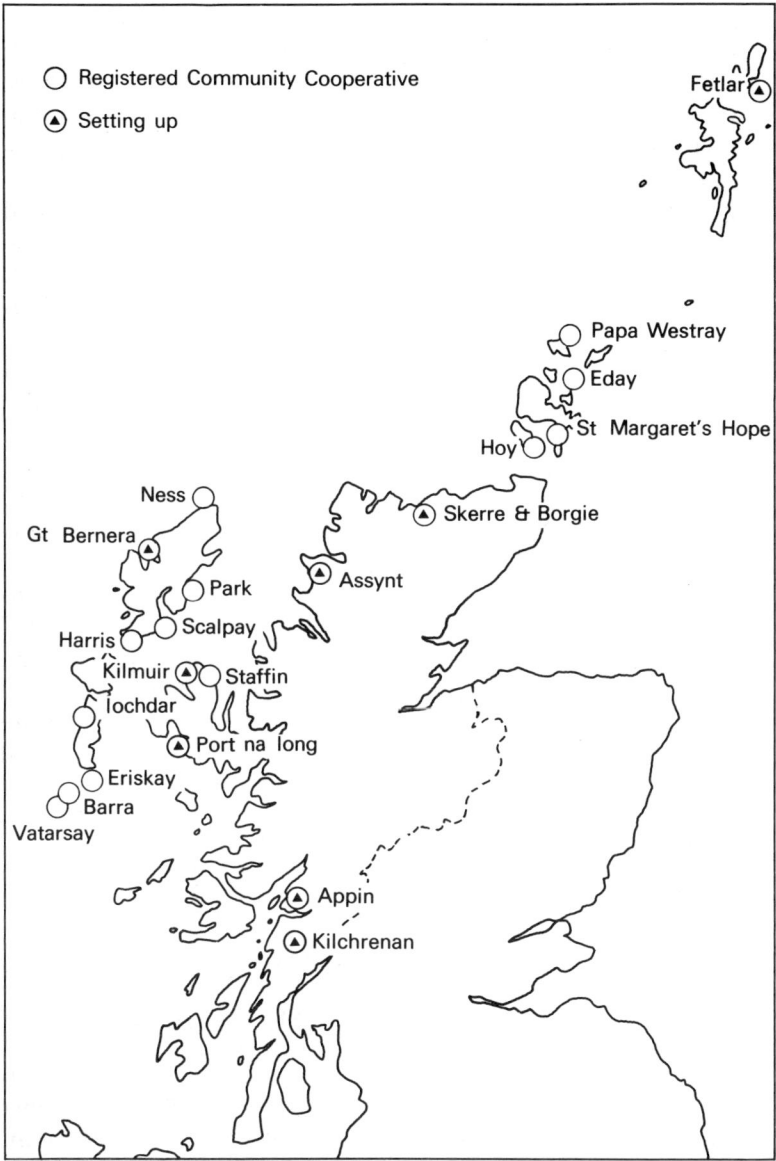

Fig. 9.1   Community cooperatives location map (May 1982)

heading 'Retail, distributive, catering and food processing' (see Table 9.1). Many of these are 'alternative' ventures in health foods and book-selling, with little likelihood of providing many jobs. The smaller number of cooperatives in engineering, footwear, clothing and textile manufacture will individually be larger and will provide more employment. The more recent ventures such as those in leisurewear, carpets, bakery and engineering suggest a shift away from 'alternative' activities into main-line business activities.

TABLE 9.1   *Producer cooperatives in Scotland, numbers by industry group, 1982*

Group	Number	Percentage
Advisory, consultative and educational	1	3
Building, house renovation and decorating, cleaning and waste recycling	5	15
Engineering, electronics and chemicals	3	9
Footwear, clothing and textile manufacture	5	15
Printing and publishing	4	12
Bicycle hire	1	3
Retail, distributive, catering and food processing	14	42
Total	33	

A SIMPLE MODEL OF A COOPERATIVE

To understand the performance and problems of cooperatives we may construct a very simple model. We assume:

(1)   that all workers have an equal say in how the firm is run and each receives the same share in the income of the cooperative after the costs of materials and of capital have been paid;

(2)   that the workers want to maximize their incomes from the

cooperative (this is different from the more usual assumption that firms aim to maximize their profits).

We shall see that the simple model predicts that; (a) in the *short-run*, cooperatives will employ fewer people than comparable profit-maximizing firms, and (b) in the *long-run*, cooperatives will be smaller and grow more slowly. While it is valid to compare theoretically the producer cooperative and the profit-maximizing firms it is important for us to recall that in practice, in Scotland at least, cooperatives have normally been set up in circumstances where private enterprise firms have in some sense failed.

The outcome for the behaviour of the cooperative of these assumptions is illustrated in Fig. 9.2 which depicts the *short run*, i.e. that period over which the capital stock is fixed but labour is variable. The curve ABC illustrates the *value of the marginal product* of labour (VMP) as employment in the firm rises. This is the *law of diminishing returns* in operation. The curve FBD outlines the relationship between the net income received by each worker and the number of workers in the cooperative. Its shape

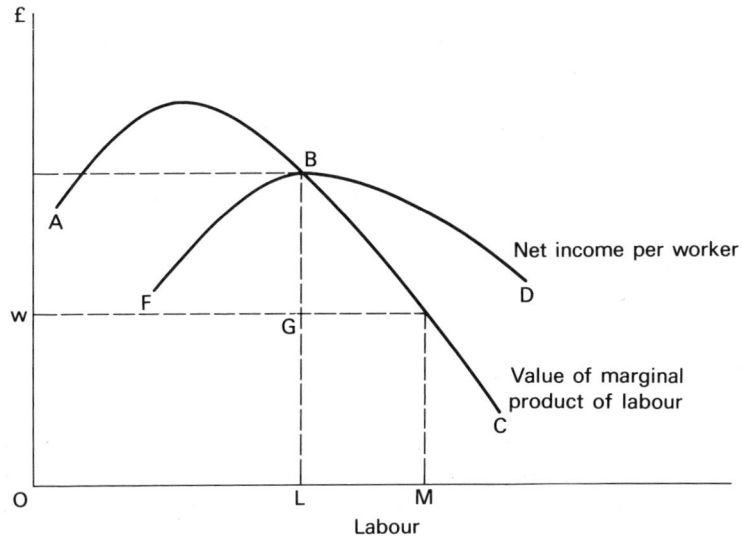

Fig. 9.2   A simple model of a cooperative

reflects falling output per worker as more workers are employed with a fixed capital stock.

If workers seek to maximize their incomes in the cooperative they will choose the level of employment OL. The reason for this can be seen by comparing the curves ABC and FBD. If employment expands beyond OL, income-per-worker will fall, e.g. if employment is expanded to OM income per worker falls to MF. Income per worker falls because each additional worker beyond L adds less to net revenue than the existing net revenue per worker, i.e. the value of the marginal product curve BC beyond OL lies below FBD. The point B, where the value of marginal product curve intersects with the net revenue per worker curve, is the highest point on FBD. Conversely, at levels of employment below B, net income per worker can be increased by expanding to the point B. Thus, because this is a cooperative controlled by workers who wish to maximize their income, the size of labour force which they will want to have, the *equilibrium* size, is OL given by point B.

This employment level differs from that of the conventional firm seeking to maximize profits. In the short-run, such a firm will operate with that labour force for which the value of the marginal product of labour equals the competitively determined wage rate. If the wage rate is w this firm's labour force will be OM. It pays the firm to expand employment beyond OL to OM because over that range each additional worker produces a greater value of output than the firm need pay him (w). Beyond OM, w is greater than VMP. Thus, economic analysis suggests that *in the short-run cooperatives will employ fewer people than a comparable profit-maximizing firm.*

Cooperatives are different from profit maximizing firms *in the long run* because they usually raise their capital in a different way. Historically many cooperatives have relied on the internal generation of funds for expansion for two reasons.

(1) Banks and other credit institutions are reluctant to lend to cooperatives because they doubt their commercial viability. This could, of course, be a self-fulfilling prophecy since the denial of capital will make any firm non-viable.

(2) Cooperatives themselves are often reluctant to raise money from such credit institutions since they feel that this will reduce

their independence and will represent a compromise with the capitalist system which many cooperative members are rejecting. Thus cooperatives rely to a large extent on generating their own funds for investment. For example, each worker initially contributed £250 in the Craigton Bakery and £100 in Randolph Leisurewear. In fact this is similar to the practice in many capitalist firms of relying on retained earnings to finance capital expenditure. However, there is a crucial difference between the cooperative and its capitalist counterpart based on the nature of ownership.

In the capitalist firm the owners are shareholders who each hold a number of shares in the firm. As the firm prospers or fails the value of these shares rises or falls. The stock market reflects the changing performance of the firm. When profits are made by the capitalist firm two things can happen; (a) the profits may be dispersed as dividends to the shareholders, or (b) some or all of the profits may be retained within the firm to finance future operations. In the latter case the shareholders receive a lower dividend. However, the retention of earnings will raise the value of the firm and, thus, the value of its shares will rise. The shareholder is giving up current dividend in exchange for an increase in the value of his long-run capital. If the stock market is a good judge in valuing companies, as evidence suggests it is, the shareholder will be indifferent between dividends and capital growth. He can always recoup foregone dividends by selling his shares.

It is unusual for shares in cooperatives to be traded in the same way as shares in a capitalist firm. The usual arrangement is that members purchase shares at a nominal figure and that these cannot be sold. Furthermore, in a 'pure' producers' cooperative share ownership is restricted to those working for the firm and dividends on shares are restricted to a nominal rate. Members are paid according to the work which they do in the cooperative. If a worker leaves the cooperative he loses all claim to income from it and his share cannot be sold to anyone else.

Consider now the cooperative in Fig. 9.2. If all net revenue is paid out to members they will each receive GB above the going wage rate w. Were some profits retained they could be used to finance new capital assets. However, these new assets might not generate higher earnings for some years to come. The workers currently employed may doubt whether they will remain members of the firm and, thus, may not reap the full benefits of their investment. This will be particularly true of workers nearing retirement or young workers who are likely to be mobile. Such groups will prefer to keep investment to a minimum and to disperse profits in higher wages. *Such behaviour will retard the growth of cooperatives* and may explain why *cooperatives remain small and relatively unsuccessful.* It may also explain why cooperatives are more prevalent in industries with a low capital : labour ratio.

If cooperatives raise more capital externally, more like profit-maximizing firms, then this model predicts that the long-run outcomes for the two types of firm are more similar.

PLYWOOD

A number of cooperatives have overcome this problem of slow growth caused by capital shortages by allowing their shares to be tradeable. The plywood cooperatives of north-western USA have tradeable shares, i.e. shares that may be bought and sold at values determined by the market. These shares entitle the holder to work in the firm, subject to the approval of existing members. However, current income from the cooperative to worker-shareholders is related to work done in the firm, not mere ownership of the share. The marketable share provides a means for workers to regain their incomes which have been retained by the cooperative. Consequently, the worker-manager in a plywood cooperative is likely to view the dividend/investment decision much in the same way as a capitalist shareholder. It is significant that the plywood cooperatives have one of the best economic records of all groups of cooperatives. One drawback with this approach is that it seems to encourage the purchase of shares held by retiring members by the other members and the hiring of non-member labour. This has been the experience of the plywood cooperatives many of which have developed to be little different from capitalist firms with a handful of worker-members and hundreds of employees. In fact, a number of these cooperatives sold out to conventional firms as the worker-owners neared retirement.

MONDRAGON

The most successful group of cooperatives is that of Mondragon in Spain. They overcome the capital accumulation problem in a compromise fashion. Some profits must be accumulated each year. The rest are retained within the firm but are credited as a form of savings account to each worker in proportion to his/her wages. Interest at a realistic rate is paid on these compulsory savings. Thus, workers do not lose all of the profits retained in the firm. When they leave the firm or retire these accumulated savings (which have in some cases come to tens of thousands of pounds) are repaid. When they join a Mondragon cooperative workers must put in significant sums of money, which may be paid in instalments. Again most of this may be withdrawn on leaving the firm. The Mondragon system has a mechanism, therefore, for assessing the worker's commitment to the firm. This may go some way to explaining the success of the group. However, other factors such as the political significance of the Basque area of Spain and the role in the group of its Banking Division may be more significant. The Bank, the Caja Laboral Popular, helps the cooperatives with their financing and with assessing their prospects and viability.

There is no organization in Scotland providing the services available to the Mondragon cooperatives through the Caja Laboral Popular. Three of the four Scottish cooperatives in 1977 were heavily financed by the Manpower Services Commission and collapsed when this funding was no longer available. Typically, the major source of funds is the workforce's contributions. Some grants and loans are available from District and Regional Councils, the Scottish Development Agency and the Industrial and Commercial Finance Corporation. To some extent shortfalls in cooperatives' entrepreneurial skills in marketing and finance can be met by assistance and advice from the SCDC.

Theory suggests that cooperatives are likely to be small and slow growing unless they adopt some means for allowing workers to capitalize foregone dividends. The American and Spanish experience shows that this can be done with apparent economic success. However, the example of the American plywood cooperatives also suggests that overcoming the economic problem may change its social structure in that the firm ceases to be a true cooperative. It would seem that it is difficult to meet the requirements of efficiency and democracy simultaneously.

PART III

Externalities, Merit and Public Goods

10

Scotland's Health

RICHARD G. BROOKS

Scotland's health record is poor compared with other developed countries. Scotland ranked thirty-first out of thirty-three advanced countries in deaths per thousand population in the late 1970s, but fared substantially better on what is perhaps a better indicator, infant mortality, being ranked twelfth (Table 10.1). Life expectation is lower in Scotland than in England and Wales: 68.2 years in 1978 for men as compared to 71.3 years in England and Wales and 74.5 years for women as compared to 76.3 years in England and Wales.

The main causes of death in Scotland are heart disease (44 per cent of all deaths); various cancers (22 per cent of male deaths, 20 per cent of female); bronchitis, pneumonia, and other lung disease (9 per cent of male deaths, 8 per cent of female). For some causes of death, for example heart disease and lung cancer, Scotland's experience is worse than that of England and Wales, although this is not the case for pneumonia, breast cancer, and bronchitis.

An unduly high proportion of deaths in Scotland result largely from habits such as smoking, alcohol abuse and poor diet, with environmental problems such as poor housing and sanitation being contributory factors. Smoking is linked with heart disease and lung cancer. In 1978 cirrhosis of the liver, caused by alcohol abuse, registered a male death rate of 88.6 per million population, and a female rate of 60.0 per million in Scotland in contrast to the rates for England and Wales of 42.8 and 35.8 per million respectively. Tuberculosis is likely to be more prevalent in poor environmental conditions, and again Scotland's male death rate at 24 per million is significantly worse than the 15.3 per million for England and Wales. The corresponding female rates are 7.82 and 5.16 per million respectively.

TABLE 10.1   *Deaths and infant deaths: International comparison*

	Deaths per thousand population	Infant deaths per thousand live births
Japan	6.0	8.9
Mexico	6.3	46.2
Israel	6.8	15.1
Canada	7.2	12.4
New Zealand	7.4	14.2
Australia	7.6	12.5
Spain	7.7	15.6
Albania	8.1	86.8
Netherlands	8.2	9.5
Yugoslavia	8.4	35.2
USSR	8.7	33.6
USA	8.8	14.0
Switzerland	9.0	9.8
Finland	9.2	9.1
Poland	9.3	22.4
Italy	9.6	17.6
Portugal	9.6	38.9
Romania	9.6	31.4
Norway	9.9	9.2
France	10.1	11.4
Denmark	10.4	8.9
Bulgaria	10.5	21.8
Irish Republic	10.5	15.7
Northern Ireland	10.5	16.1
Sweden	10.8	7.7
Czechoslavakia	11.5	18.7
Belgium	11.7	11.9
West Germany	11.8	14.7
England and Wales	11.9	13.2
Austria	12.5	14.9
Scotland	12.6	12.9
Hungary	13.1	24.3
East Germany	13.9	13.2

Note: With the exception of Albania (deaths 1971, infant mortality 1965), Portugal (infant mortality 1975) and Romania (both figures 1976) figures for all countries are for 1977 or 1978.

TABLE 10.2   *Beds and health personnel by Health Authority, 1979*

	Beds per thousand population	All staff and practitioners per ten thousand population
England	7.8	178.3
Wales	8.4	195.4
Scotland	11.3	240.3
Northern Ireland	11.1	241.5

Social classes IV and V (semi-skilled and unskilled manual occupations) fare much worse than classes I and II (professional, managerial, supervisory and skilled clerical occupations): this situation has remained unchanged for many years.

Scotland is well-provided with health facilities in UK terms. In 1979/80 Scotland had more beds per thousand population than any other region, the smallest average list size (number of registered patients) for general practitioners, and the second largest number of health personnel per 10 000 population, and was also second largest in expenditure at £198 per head (£163 UK average), or £1062 million in total (see Tables 10.2 and 10.3). However, the relative abundance of health facilities may simply reflect Scotland's poor health record and the need for more facilities and more spending.

The biggest change foreseen for the health service in Scotland is increasing demand for institutional care resulting from an increase during the 1980s in the number of people over seventy-five years old. Geriatric (old and infirm) patients tend to stay longer in hospital and it seems that fewer old people are cared for at home by their families.

TABLE 10.3   *General practitioners: List sizes, 1980*

	General medical practitioners, average list	General dental practitioners, persons per dentist
England	2247	3725
Wales	2086	4440
Scotland	1831	4006
Northern Ireland	2097	4105

There are two main economic mechanisms which can allocate resources among competing needs and adjust to a changing pattern of demand: the *market* or *planning and administration* by, or on behalf of, the government.

A market is a system of buyers and sellers who have come together to exchange a good or service. The price set by the market; (a) *transmits information* about what producers will accept and so about the cost of supply of products and about what customers are prepared to pay and so about their preferences, (b) *rations* the available supply among the purchasers, and (c) *rewards* the sellers and *satisfies* those who buy.

Health care may be provided through such a market. On the demand side, for example, patients could pay for surgery consultations, X-rays, laboratory tests, and room and board in hospital. The supply of doctors, nurses, clinics and hospital services would then respond to this demand.

There are four major drawbacks to market provision of health care.

Imperfect information. Demand for health care usually arises when a person feels ill and attends a doctor's surgery. The doctor then recommends the next step, which could range from 'do nothing' to arranging for the patient to enter hospital. The doctor is, thus, largely directing the nature of demand in the health-care system. Knowledge about an illness can be hard to obtain or understand by a patient, and doctors themselves may have difficulties in diagnosing illness. With such problems of information and uncertainty it is argued that health care is 'different' and it is thus inappropriate to adopt the private market approach that would prevail in, say, the provision of food or hair care, where knowledge of the product or service is readily available and easily understood.

Myopia. People tend to be short-sighted about their health when they are young and fit and to make inadequate provision for later years when they will be old and less fit. A caring society is unwilling to turn away the sick and needy from help.

Public goods. Some responsibilities for health care are clearly collective and cannot be parcelled out among individual consumers. While one could conceive of individuals making their own market arrangements for, say, sewage collection, the integrated nature of modern urban life makes it unlikely that such a system would lead to adequate provision of this service. This argument applies even more to infectious diseases, such as measles, whooping cough and chicken pox, where we *all* benefit from *individuals* being protected, for example, through vaccinations. Moreover, a 'free-rider' problem may arise: if I expect that you will pay for a collective service from which I will also benefit, it is in my interest to understate the amount I am willing to pay for the service.

Inequality. Provision of health care through the private market clearly means that you must be able to pay for it. Thus, rich people will be able to obtain more, and possibly better, health care. This, it is argued, is inequitable.

Thus, governments, including that in the UK, are often motivated to consider health care to be a good whose provision by the market would be inadequate and is more appropriately financed within the Welfare State through compulsory insurance contributions and taxation.

HEALTH CARE EVALUATION

Whether health care is publicly or privately provided it is important to assess the value of expenditures. Perhaps the need for formal evaluation is stronger in a publicly financed system, as a private market would respond to competitive pressures and provide the services that those who can pay want and require. In the public sector this direct market link between payment and provision does not exist, as health provision is largely financed independently of consumption, with the notable exceptions of prescription charges and dental and optical care.

There are two major aspects of evaluation. What does health care *cost* individuals and society in general? What are the likely *outcomes* of health interventions, whether curative, promotive or preventive? (See Box 10.1.)

BOX 10.1   *Health interventions*

Preventive medicine. Public measures aimed at preventing ill-health, for example, clean-water provision, adequate environmental sanitation, vaccinations.

Promotive medicine. The encouragement, through *health education,* of anything promoting good health, for example, campaigns to clean teeth, give up smoking, cut down on drinking. The Scotland 1982 World Cup Squad supported an anti-smoking campaign promoted by the Scottish Health Education Unit.

Curative medicine. The provision of facilities, personnel, drugs etc., to cure persons already ill. Typically, most hospital treatment is of a curative nature.

Curative medicine in the UK is overwhelmingly the responsibility of the National Health Service, though there is a relatively small, but growing, private-market sector. Preventive medicine is generally financed by local authorities. Promotive medicine is undertaken by specialist government agencies which are small and notoriously under-financed.

Costs

If, say, it is decided to provide more facilities for heart transplants then the *opportunity-cost* of this activity to society is the value of the next best use of the resources so provided. Every £100 000 spent on heart transplants is £100 000 *not* spent on something else. The opportunity-cost may be, for example, the inability to treat twenty mentally-ill patients. Clearly every health-care decision should be viewed in the light of other ways of spending money and using resources, including options *outside* the health system; £100 000 spent on health care is £100 000 not spent on, for example, schooling or submarines.

There are two types of costs: the *direct costs* of health care provision imposed directly on the health system, and the *indirect costs* of ill-health to society more generally.

Direct costs. The greatest *efficiency* of spending and resource use is usually a goal of any society. We would not want the health sector to use techniques which are unnecessarily costly (if cheaper alternatives are available to do the same task), or, perhaps, obsolete. We would not wish three persons to be doing a job capable of being done by two, or facilities and equipment to be unnecessarily duplicated. There is some evidence that some hospitals are too small, particularly for the provision of specialist care: they do not reap *economies of scale.* Specialist care typically involves high costs in terms of physical capital – often highly specific equipment and machinery – and human capital – the expertise of highly trained medical staff. Consequently, specialist units are often concentrated in particular hospitals, e.g. in Glasgow, cancer treatment is largely concentrated at the Western Infirmary, neurosurgery at the Southern General and cardiac surgery at the Royal and Western Infirmaries; in Edinburgh, renal transplants and neurosurgery are concentrated at the Western Infirmary and cardiothoracic surgery and respiratory intensive care at the Royal. On the other hand, large general hospitals can be too large, exhibiting *diseconomies of scale,* particularly in the management of such complex organizations but also in the provision of care. Currently, there are plans to decentralize the provision of paediatric care and move it away from large specialist children's hospitals in Glasgow and Edinburgh to smaller local hospitals and so cause less family separation and disruption.

Indirect costs. Ill-health has important *indirect* costs, in particular the opportunity-costs of time lost at work (society loses a sick person's output of goods and services), of reduced capabilities at the workplace, and of additional burdens placed on family and friends.

Outcomes

What does a country get for its health spending? Primarily, it is hoped, a healthier society. A healthy society should mean happier people, less suffering (from pain, for example) and greater outputs of goods and services. Thus, we are not concerned solely with the costs of ill-health and the costs of reducing it, but also with the outcomes of health care. We need this information in order to help make decisions about the allocation of resources to, and among, health care needs. Priorities are assessed in two main ways.

Effectiveness

If we have fixed sums of money available in any time period, this money should be used *effectively*. The greater reductions in death (mortality) and sickness (morbidity) we can obtain for the use of this money, the better. Alternatively, we could select a target, say, a reduction in infant mortality by a given figure, and investigate ways of achieving this reduction. The cheapest way would then be the most *cost-effective*.

Cost-Benefit Analysis

A more ambitious evaluation method, which explicitly attempts to value over time, and usually in money terms, both inputs and outputs, is *cost-benefit analysis*. It is more ambitious because, unlike cost-effectiveness analysis, where outcomes will often be expressed in physical terms (e.g. reduced sickness days as a result of treatment), cost-benefit analysis assesses health sector projects by comparing the money valuations of costs and *benefit* (*value* of outcomes) and compares them in the context of allocation of resources which might increase social welfare (see Box 10.2).

Despite criticisms, some methodological, and some moral or ethical, of the various approaches to health-service evaluation, few doubt that *some* attempt has to be made to relate costs of health services to outcomes.

Difficulties in health care provision, particularly in the National Health Service (NHS), which is most directly concerned with 'customers', are well known – long waiting lists for operations, queues at clinics, old and outdated buildings. However, these problems are more likely when the provision of any service is removed from the discipline of the competitive market, whatever other advantages that removal may have. *Excess demand* is likely when a service is free to the patient at the time of consumption and so the rationing function of price changes cannot operate (though, of course, the need to queue or wait may be an alternative partial form of rationing). Organizations which are not

---

BOX 10.2   *Cost-benefit analysis*

Cost-benefit analysis (CBA) has its origins in the USA in 1902 when it was seen that US Army engineering projects, such as harbour and river improvements, had benefits for the civil population who, it was argued, should therefore pay part of the cost.

During Roosevelt's 'New Deal' in the 1930s the method provided broader justification for vast public expenditure on large water resource projects such as irrigation and hydroelectric power schemes which could not satisfy commercial criteria but had extensive external benefits on employment and economic infrastructure.

Cost-benefit analysis is a practical way of assessing the desirability of public expenditure where it is important to allow for side effects and to look at repercussions in the further, as well as nearer, future. It implies the enumeration and evaluation of all the costs and benefits which will affect the economic welfare of society. Thus CBA provides a method of appraisal for *public* projects when the criteria for assessing private investments — profits or sales — are inappropriate.

In the UK, CBA was first applied to Britain's first motorway, the M1, in 1960 and since has mainly been applied to transport projects.

In the health sector there have been assessments of, for example, heart surgery, joint replacement, kidney disease programmes, BCG vaccinations, care of the elderly and water fluoridation.

The biggest problem is how to value the *benefits* of health care. Even items which could have a market generally do not in our system of public provision. There are very important *intangible* benefits too. What value can we place on saved (or lost) lives or reduced pain? Much ingenuity is now being shown in the development of *health status indicators* which give the promise of providing measures of changes in health status for individuals and society from health interventions.

---

required to earn profit in competitive markets can be inefficient in the *supply* of the service.

Such excess demand and potential supply-side inefficiencies offer opportunities for private medical care provided for profit. However, in Scotland, this market sector has traditionally been fairly small. In January 1981 there were ninety-five 'pay' beds in Scottish NHS hospitals available, though not exclusively reserved, for private patients. As a proportion of the total population this is a less intensive provision than in England where there are 2402 such beds. Not surprisingly, this is largely because NHS waiting lists are shorter in Scotland.

II

How Much is Enough?
Defence in Scotland

GAVIN KENNEDY

Scotland has a very important location and role in the defence of the UK and Western Europe. Her importance in the military 'frontline' follows from several inter-related factors:

(1)   Scotland is close to the 'Faroes Gap' – through which the ships, submarines, and aircraft of the Soviet Union must pass en route to and from their military bases in the Murmansk region. An ability to patrol that air and sea space, to monitor all movements through it and to intervene there effectively, if necessary, is a prime need for the defence of Britain and its allies.

(2)   Scotland is the home base of the British nuclear submarine Polaris missile fleet – the strategic deterrent – and this is prepared for service from the Clyde Submarine Base at Faslane and the Naval Dockyard at Rosyth. The US Navy has a similar facility in the Holy Loch for its Polaris and Poseidon submarines.

(3)   Scotland has three important airforce bases at Lossiemouth, Kinross and Leuchars, soon to be joined by a fourth at Stornaway, all with active roles in UK air and maritime defence.

(4)   Scotland also has an important Command and Control facility, without which no pilot could find his way to his targets and no ship could co-ordinate its activities with others. The radar and other communications centres located in various parts of Scotland, linked to their headquarters at Pitreavie, Fife, are integral links in NATO's Early Warning System.

The deployment of servicemen and women reflects Scotland's

TABLE 11.1   *Defence employment in Scotland*

Armed forces		18 000
of which (approximately):		
Royal Navy	9000	
Royal Airforce	4500	
Army	4500	
MOD civilians		22 000
MOD contractors		13 000
Total		53 000

military importance. Most – about three quarters of the total – are engaged in *maritime* and *air defence* roles. The rest are in the army, mainly on a 'home posting' or training tour (see Table 11.1).

About 37 000 Scots serve in the British Armed Forces. This is more than twice those stationed in Scotland at any given time. Most of the 37 000 Scots are based outside Scotland, mainly in the British Army of the Rhine, in garrisons in England or in Hong Kong, Belize, Falkland Islands, Gibraltar, Northern Ireland or Norway. Effectively, Scotland 'exports' manpower, i.e. the Scottish Regiments, and 'imports' navy and airforce personnel from the rest of the UK for the *maritime role* in which Scotland specializes.

DEFENCE: A PUBLIC GOOD

Defence is the oldest activity undertaken by the state – in earlier centuries it was often the *only* activity for which taxes were raised. Adam Smith, in 1776, identified defence as the 'first duty' of the government. Indeed, he went further and suggested that if there had to be a choice between 'opulence and defence' a prudent people would always choose the latter, because without a credible defence against the depredations of neighbours there would soon be an end to opulence (see Chapter 4).

Defence, it is argued, can only be provided at a sufficient and credible level if provided by the state. The benefits of defence spending go automatically to all members of a community and not just those prepared to pay. Thus, individuals would be unwilling to exercise their demands in the market. Defence is, at least in its deterrence role, a *pure public good* (see Box 11.1).

BOX 11.1 *Public goods*

When a good is bought or sold there is a change of *ownership*. The handing over of money is accompanied by a simultaneous transfer of ownership from the seller to the buyer. For most everday items, such as newspapers and groceries, this is taken for granted and physical possession is enough to indicate ownership. Some more important items, such as houses, land, cars, have a much more formal change of ownership, requiring the exchange and registration of legal and official documents. This is because ownership in our society carries with it a very important *right*; the right to the exclusive use of the good.

The efficiency of the *market mechanism* depends upon the transfer of ownership. When I buy bread it is so that *I* can eat it, or *I* can give it to somebody else. If somebody else was allowed without my permission to eat bread that I had bought, I would not want to buy it in the first place. If it was the same for everybody, the market mechanism would not work.

Defence is the most important good for which the market fails. A person who would be willing to purchase those goods and services which would deter an external threat could not have the right of exclusive use. By their nature, these goods and services would also provide protection for others. Realizing that he or she could benefit from neighbours' spending, a rational individual would reduce spending on defence. As every person would do this the market mechanism would not allocate sufficient resources to this need. Consequently, defence must be provided collectively and organized by the state.

Apart from defence, few goods and services are like this. Other important ones are the maintenance of law and order (parliament, justice, police, prisons); the regulation of industry; environmental controls and preventive medicine (e.g. sewage and pollution regulation, vaccination programmes); overseas aid and representation, export and tourist promotion; tax collection; and the fire service.

Deterrence can be measured by the probability of non-attack. The objective of a deterrence defence policy is to make the probability of non-attack as low as possible by either: (a) maximizing the deterrence value of any given defence expenditure, or (b) minimizing the cost of securing a given probability of deterrence.

Deterrence is achieved by convincing a potential aggressor that the country concerned has the *capability* and the *will* to inflict damage on the aggressor greatly in excess of any likely gains to him if he attacks the defended territory. In defence jargon this is known as threatening *unacceptable damage* upon an aggressor if he attacks. If he does not attack because he is deterred by the possibility of unacceptable damage, or for any other reason, the policy requires that the defence capability is not used, i.e. it is for defensive purposes only.

In the event of deterrence failing, the objective of defence policy shifts to ensuring the highest probability of survival. War, unlike deterrence, does not affect everybody equally. Some people do not survive – they are the casualties of war. Prospects for the survival of 'consumers' vary according to circumstance and the 'accidents' of hostilities. In war, defence cannot be regarded as a *pure* public good, but must be regarded as an *impure* public good.

This distinction is not just confined to defence. Consider a public road system where one user's consumption does not interfere with another's. For each individual the road system is a pure public good – as long as there is no congestion by other users!

Defence is an impure public good if war occurs but the fact that the probability of survival may be different for individuals does not detract from the view that the survival of *the majority of the people in a country* may still justify a defence capability, and a willingness to use it, as a worthwhile use of scarce resources.

DEFENCE EXPENDITURE IN SCOTLAND

The UK defence budget in 1981/82 was £12.3 billion. It was spent in three broad budgetary categories: (a) pay for personnel, (b) purchase of equipment and (c) administration and stores. Estimates vary as to how much of defence expenditure is made in Scotland each year. The conceptual and statistical issues are complex and we are also short of hard evidence. Hence, we must be careful in applying our economics principles (it being better to be approximately right than absolutely wrong!).

Scotland's Share

One way to calculate Scotland's 'share' of defence expenditure is to simply take a percentage of the UK total defence budget and attribute it to Scotland. We might for example, take Scotland's population as a percentage of the UK population, i.e. 9 per cent, and estimate 9 per cent of £12.3 billion, i.e. £1.11 billion. This approach offers a guide to what the region 'should' pay in taxes to the government for its share of common defence costs or what it would pay if it were an independent country carrying out the same level of defence activity.

Scotland's Economic Benefit

However, if we wish to estimate the economic benefits of defence spending in Scotland then we are concerned with the actual expenditure that occurs *within the region* as a result of the UK's defence activity. For example, the original construction costs of the Nimrod maritime reconnaissance aircraft, or of the Phantom and Lightning interceptors flying out of Scottish bases, are not relevant to the economic effects of defence expenditure in the Scottish economy. As the aircraft were built elsewhere in the UK, the economic effects of that expenditure occurred in the localities concerned. Only the incomes of the personnel flying, maintaining, guiding and servicing the aircraft and any local purchases of fuel and spare parts are relevant. The same is true of the nuclear submarines, frigates and carriers built in yards in other parts of the UK.

To gauge the impact of equipment expenditures on the Scottish economy we take account only of the defence contracts that are currently underway in Scottish industries. This requires that we calculate the incomes of the 13 000 employees of the Scottish-based defence contractors (see Box 11.2), plus the receipts of those defence subcontractors supplying other regions who are located in Scotland, and any local purchases of fuel, accommodation, vehicles, and so on that are charged to MOD's budget.

BOX 11.2   *Some Scottish defence contractors*

Ferranti, Edinburgh — electronics for aerospace

British Shipbuilders (Scott-Lithgows, Yarrows), Clydeside — naval combat and support vessels, coastal submarines

Hall Russell, Aberdeen and Robb-Caledon, Leith — patrol vessels

Mactaggarts, Midlothian — hydraulics

British Aerospace, Prestwick — pilot trainers, light combat aircraft, engine maintenance and refitting

Marconi–GEC, Fife — electronics for aerospace and communications

Barr and Stroud, Glasgow — submarine periscopes and optical equipment

Many smaller firms are also active in defence supplies covering industries as varied as electronics and ship victualing.

Thus, the most satisfactory method of calculating the direct contribution from the defence budget to the Scottish economy is to estimate the number of defence personnel stationed in Scotland, the share of the UK defence contracts going to Scottish companies, and the share of the Administration and Stores budget (see Table 11.2).

It appears that annual direct expenditure from the UK defence budget into the Scottish economy amounts to about £770 million. This is an *estimate* figure which does not take account of 'leakages' from the attributed Scottish expenditure of such things as:

(1)   Personnel remittances to families who may not be stationed with the recipient in Scotland (families with children of school age may prefer not to keep changing house and schools with father's postings).

(2)   Subcontracting by Scottish firms to suppliers in other parts of the UK, or abroad, for example, Yarrows on the Clyde receives electronic equipment manufactured in England and Wales for the frigates it builds, and the value of these inputs, given the nature of the modern fighting ship, can be as high as 60 per cent of the ships' construction costs.

TABLE 11.2　*Estimated defence expenditure in Scotland*

Principal headings UK defence budget	UK totals £ billion	Scottish share £ million
Personnel costs	4.9	338
Equipment	5.4	297
Admin & Stores	2.0	135
Totals	12.3	770

However, against the unmeasured leakages there are similar, compensating injections.

(1) Remittances from Scottish servicemen, temporarily stationed elsewhere, to their families in Scotland.

(2) The receipts of Scottish subcontractors supplying firms in the rest of the UK, or MOD directly, with defence products; for example, Ferranti, Edinburgh, supplies electronics for combat aircraft and helicopters assembled in England.

These have not been included in the estimate of £770 million defence expenditures in Scotland because of lack of data. The *net* effect of the defence expenditure flows into and out of Scotland would have to be considered if we were interested in the 'second round' or 'regional multipliers' effects of UK defence spending (see Chapter 15). Given these caveats, we may accept that defence expenditure in Scotland in cash terms was about £770 million in 1981/82. In employment terms this represents about 53 000 jobs. In strategic terms – Scotland's role in UK defence – the importance of Scotland to the UK, and through the UK to NATO, is very considerable.

DEFENCE EXPENDITURE OPPORTUNITY COSTS AND ALLOCATION

The public debate about defence in the democracies is a proper activity for its citizens. Individuals have the right to differ in their often very deeply held ethical and moral views, particularly about nuclear deterrence. Important to any debate on how much defence is 'enough' is an awareness that resources allocated to defence have an *opportunity cost* in the foregone alternative uses of the scarce resources. The £12 billion spent on British defence has other possible uses in industrial, social and welfare programmes or in private consumption and saving.

Against the argument that defence spending should be severely cut we must consider the implications for the preservation of our way of life. If that is not worth defending, or we believe it would not be threatened by others, the case for reducing defence expenditures is likely to prove overwhelming. However, majority opinion in the UK believes that defence is a necessary activity. Therefore successive governments have voted the resources, knowing fully the sacrifices involved.

EFFECTIVENESS OF DEFENCE

Once society has committed resources to defence, decisions have to be taken on the allocation of resources among competing military options. A functional cost budget, which identifies the costs of each function, i.e. the military outputs obtained for the cost of the inputs, provides a basis upon which to make judgements about 'value for taxpayers' money'. Table 11.3 shows a broad functional cost budget for the UK (in reality we would

TABLE 11.3   *Functional cost budget for UK*

Function	Cost (£ billion per year)
Nuclear strategic	0.3
Navy general purpose	1.7
European theatre army	1.9
Air Force general purpose	2.2
Reserve forces	0.3
Research and Development	1.7
Training	1.1
Repair, maintenance	0.8
Contingency war stocks	0.3
Other support functions	2.0

breakdown the functions into more specific activities rather than leave them in aggregate form as shown here).

The entire operating cost of the strategic nuclear deterrent, the Polaris force, in 1982 was £300 million, i.e. if this activity was terminated the defence budget would save £300 million a year. The cost of developing Polaris, and building the huge submarines for the weapon system, is now a 'byegone'. What is spent cannot be recovered and there is no possibility of saving the past costs of the system if we scrap Polaris. Only the saving of the operating costs is relevant to a financial decision to abandon the Polaris deterrent force.

Other activities can be analysed in the same way using the functional cost approach.

The British Army of the Rhine costs £1.9 billion a year, the air defence of the UK costs £2.2 billion and the Royal Navy's maritime role, mainly in the North Atlantic and the Channel, £1.7 billion.

To decide how much to spend on a particular function, it is necessary to compare these budget costs, i.e. what the tax payer provides, against the military benefits considered to be appropriate by the community, its representatives in parliament and the government of the day. For instance, in the continuing review of defence policy in Britain, it could be argued that as it costs nearly £2 billion to defend a 65-kilometre strip of the Federal German border the debate ought to concentrate on whether that money could be better spent in defence elsewhere, perhaps on more maritime cover or a larger airforce. Functional costing enables MOD to examine closely the operating costs of BAOR. Explicitly identifying the costs of alternative defence policies improves defence decision-making.

The message from economics is clear: Governments and Oppositions ought not to enter into, or abandon, particular defence commitments without considering the comparative opportunity costs of the various options.

BOX 11.3 *Defence jargon*

NATO – North Atlantic Treaty Organization, set up in April 1949, for collective defence as defined in Article 51 of the Charter of the United Nations. It has sixteen sovereign states as members:

Belgium, Canada, Denmark, Federal Germany, France, Greece, Iceland, Italy, Luxembourg, Netherlands, Norway, Portugal, Spain, Turkey, the UK and the USA.

WARPACK – Warsaw Pact – or Treaty of Friendship, Co-operation and Mutual Assistance, set up in May 1955. Originally it had eight members: Albania, Bulgaria, Czeckoslovakia, German Democratic Republic, Hungary, Poland, Rumania and Soviet Union. Albania left the Pact in 1968.

MOD – Ministry of Defence. Responsible for the employment of 332 000 service personnel and 267 000 civilian employees.

BAOR – British Army of the Rhine. Under the Brussels Treaty of 1955 Britain agreed to station 55 000 troops in Germany as part of the NATO defence force. All the Scottish Regiments are rotated through tours in BAOR.

Functional Costing – a budgetary technique that sets out the costs of providing specific defence functions – BAOR, Air Defence, Maritime defence and so on – to assist in defence decision-making.

Billion – to get an idea of what a billion means, think of yourself earning £10 000 a year – it would take you 100 000 years to earn a billion pounds.

Deterrence – a policy aimed at preventing someone doing something specific, i.e. attacking you – he can do almost anything else. Deterrent defence aims to deter an attack by an aggressor.

12

Housing Schemes and Schemes for Housing

ROGER J. SANDILANDS

Most of us who live in urban Scotland, especially in Clydeside, cannot fail to appreciate the scale of urban deprivation suffered by large numbers of our fellow Scots. The evidence is all around us whether or not we ourselves live in one of the many thousands of dwellings below the official 'minimum tolerable standard' (concerned with structural stability, freedom from damp, and the provision of a WC, sink and hot and cold water). The most recent official data are for 1971 when 160 000 such dwellings existed. Perhaps twice that number were at or a little above the minimum standard.

In some respects there has been an improvement in housing in recent years (see Table 12.1). Between 1970 and 1980 400 000 improvement grants were approved for the public sector and a further 130 000 for private dwellings. But these figures are themselves a reflection of the scale of the problem of poor housing standards in Scotland. The 6 per cent of all households still lacking at least one basic amenity in 1976/7 represents around

TABLE 12.1 *Percentage of households lacking basic amenities, 1965–1976/7*

Percentage of households	All tenants		Private rented etc.	
	1965	1976/7	1965	1976/7
Without WC inside dwelling	13	2	34	12
Without fixed bath (or shower)	21	6	58	27

114 000 households, mainly in the private rented sector, most of which was built before 1919.

A further indication of the poor quality of Scottish housing is that in 1976/7, 37 per cent of Scottish housing had an annual rental value of less than £100. In addition 9 per cent of all Scottish households, or around 170 000 families, suffer from overcrowding, measured in terms of the number of bedrooms considered appropriate to the sex and age composition of the household.

When we consider also the unimaginative design and layout of many major housing schemes constructed for low-income families in the 1930s (for example Blackhill in Glasgow and Ferguslie Park in Paisley) and the 1950s (Drumchapel, Easterhouse and Castlemilk, all on the outskirts of Glasgow and Craigmillar and Wester Hailes in Edinburgh) the scale of Scotland's housing problem assumes even greater proportions. For it is not simply the number of housing units with the basic facilities that is important in providing a sense of dignity and well-being for a community, but also the variety and quality of internal and external design, the quality of building materials used, the standard of insulation to conserve heat and avoid damp, and the provision of community facilities and attractive landscaping.

BRITAIN AND EUROPE

Many Scots do not appreciate the degree of housing deprivation unless they visit other parts of the UK and Europe. By European standards the quality of Britain's housing, especially its municipal housing, compares badly. But parts of Scotland are grim even by British standards. The comparison with Scandinavian countries, which are not dissimilar to Scotland in terms of population, climate and, until recently, income per head, is especially telling. It is only quite recently that Scandinavia overtook Britain in income per head. Even before then, housing was given a much higher priority than in Britain. Low-quality housing was regarded as a poor long-run investment even when that region was much poorer than Scotland is today.

The reasons for poor housing in Scotland are largely economic and financial. It is not because we lack the architects, engineers and builders, though these groups must probably accept some of the blame. Much more importantly it is a question of priorities and the allocation of scarce resources by those people and institutions that have the power to decide such things. The study of economics is the study of resource allocation among competing ends. The economy can be national or local and it can be subject to the control of state or local government, as well as to the individual enterprise as producer and the household as final consumer. The provision of housing is subject to control at all these levels but the political balance between them varies greatly in different countries at different times.

PUBLIC HOUSING

Of nearly 1 million dwellings built in Scotland since 1945, 82 per cent were built by the public sector, compared with 52 per cent in England. Only 33 per cent of Scottish housing is owner occupied. This is a lower proportion than almost any other Euro-

TABLE 12.2 *International comparison of tenure patterns*

Country	Percentage owner-occupied	Percentage rented from public sector	Percentage rented from private sector
Scotland (1978)	33	56	11
England (1978)	56	30	14
Wales (1978)	59	29	12
Czechoslovakia (1970)	50	50	
France (1968)	43	57	
German Democratic Republic (1971)	23	77	
German Federal Republic (1972)	34	66	
Ireland (1971)	69	31	
Sweden (1970)	35	65	
Yugoslavia	71	29	
USA (1970)	63	37	
Japan (1970)	58	42	

pean country. In the rest of Britain the share is around 57 per cent (see Table 12.2). Although owner-occupation is also relatively small in West Germany and Sweden, most of their housing stock is privately owned. A very large number of dwellings there are owned by private housing associations, with the occupiers having some equity stake in the property. In Scotland this form of tenure is still very uncommon.

The dramatic increase in municipal housing has coincided with a similar decline in the private rented sector. In 1914 around 90 per cent of Scotland's housing was rented from private landlords; today the proportion is only 11 per cent and caters mainly to groups such as single persons, childless couples (including the elderly) and students. Rent controls, increased security of tenure and tighter building and public health standards have combined to reduce the profitability of this sector. This has induced private landlords to sell off their property when it became vacant and to reduce spending on upkeep. Low, heavily subsidized rents to tenants of municipal housing have also attracted families away from the private sector where rents are not directly subsidized.

Why Public Provision?

It is impossible to discuss the housing problem in Scotland without raising several unpopular and sensitive questions about the unusually important role of public-sector housing here. In the face of overcrowding in urban areas at the end of the first world war, it is understandable and laudable that central and local government should have embarked on various crash programmes to rehouse people in the worst slum areas. Those who were living in the most squalid housing – if, indeed, they were housed at all – were, naturally, mainly the poorest-paid section of the community. Unfortunately, their incomes were so low that they could afford only a small fraction of the cost of new housing, no matter how basic it was. No commercially-minded private builder would build new houses for them. That would have been a recipe for instant bankruptcy. In the public domain, however, similar considerations were no thought appropriate or moral. If the public sector was to build new houses, who were more deserving of them than the most under-privileged, the most needy, the most poor?

Thus, in the 1930s and the 1950s a number of huge housing schemes were constructed on the edge of cities and towns at the lowest possible cost. The sites themselves were very cheap per acre, but this was itself a reflection of their relatively undesirable, peripheral location. Each housing unit was designed to a specified minimum tolerable standard. This minimum standard included more of the basic amenities (such as an inside WC and fixed bath) than were found in many of the slum dwellings that they replaced. However, these new housing units were usually built with the cheapest materials, with little or no spending on landscaping and few communal facilities. Despite this, it was impossible to charge more than a fraction of the economic cost of these basic dwelling units to the low-income tenants who were housed in them. Even today, barely 40 per cent of local authority housing expenditure is covered by rents to tenants, with many tenants paying a much smaller proportion of the cost of their housing. In 1980/81 annual rents charged on each public sector dwelling averaged only £305.

As a result, large deficits were incurred by local authorities. In the financial year 1980/81 the deficit on the Housing Revenue Accounts of all local authorities in Scotland was over £320 million. Rents accounted for around £290 million out of total housing expenditures (on loan charges, management, and repairs and maintenance) of more than £615 million. Such deficits reduce the ability of local authorities to spend more to improve housing conditions in the future. There was a limit on the extent to which the deficit could be covered by central government subsidy (in turn constrained by competing claims on government revenues and by the ability to impose higher taxes) and higher local rates. Higher rates on commercial establishments and private dwellings threaten to drive these ratepayers away from the cities. The rateable base declines and if further rates are levied on this diminished base, a vicious circle can arise. Inadequate financial resources force a continued policy of providing the cheapest possible housing in soulless schemes, to the despair of architects and residents alike.

In Scandinavia a policy of building houses directly for the very poor has never been embraced in the way it has in Scotland. There the emphasis has been on building houses to a much higher standard, despite the higher cost, in both the public and the

BOX 12.1   *Housing: an analogy with car markets*

Even in some of the worst housing schemes in Scotland many cars are parked in the streets. Most are probably five or six years old and are worth perhaps £500 each. But most are also in good working order and, when new, cost perhaps £4000 each. Today it is probably impossible to build a new car, no matter how basic the design, for less than about £3000. Such basic cars might be considered less desirable than many much cheaper, second-hand cars. Because the government does not provide massive subsidies to low-income families to buy new cars, new cars are built almost exclusively for the relatively rich, who usually trade in their old cars in part exchange. The rest of us, including some quite low-income families, happily purchase these second-hand cars at low prices. If tomorrow the government were to decree that families with no car, or very old cars, should be given subsidies to allow them to buy new cars of a very primitive design, it is unlikely that in ten years' time the British would be better provided with cars than they are today. But local authorities operate by subsidizing the building of basic housing units and this, by analogy with the car market, has clear, and not very encouraging, implications for the housing stock.

private sectors. The new housing has been occupied mainly by higher income families, with some lower income families also moving in with some rent subsidy. This has ensured a much better social mix in new residential areas. Equally important, however, is the fact that lower income families have been able to occupy the housing that the richer people have vacated and in this way a better social mix has been achieved in the older residential areas. In most of Europe the poorest urban housing may be of antique vintage but it is invariably of a much higher standard than the worst housing in Clydeside, much of which is relatively new.

As a nation we spend, despite the subsidies to both council tenants and owner-occupiers, a lower proportion of our national income on housing – less than 4 per cent – than most other developed countries including our European neighbours (see Table 12.3). This must be due at least in part to the policy of building relatively new housing for families who can afford to

TABLE 12.3   *Gross fixed investment in housing*

Country	Gross fixed investment as percentage of GDP	Year
Australia	4.6	1974
Belgium	6.2	1975
Canada	4.9	1974
Denmark	5.5	1974
France	7.2	1975
West Germany	5.3	1973
Italy	6.7	1975
Japan	8.4	1975
Netherlands	5.3	1975
USA	2.7	1975
UK	4.4	1975

pay only a small fraction of the economic rent, with the result that fewer funds are available to local authorities for further housing programmes. At the same time, the subsidy programme has tended to be unselective, so that even those who could afford to pay a higher fraction of the economic rent are not asked to do so.

'Points' Rationing

If the market is not allowed to ration the available housing then some alternative rationing mechanism must operate. An effect of the heavy emphasis on subsidized municipal housing in Scotland has been a complex 'points system' for rationing available housing to families on the waiting lists. To obtain the more desirable public-sector properties can mean remaining on the waiting list for ten years or more. Newcomers to an area in Scotland may have to wait a long time even for some of the less-desirable houses. The points system is less rigid in England and it has been said that it is easier for a family to move to England than from one part of Scotland to another.

The ability to move house freely and cheaply is a vital part of the smooth functioning of *labour markets*. It is the mobility of labour, between jobs and regions, which ensures that income differences are narrowed. Labour movement also plays a vital role in reducing the hardship caused to specific groups of workers who are displaced by technological change and productivity increases. Only if housing is readily available in areas where new jobs are being created can full advantage be taken of our economic growth potential. Thus it is evident that an improved housing policy can play a key role in the successful management of the whole economy.

A PRIVATE MARKET FOR HOUSING

A variety of factors have restricted the growth of private-sector housing in Scotland. First, low rents in the public sector reduce the rents that private landlords can charge, thus reducing their supply of accommodation. These low rents also reduce the demand for and supply of owner-occupied housing. In addition, some local authorities have viewed the activities of the private sector as working against their own operations, for example, by depriving the local authority of suitable land. This has also been given as a reason why private housing associations (or co-ownership schemes) have made little headway in Scotland compared with England and other parts of Europe.

Mortgages

The supply of private-sector housing is also heavily influenced by the supply of mortgage finance. In Britain, this has been characterized in the past by a 'feast and famine' cycle which has prevented builders from planning a stable, long-term housing programme.

The commercial banks recently became involved in housing finance (see Chapter 5) but the building societies have been the traditional source of funds to the private housing market. There has been considerable year-to-year variation in the real value of building society loans in Scotland (see Table 12.4). Although a considerable increase in average annual lending took place during 1976–80, this was not matched by a corresponding increase in housing construction, because a large percentage financed the purchase of older houses. In 1980 only 18 per cent of all building society lending in Scotland was for the finance of new housing. Although there was some slight increase in the average annual

TABLE 12.4 *Building society flow of funds in Scotland (£ million)*

Year	Real lending
1970	83
1971	112
1972	125
1973	110
1974	95
1975	139
1976	153
1977	158
1978	179
1979	154
1980	158

number of private-sector houses completed in 1976–80 this did little to offset the considerable decline in the public-sector building programme (see Table 12.5).

British building societies are non-profit-making bodies which form a cartel to fix interest rates paid to investors (depositors) and charged to borrowers. Thus, especially when the building societies had the field to themselves, normal competitive principles have not applied in this market. The Building Societies

TABLE 12.5 *New houses completed, Scotland*

Year	Public sector	Private sector	Total
1970	34 906	8 220	43 126
1971	29 169	11 614	40 783
1972	20 157	11 835	31 992
1973	17 818	12 215	30 033
1974	17 097	11 239	28 336
1975	23 952	10 371	34 323
1976	22 823	13 704	36 527
1977	15 188	12 132	27 320
1978	11 316	14 443	25 759
1979	8 603	15 069	23 672
1980	7 964	11 623	19 587

Association has usually been more concerned to stabilize interest rates than constantly to vary them in response to changing conditions in the financial markets as a whole (see Chapter 5).

In some ways this would seem to have been a reasonable policy. Building Society customers who have borrowed large sums long term to help purchase a house can be seriously embarrassed by a sudden jump in interest rates from, say 8 per cent to 12 per cent, since this would increase their monthly interest payments by 50 per cent. However, if the building societies do not raise their charges to borrowers at times when interest rates paid on other financial assets (for example, bank deposits or local authority bonds) are rising, they will experience a sharp decline in their deposits as existing or prospective building society investors shift their savings. This problem can be particularly acute in times of inflation which pushes up the general level of interest rates, since building societies then find it increasingly difficult to compete for funds except by imposing strains on borrowers.

The supply of mortgage finance has often tended to fall short of potential demand. Since the demand for housing is heavily dependent on the supply of mortgage funds this feeds through to the building industry which curtails its own level of activity. When the private building industry is depressed there is no guarantee that the public sector will be expanding to take up the slack. On the contrary, in times of inflation, when the building societies may be having difficulty obtaining funds to lend, the government often curtails public spending on housing as a counter-inflationary policy. This has certainly been the case in the period 1979–81 when the building industry suffered its worst recession for decades, with hundreds of thousands of jobs lost as a direct consequence.

To a very large extent industry finances its own production and investment from sales proceeds, profits and shares issues. The situation is very different, however, for home buyers. A house is generally the largest single purchase any of us ever makes and for the vast majority it is not feasible to finance this purchase out of accumulated savings, at least not the first house we buy. Instead it is usual to save up for, say, a 5–15 per cent down-payment and to borrow the rest over 20–25 years. The mortgage of a first-time buyer is typically two to three times his annual income. Until April 1983 interest often represented the bulk of total monthly payments in the early phase of the mortgage period with capital repayments becoming more important in later years. The present scheme spreads the capital repayments more evenly over the mortgage period.

Clearly, however, the interest rate, is crucial in determining the size of the loan that can comfortably be serviced with a given income. For example, a £15 000 mortgage at 7 per cent interest over twenty-five years would involve around £1050 interest payments a year which would be reasonable for someone earning about £5000 a year. But if the interest rate were 14 per cent the same mortgage would involve £2100 interest payments and absorb a greater proportion of the person's income. In times of inflation such as we have been experiencing over the last ten years, nominal interest rates rise to very high levels, effectively excluding thousands of young couples from the chance to own their own homes. This weakens the private housing market, especially when the flow of savings into housing finance is curtailed because inflation is eroding the real value of these savings.

Competition from commercial banks may now have introduced a greater degree of flexibility into building societies' policies but in the past the inadequate supply of mortgage finance relative to the demand placed building society managers in a position to pick and choose the people to whom they will lend money and the properties they will allow them to buy. The customer's income and ability to repay a mortgage could often take second place to the building society managers' subjective opinions of the personal characteristics of the applicant as the criterion for a loan approval. Similarly, by taking an overly conservative view of properties suitable for mortgages they became notorious for 'red-lining' (that is, refusing to lend on properties in) certain older city districts which have consequently fallen into disrepair, eventually to be demolished unnecessarily.

In some countries suffering chronic inflation the problems that Scotland has faced with its inadequate supply of housing finance have been solved by 'inflation-proofing' or 'index-linking' savers' deposits on the one hand and mortgage lending on the other. This involves periodically writing-up the value of the assets (mortgages) and liabilities (savers' deposits) of housing finance institutions in line with an inflation index such as the cost-of-living index. Interest is then paid on the indexed value of these assets and liabilities. This protects savers' assets from the ravages of inflation, and also ensures that a positive real rate of interest is earned. This has helped attract a larger and steadier flow of funds into the housing market.

Such schemes are also attractive to borrowers, however, in that the schedule of payments is spread much more evenly throughout the entire repayment period. This is because it is the outstanding debt that is indexed, to preserve its real value, while current repayments consist only of the relatively much lower interest payments together with amortization payments (repayments of principal) that are spread evenly, in real terms, over say 20 years. By contrast, conventional non-indexed debts tend to concentrate the burden of repayments, in real terms, into the early years of the contract period. When the outstanding debt is not index-linked this 'front-loading' problem is more acute the higher and more variable the rate of inflation, since the nominal interest rate tends to fluctuate in sympathy with the inflation rate.

Of course these problems would not arise if we were more successful in controlling inflation in the first place. Either we must act more decisively on inflation or we must be prepared to introduce appropriate new models of housing finance to protect this sector from inflation's very harmful side-effects. Otherwise the prospects for a steady improvement in the quality of Scotland's housing stock will not be bright.

13

Education in Scotland

T. D. WILLIAMS

Unlike most of the goods and services we consume, education is compulsory. Parents in Scotland, as in other countries, are required to send their children to school to 'consume' primary and secondary education and provision of this service is expensive. Why is education so important? How are its aims achieved in Scotland? How do we assess the value of education?

THE AIMS OF EDUCATION

Some of the main aims of education are:

(1) to instil the skills and attitudes which will enable people to play a useful, productive role in the labour force, both enabling them to earn a reasonable living and providing the community with the benefits of efficient provision of goods and services;

(2) to increase the social awareness of students, enabling them to make a constructive contribution to the social and political life of the community;

(3) to improve the individual's chance of leading a 'fulfilled' life by developing talents, imagination and ambition, so that each person can become aware of and develop his or her natural abilities.

Except perhaps for the first of these objectives, which might be called the economic objective, it is difficult to agree on criteria which would tell us whether or not the results of education are satisfactory. There are many differing views about what sort of social and political behaviour is desirable.

TABLE 13.1   *Number of primary pupils on the register of education authorities and grant-aided schools in Scotland*

1951/52	1961/62	1966/67	1971/72	1972/73	1973/74	1975/76	1977/78	1978/79
561 800	581 200	606 100	642 800	644 400	643 100	628 700	601 400	575 600

Also educational success (however measured) of students depends in part upon the ability, motivation and background of the students themselves, together with the facilities and support available to them outside of school hours. 'Good results' in a particular school may have less to do with the methods used in that school, or with the facilities provided within it, than to the fact that the school has attracted a relatively large number of highly motivated students who also have the type of ability required for good performance in examinations.

The amount and type of education provided depend largely upon judgements made by the community about the value of education. These judgements, however, are made in conditions of uncertainty about what is really being achieved.

THE PATTERN OF EDUCATIONAL PROVISION IN SCOTLAND

Numbers of Students and Student-Teacher Ratios

Scottish population growth was very low during the 1960s and the population declined during the seventies, due in part to the fall in the birth rate since the 1960s and in part to outmigration.

As a result of these changes there has been a fall in the number of children in *primary* schools since 1972 (see Table 13.1). There will be a large drop during the eighties and numbers are expected to continue falling until at least the end of the century. In primary schools the number of students per teacher has fallen since enrolment began to fall, but there had already been a large reduction in earlier years when enrolment was rising (see Table 13.2).

TABLE 13.2   *Number of students per teacher in primary schools*

1966/67	1972/73	1974/75	1977/78	1978/79
30.2	25.7	23.4	22.4	21.4

TABLE 13.3 *Number of students per teacher in secondary schools*

1966/67	1971/72	1973/74	1975/76	1977/78	1978/79
16.2	15.6	15.5	15.1	14.7	14.6

The number in *secondary* schools continued to increase until the end of the seventies, but did so at a declining rate (see Table 13.3). Falling enrolment is expected during the eighties as the smaller age groups move up from the primary schools.

Student-teacher ratios fell, even though there was increased student enrolment, reflecting – as with the primary schools – a more than proportional increase in the numbers of teachers employed in the educational system.

We might have expected the increase in the number of teachers to have led to an increase in the cost per student of teachers (in real as well as nominal terms), but the real cost of teaching staff per student remained at approximately £450 (at 1980 prices) throughout the period. This appears to have been due, at least in part, to a change in the age-distribution of teachers, which meant that there was a higher proportion of teachers at the lower end of the pay scale. The economies gained in this way are, however, of a short-term nature, and it seems certain that (unless there is some change in conditions of service) there will be a large increase in the real cost of teaching staff per student as teachers move up the pay scale.

There have been increases of almost 40 per cent in expenditure per pupil on property and about 22 per cent in expenditure per pupil on non-teaching staff, due in part to falling numbers in many schools. It may be possible to reduce these costs by closing schools when numbers fall below a certain level and transferring pupils to some other school which is reasonably close to their homes.

Spending per pupil on supplies and services, including books has fallen, in real terms, by about 15 per cent during the same period. These expenses are relatively easy to cut, because they do not directly affect sensitive areas such as employment practises, but reductions below an appropriate level may have severe adverse effects upon the quality of education.

Regional Variation in Educational Provision

(1) Population densities have a considerable effect on the cost of education. Urban areas are cheaper because they are able to draw a much larger number of pupils from any given area (see Table 13.4). The relatively favourable teacher–student ratios in rural regions may be largely due to small numbers of pupils in each catchment area.

(2) The proportion of students who remain in full-time education after secondary school was, in 1979, highest in the Highland Region, followed by the Islands Region. The lowest proportions were in Strathclyde, Central, Dumfries and Galloway and Fife.

(3) The influence of fee-paying schools in Scotland has, at least in numerical terms, been particularly strong in Edinburgh, which has also had a tradition of fee-paying and academically selective schools in the public sector. The latter are now part of the public comprehensive system, but in many instances they are in areas which contain a high proportion of middle-class and skilled artisan parents so they have probably continued to provide many more children for higher education than other schools in the city.

The presence of fee-paying schools may make it difficult for some comprehensive schools to develop effective academic

TABLE 13.4   *Numbers of students per teacher in the regions of Scotland*

	Primary *31 December 1979*	Secondary *31 December 1979*
Islands	17.7	12.6
Highland	19.7	14.5
Borders	19.1	14.1
Grampian	19.7	13.6
Dumfries and Galloway	20.2	14.2
Central	20.0	14.5
Tayside	21.1	14.0
Lothian	19.7	13.9
Fife	21.7	14.6
Strathclyde	22.9	15.1

streams. However, if there were no fee-paying schools, some parents would probably move to the catchment areas of the 'better' education authority schools.

It may be that the major differences in examination performance are not between the private schools and the 'best' education authority schools, but between those local schools in a 'good' catchment area and those in a 'poor' one. To remedy this, it would probably be necessary both to change present catchment areas *and* to make it very difficult for pupils to attend a school outside their area.

It has proved difficult to specify performance criteria in terms other than Ordinary (O) grade and Higher (H) passes and it is then important to consider evidence on examination performance.

Proportion of School Leavers with O and H Grade Passes

At present, about 40 per cent of pupils leave school without having gained any passes at O grade. However, during the past thirty years there has been a very big increase in the proportion of school leavers who have acquired passes at O grade and at H grade (see Table 13.5).

In 1978, approximately 20 per cent of school leavers went on to some form of further education. The numbers going to universities in Scotland increased substantially (as elsewhere in the

TABLE 13.5 *Proportion of school leavers in Scotland with O or H grades*

	1950/51	1960/61	1970/71	1976/77	1977/78
1–2 O grade (no H)	0.6	0.8	6.2	15.1	14.9
3 or more O grade (no H)	0.3	0.9	10.6	16.9	17.4
1–2 H grade	3.0	5.4	8.3	9.2	8.8
3 or more H grade	3.7	6.6	18.2	17.6	17.2

Note: Until 1970/71, the figures included some GCE O levels. Since then they include only SCE results. The real increase is, consequently, higher than indicated in the table.

UK) in the late 1960s. Expansion continued, although at a slower rate, in the seventies, and with an increase of almost 16 per cent between 1970 and 1977. Other forms of further education increased more rapidly, but it is not clear to what extent this reflected a belief in the merit of alternative forms of further education and to what extent it was due to the availability of more-or-less conventional degree courses for which the entrance requirements were less exacting than at university.

Unemployment among School Leavers

The number of school leavers unable to obtain work has increased substantially, with registered unemployment in Scotland among people under the age of 20 rising from less than 20 000 in the early seventies to almost 70 000 in 1981. Moreover, school leavers have accounted for an increasing proportion of this total – 28 per cent in July 1970 and 51 per cent in 1981. This increase may be a slight overstatement because there has been an increasing tendency for leavers to make use of employment offices during the seventies. There is no doubt, however, that the problem is now very severe.

People with higher formal qualifications are more likely to get a job than those with weaker paper qualifications. There are two views on why this is so.

One view is that the qualifications reflect an education that has increased the capacity of the individual and improved his or her ability to work effectively. If this is correct, there would be a strong case for increasing the level of education offered to pupils who presently have very meagre qualifications, though this need not always be of an 'academic' kind.

An alternative view is that employers use formal qualifications as a 'screening device': they assume that qualifications do reflect, albeit rather crudely, qualities that they seek in an employee such as intelligence, self-discipline and ambition, and they offer jobs to those who are best qualified according to their views about the type of person required to do the job. If this view is correct, then employment prospects overall will not be improved by increasing the level of education; it will simply increase the level of qualifications required for any particular job.

ECONOMIC EVALUATION OF EDUCATIONAL EXPENDITURE

Basic Principles

If education was a *free good*, to society as well as to the individual, almost everyone would agree that we should have a lot more of it. It has, however, a high *opportunity cost*, and forms a large part of public expenditure: it uses a great deal of skilled labour which could otherwise be employed in the production of goods and other services. It uses land which could be put to other uses. It requires construction and maintenance which could be devoted to, for example, houses and hospitals. The pupils themselves might be employed in productive activities.

The cost is, however, offset at least in part by the fact that appropriate education increases the productivity of the labour force. It, thus, provides an opportunity to increase national (and individual) wealth beyond what it would otherwise be.

If we are to assess the worth of spending on education then we must compare the value of additional wealth produced *in future* with costs incurred *now*. This is often done by using the techniques more commonly employed to assess productive investment schemes in private firms and public corporations (see Box 13.1). This is perhaps not inappropriate as education – investment in human capital – may be analogous to capital investment.

In assessing costs and benefits it is usual to distinguish between *private* and *social* costs and benefits. Private costs are those actually met by individuals – for fees, book, uniform (if more expensive than the clothes which would otherwise be worn) – together with the *opportunity cost* of a loss of wages which could have been earned if the student had been in the labour market instead of at school or college. The benefits are those which the individual actually receives – additional income, after deduction of tax.

The assessment of social returns is of a broader nature. If education is (as is usually the case) subsidized, the cost of the subsidy is added to the private cost borne by the individual on the assumption that this is society's evaluation of the benefits to it of this individual's education. The total, private *plus* social, benefit is the total additional income because society is held to benefit from the amount collected in tax. However, if the income that people earn

---

BOX 13.1   *The return on education*

Assuming for simplicity that £100 is invested today at a rate of interest of 10 per cent we would receive £110 next year: £110 next year has, therefore, the same value as £100 today – that is its *Present Value*. For any sum in the future (say £200 in five years time) one can find its present value by finding the amount which if invested today, at the standard rate of interest, would produce £200 in five years time. This procedure is known as *discounting future income*.

The *Net Present Value* of education thus involves:

(1)   identifying all the *costs* of education incurred in the first year, second year, and so on;

(2)   estimating the *returns* which normally occur several years into the future after the student has entered the labour force;

(3)   subtracting costs from returns to get the *net* returns in each year and discounting;

(4)   the *sum* of these discounted values will give a single value in money terms of the Net Present Value of the education;

(5)   if this Net Present Value is positive then this education spending is said to be worthwhile.

The *Rate of Return* is the interest rate which would equalize the value of the stream of costs and the stream of benefits.

With higher levels of education the benefits may not really become apparent until the engineer, doctor or whatever acquires a considerable amount of experience and is able to take full advantage of his or her training.

There are, however, many factors which affect the income that a person may earn, and several of these are also associated with the level of education that is attained.

Ability, motivation and social status are likely to influence the amount of education a person obtains. These factors would also be expected to affect the type of job that a person would get, even if he or she did not have additional education. The problem is to distinguish between the *effect of education* and the *effect of other factors* on the level of income earned.

An American study which examined the effect of many factors, including education, on earnings, suggested that about 35 per cent of income differentials were due to ability, social status and so on. It has been usual for economists making rate of return estimates to assess about 65 per cent of differentials related to additional education as being *due* to education rather than to other factors. It is this adjusted estimate that is used in these calculations.

One drawback to this method, as normally used, is that it only provides a means of assessing the value of additional education beyond the compulsory level. Information is obtained about the average life earnings of people with various levels of education.

In its simplest form, it would give the average life earnings for ten years, eleven years, twelve years and so on (together with the normal pattern over the lifetime of earnings – which typically shows people with relatively little education reaching something close to their maximum earnings fairly early in their working life, while those with higher education continuing to increase their earnings until middle age – see Chapter 14). It is quite possible to take account of the type of education received.

The method enables one to compare the rate of return on additional years of education with that of the minimum required level. It might indicate that it would be desirable to increase the level of education – if for example the rate of return on an additional year were higher than the standard rate of interest. It cannot give any guide as to whether the minimum age should be lowered. In practice that is not a serious matter because it is unlikely that the community would regard lowering the compulsory age as a serious option.

---

does not reflect fairly accurately the real value of their productive contribution, there is no point in the community subsidizing their studies simply so that they can make a great deal of money.

It is generally believed that, in most countries, the private rate of return is a good deal higher than the social rate of return. This is because there is a high rate of subsidy on education, so the cost to the individual is relatively low, while the difference between pre-tax and post-tax incomes is much less substantial. This means that the private demand for higher education is typically a good deal larger than the level which would appear justified if the costs to the community were taken into account.

Externalities

Calculations based on income do not, however, take into account the value of the non-economic benefits of education. Neither do they take into account the possibility that there may be substantial *external benefits*.

External benefits may arise from educational investment when education increases the general level of efficiency and so enables some people to make a technical or administrative 'breakthrough' of economic and social benefit which would not be possible if the general level was lower. A new technique is rarely due solely to the work of those most closely associated with it. Informed discussion, competent appraisal, awareness of the possibility of creative change may combine to create a 'climate' in which the prime innovators are able to take advantage of accumulated insights and apparently minor technical advances made by many other people who play a small, but cumulatively vital, role and may receive no reward themselves.

Unfortunately, however, there are no clear guidelines as to when the general level of efficiency is at the critical level where an increase – created through extra spending on general education – could make it possible for a breakthrough to occur. There may be many occasions when an increase in the level of education would have no important external effects.

Who Should Pay for Education?

In so far as education is compulsory to a certain level, it would appear that the community should be responsible for the costs to that level. There may, however, be provision for private payment when parents prefer some form of education outside the provided education.

The principal arguments in favour of compulsion are that; (a) parents may have an insufficient awareness of the benefits of education, and children have to be protected from the ignorance of their parents, and (b) education – at least to that level – provides external benefits in the form of social training which is valuable to the community, even if not seen as such by all parents or their children.

With respect to education beyond the compulsory level, it may be argued that the greatest benefit goes to those who receive it.

As a consequence of better education, they will earn higher incomes. Would it not then be just if they or their parents were to meet the costs of that education? However, many people would perhaps not be able to afford such education, and it would be unfair if opportunity were to be denied to young people simply because their parents had low incomes.

A cynic might argue that the children of people with low incomes are denied all sorts of opportunities, so why should one make a particular point about education opportunity? Besides, if the community is really concerned about the unfairness of income distribution, why not redistribute income and let people decide for themselves how they wish to spend their money? But, we live in an imperfect world, and re-distribution on a major scale appears to have been beyond the capacity, or perhaps the will, of political parties in all countries. If we start from an acceptance of the fact that income is very unequally distributed, there would seem to be a case for making special provision in some 'key' areas.

Loans?

It might, however, be possible to meet the needs of students from low-income families by providing loans rather than outright grants. The loans would be repayed from the higher incomes that the students would subsequently earn.

There are some practical problems involved in a loan scheme. Even though students will, on the average, earn higher incomes than their contemporaries with less education, some will be unlucky. The risk might be too great for a student from a low-income family to accept. If he (or she) does not earn a higher income, he (or she) will be saddled with a heavy debt and no means of paying it off.

Most loan schemes do, in fact, make some provision for this, by specifying an income level below which no repayment is required. Such a scheme may, however, involve heavy administrative costs and would add to the already familiar problem of the 'poverty trap'. As income increases, entitlement to benefit or exemption from tax or repayment is lost, and one may be worse off or only slightly better off with what appears to be a considerably larger income.

Even with a grant system, disproportionate numbers of students in higher education come from relatively well-to-do occupational groups (i.e. from skilled artisan upwards). As a consequence, the well-to-do benefit more than proportionately from a grant system, while people in low-income groups pay larger taxes (mainly indirect taxes) than would otherwise be necessary and gain few compensating benefits.

Perhaps the practical problems of introducing a fair and efficient loan scheme are too great to overcome, but if it were possible to develop such a scheme it might be more advantageous to the majority of low-income families than a grant system which subsidizes the relatively affluent.

14

'Rich Man, Poor Man . . .' (Distribution of Income)

KAREN HANCOCK

Income in Scotland is far from evenly distributed. In 1977 the poorest 20 per cent of households received less than 1 per cent of total Scottish income while the richest 20 per cent received almost 50 per cent. Income largely determines material welfare (well-being) and in Scotland, as elsewhere, the distribution of income between the rich and the poor is an emotive issue. What is the evidence on income distribution for Scotland? How far can the government affect income distribution? Why does income remain unequally distributed?

INCOME DISTRIBUTION IN SCOTLAND

The poorest 20 per cent (or quintile) of Scottish households received an average income of £2.30 in 1977 (see Table 14.1). This contrasts sharply with the average of £176 per week received by households in the richest quintile. Only 0.6 per cent of total income was shared among the 20 per cent of poorest Scottish households. The share going to the next group (8.5 per cent) was more than fourteen times greater while that going to the richest group (46 per cent) was about seventy-five times greater. These comparisons are based on *weekly original income per household*.

Original income is income from employment, self-employment, investments and private pensions schemes.

Weekly rather than monthly or annual data are used because poorer households, for whom even small changes in income can

TABLE 14.1   *How Scotland's income is shared, before and after direct taxes and benefits, 1977*

(1) Quintiles of households	Original income			Net income		
	(2) Average income per household (£ per week)	(3) Shares of original income (%)		(4) Average net income per household (£ per week)	(5) Shares of net income (%)	(6) Implied average tax rates (%)
Bottom	2.30	0.6		23.90	6.8	−939.1
Second	32.60	8.5		43.23	12.3	−32.6
Third	72.11	18.8		59.39	16.9	17.6
Fourth	100.11	26.1		90.67	25.8	9.4
Top	176.44	46.0		134.25	38.2	23.9
		100.0			100.0	

be of great importance, often find it difficult to obtain credit facilities and are generally concerned about income in the short period.

Households rather than individuals are used as the income-receiving unit. Distributions based on individuals' incomes are not very meaningful since there are large numbers of people who have no income. Most of these are children, who depend on their parents' incomes, and housewives, who depend on their spouses' incomes. The incomes received by individuals are assumed to be shared within households.

Estimating the distribution of income is a difficult and expensive exercise. However, although many incomes will have risen since 1977, it is unlikely that the shares of each group will have changed much since the distribution of original income changes only slowly over time.

Income distribution is frequently illustrated using a Lorenz curve (see Fig. 14.1). The diagonal represents 'complete equality' with each household having the same original income. The actual distribution of original income in Scotland is shown by curve A. The shape of the distribution for Scotland is typical of that for many industrialized countries with large numbers of people

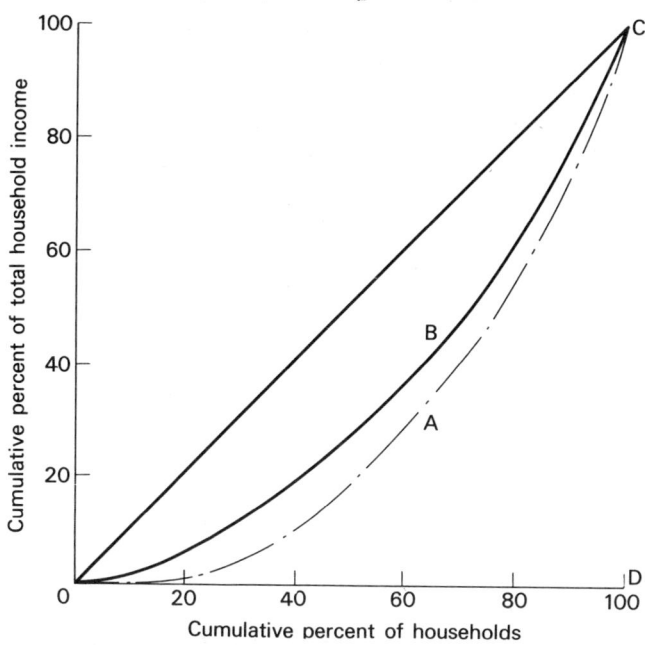

Fig. 14.1   Lorenz curves for Scotland, 1977. A: Original weekly income per household. B: Net weekly income per household

receiving low incomes and a small number receiving very high incomes. The area between the diagonal and curve A highlights the extent of income inequality and amounts to 0.45 of the area OCD. This simple numerical measure of inequality is known as the Gini coefficient. The Gini coefficient for original incomes in Scotland is very similar to that for the UK as a whole, although the levels of money income for each quintile are lower.

CAUSES OF INEQUALITY

Differences in earnings from employment are the main source of inequality in original incomes. In general, non-manual workers earn more than manual workers and full-time males earn more than full-time females. Within occupational groups pay tends to vary with the age of the worker. Workers in their early twenties generally earn less than workers aged between 30 and 40. Non-manual male workers in their twenties usually earn less than manual male workers of the same age, but manual workers' pay increases little after that age. Peak earnings for non-manual male workers are not reached until the 40–49 age range. Such differences in workers' earnings are determined by the following.

Differences in human capital. Education and training represent investment in human capital or potential life-time earning power. A young doctor undergoing a lengthy period of training would expect to earn less than a manual worker of the same age. The same is true for apprentices training to be skilled workers such as joiners, electricians and mechanics. Acquiring skills, i.e. investing in human capital, brings rewards later in the form of enhanced earnings power.

Differences in employment status. Although there is a well-known tendency for the self-employed to understate their incomes for tax purposes, the average recorded income for this group in the UK is about 70 per cent higher than for non-self-employed workers. Part of these higher earnings represents the reward for entrepreneurial ability and risk-taking, part represents a return on capital invested in the business and part is the return to their labour which often embodies considerable human capital. The highest paid self-employed workers are those providing professional services, e.g. architects and lawyers.

Changes in market conditions. Wages for workers with particular skills or for workers in a particular region may change relative to the wages of other workers as market conditions change. The resulting *dynamic differentials* tend to disappear as the labour market adjusts. After the discovery of oil in the North Sea, for example, wages rose in the north-east of Scotland. These higher wages attracted labour from other parts of Scotland such as the Strathclyde region where traditional activities such as shipbuilding and steel-making were declining.

Barriers to entry. The numbers of people able to enter certain occupations are limited by the educational standards required and/or by the availability of apprenticeships and places on specialist courses. These barriers to entry restrict the supplies of particular skills and allow those completing their training to earn relatively high wages. Perhaps the best example of barriers to entry and their effects are in the medical profession. The high educational standards needed for admission and the few places available in medical schools restrict the number of graduates in medicine and helps explain the relatively high earnings of qualified doctors.

Trade union power. Trade unions may be able to raise their members' earnings by bargaining on their members' behalf and by using the threat of strikes to exercise industrial 'muscle'. A union's 'muscle' is greater, the more highly organized is the workforce in terms of union membership and the more important is the industry in which members are employed. Organized 'key' workers in the electrical power industry have considerable 'muscle'. In contrast, the threat of a strike by university teachers is a much less potent weapon. Although fairly well organized and providing essential services, health workers have done badly in terms of pay awards because of their traditional unwillingness to withdraw services from the sick.

Special talents or abilities. Some individuals have talents or abilities which attract high rewards. Most notable examples are some pop-stars and professional footballers. Sheena Easton, for example, probably earns far more as a pop-singer than she would earn in the alternative occupation to which she is next-best suited. The difference between her actual earnings and the income she could obtain elsewhere is her *economic rent*.

Overtime hours and payments. Even in the same occupation individuals may have different earnings because of differences in hours of overtime and in overtime rates of pay (see Chapter 6).

Unpleasant working conditions. Certain groups, for example miners, have to be rewarded for working in unpleasant, and often dangerous, conditions.

These factors help to explain differences in earnings, but differences in original incomes may also arise from *differences in wealth*.

Income may be obtained from owning a stock of wealth. Wealth can be accumulated in one's own lifetime or it can be obtained through marriage or inheritance. If wealth is defined in terms of marketable assets then the distribution of marketable wealth among the adult population in Britain is much more unequal than the distribution of income. The top 1 per cent of the wealth-owning population own around 25 per cent of total marketable assets, while the bottom 80 per cent own less than 25 per cent. In total the top 10 per cent owns 60 per cent of the wealth.

These factors help explain the relatively high original incomes received by some and the relatively low incomes received by others. But the low pay received by some individuals is not, at least in the short-run, an important source of poverty for households. Less than 20 per cent of all low-paid workers in the UK find themselves in the bottom 25 per cent of households. This is for two reasons. First, most low-paid workers are not the main earners in their households. Secondly, poverty is due more to absence of earnings than to low levels of earnings.

A low-paid worker may be defined as someone who works at least 30 hours per week, while earning less than someone one-tenth of the way up the male manual-workers' earnings distribution. On this definition, about 72 per cent of the low-paid workers in the UK are women. These low-paid women tend to have relatively unskilled jobs and to be concentrated in particular industries. Large numbers of the low-paid are to be found in agriculture, clothing and footwear, the distributive trades, public administration, the health service and defence.

There are several explanations for the predominance of women among the low paid:

(1) There is usually a low degree of unionization among women.

(2) Women are often geographically immobile. They cannot move to better-paid jobs in other areas because they are tied to the areas in which their husbands work.

(3) Women find themselves in low-skill occupations partly because they often take time out of the labour force to raise families and partly because of inequality of opportunity (see Chapter 6).

ROBIN HOOD AND REDISTRIBUTION

Original incomes are low for many households because these households contain few wage-earners. Many of the households in the poorest group are pensioner households which, unless they benefit from a private pension scheme, have no original income. Even in 1977 £2.30 (see Table 14.1) would have bought little and certainly not enough to sustain even a one-person household. The government, however, intervenes to redistribute income through the tax and transfer system.

A large number of households in the poorest group rely on state transfers such as pensions, unemployment benefits and Family Income Supplement. These transfers meant that in 1977 the typical household in the poorest group had a *net income,* i.e. income after taking account of redistributive measures ten times as great as its original income (see Table 14.1). In contrast, richer households find themselves worse off. Households in the richest group received an average net income £32 lower than their average original income.

Ideally, analysis of the impact of taxes and transfers should include the effects of indirect taxes, e.g. VAT, and of government expenditure on, for example, health and housing. However, there are conceptual problems in determining the *incidence* of these items and their effects cannot be considered here. For those taxes and benefits whose effects we considered in Table 14.1, implied average tax rates have been calculated as:

$$\frac{\text{average original income} - \text{average net income}}{\text{average original income}} \times 100$$

The average tax rates for the bottom two groups are negative because these groups are net recipients of cash benefits. Average tax rates rise with original income, reflecting the progressive nature of the tax and benefit system.

The system of taxes and benefits gave the two poorest groups higher shares in net income than in original income. This reduction in inequality shifts the Lorenz curve for Scotland inwards to B on Fig. 14.1 and reduces the Gini coefficient to 0.31.

However, even after the government has taken redistributive measures, considerable inequality remains. For example, the richest group still receives about six times as much income as the poorest group. The question of whether the government ought to redistribute further is largely a political issue.

A fundamental issue when considering redistributive policies is the trade-off between equity and efficiency. It may be the case that if incomes were made more equal some individuals would wish to work less, would have less incentive to save and invest and would take fewer entrepreneurial risks. The total income to be redistributed might then be reduced. The relative importance attached to equity as against efficiency differs among political parties and over time.

But however much equality is thought desirable there are important limitations on achieving targets.

(1)   Not all households have identical needs. If attempts were made to equalize households' net incomes, individuals would still not have identical living standards. Smaller households require lower incomes to achieve a given living standard.

(2)   The relationship between household size, household income and individual living standards is not a simple proportionate one. Larger households can achieve economies of scale in their purchases of, for example, housing. A two-bedroomed flat costs less than two one-bedroomed flats of similar quality. Thus, a two-adult household does not need twice the income of a one-adult household for its members to achieve the standard of living enjoyed by the one-adult household.

(3)   Some households receive 'unrecorded' income from the 'black' or 'informal' economy. It is not known whether such incomes make households' incomes more or less equal.

(4)   Households differ in the extent to which they receive 'unrecorded' income through government expenditure. The benefits to households of public expenditures on health and education, for example, are only felt indirectly. Again it is unclear whether their impact is progressive or regressive.

(5)   The transfer and income-tax system does not directly affect the distribution of wealth.

INCOME AND WEALTH

Rather than the narrow definition in terms of marketable assets, wealth may be defined to cover all assets capable of producing income including human capital, durable consumer goods and state and occupational pension rights. Income derived from human capital and durable goods is difficult to measure but if wealth is defined broadly to include the present values of pension rights the distribution becomes more even. Nevertheless the share of the top 1 per cent is still about 14 per cent of total UK wealth while the share of the bottom 80 per cent is about 45 per cent.

Differences in individuals' abilities to acquire wealth may be related to differences in income. Life-cycle theories suggest that while their incomes may vary over time, individuals wish to maintain a steady flow of consumption expenditures. During their working lives individuals finance consumption expenditure out of current income but some part of their income is saved to finance consumption during retirement. These savings are used to accumulate assets and the individuals' stock of assets reaches a peak at retirement age. Thus, individuals nearer retirement age will have greater stocks of wealth. Clearly individuals with higher incomes will be able to save more and acquire greater stocks of wealth.

Much of the distribution of wealth may be related to factors other than income. Inheritance and gifts made by living relatives may account for about 25 per cent of total UK wealth. Generally, wealth is more equally distributed now than at the beginning of the century. In part this is due to a rearrangement of wealth holdings among the wealthier families rather than to a redistribution from wealthy to poor families. Some redistribution has taken place because of the spread of home ownership and the relative rise in house prices. Those individuals who hold their wealth in company shares have experienced a fall in the real value of their assets during the 1970s and this will also cause a move towards greater equality in wealth distribution.

HOW TO BECOME WELL-OFF

There seem to be several important steps to becoming well off. It is important to pick the right job: become a hospital doctor, solicitor or higher executive rather than a farm worker or shop assistant. It helps if your spouse works and if you do not have a large number of children. And when you retire, make sure that you and your spouse have contributed to good occupational pension schemes. To avoid being poor, ensure that at least one adult in your household works full-time, and for preference two. But if you want to be really well-off, it is a matter of choosing your parents or spouse carefully, earning a lot when you are younger so that you can live off investment income later, owning your own business, although that can be risky, or winning the football pools.

PART IV

Economic Role of the Government

15

Government Expenditure and Revenues

J. K. SWALES

Public Expenditure in Scotland in 1979/80 was at least £6.9 billion. This does not include certain spending, notably on defence, which is difficult to allocate to specific regions. Important grants to industrial investment and private house purchase which take the form of tax rebates are also excluded. Even so, the sums of money involved are very large, amounting in total to almost half of Scottish Gross Domestic Product.

GOVERNMENT EXPENDITURE

Government expenditure has two important functions in the Scottish economy. First, it provides goods, services and welfare payments which directly benefit the Scottish population. Secondly, government expenditure is an injection of aggregate demand, and its absolute size partly determines the overall level of Scottish unemployment. The money for these activities is raised by either taxation or borrowing.

Public expenditure is very diverse (Fig. 15.1). The government; (a) provides certain goods and services free, (b) subsidizes and regulates certain activities, and (c) also attempts to redistribute income via social security payments and pensions.

Social security, which accounts for over 25 per cent of Scottish public expenditure, includes pensions, social-security payments and unemployment and child benefits. Overall spending on these tends to vary counter-cyclically. That is, as employment falls, social security and unemployment payments rise simultaneously. In the second half of the 1970s real expenditure under this heading increased by 25 per cent in Scotland. There were three main reasons for this: an increase in unemployment, an increase in the number of pensioners and a rise in child benefits.

Health expenditure has remained fairly constant in real terms in the recent past and makes up around 18 per cent of total public expenditure in Scotland. Over half of this is on hospitals. Projections for the future are that health expenditure will rise to meet the expected increase in demand from the larger number of elderly people in the population (see Chapter 10).

Education expenditure is very similar in absolute size to the health budget. It comprises spending on schools, further education, research, administration, arts and libraries. Whilst in the recent past expenditure on education has been fairly stable in real terms it is expected to fall in the period up to the mid 1980s. This is due partly to a smaller school population, and partly to tightening university budgets (see Chapter 13).

Housing. Just over 11 per cent of Scottish public expenditure is allocated to housing. This comprises grants to council housing, the New Town Development Corporations, the Scottish Special Housing Association, Housing Associations working on a non-profit basis and government departments who provide housing for families of police, prison staff, the armed services and certain other services. The subsidy to council housing comes in two forms: a payment from central government in the form of the Housing Support Grant and a payment from local rates. In the past decade these subsidies have averaged about 50 per cent of council-house expenditure in Scotland. However, this is not to imply that council-house tenants are a particularly favoured housing-tenure group: substantial subsidies are paid to private house owners, mainly in the form of income tax relief on mortgage interest payments (see Chapter 12).

Trade, industry and employment includes the various temporary employment schemes such as the Youth Opportunities Programme, and grants to industry from regional and industrial policy (see Chapters 16, 17). The amounts spent on these prog-

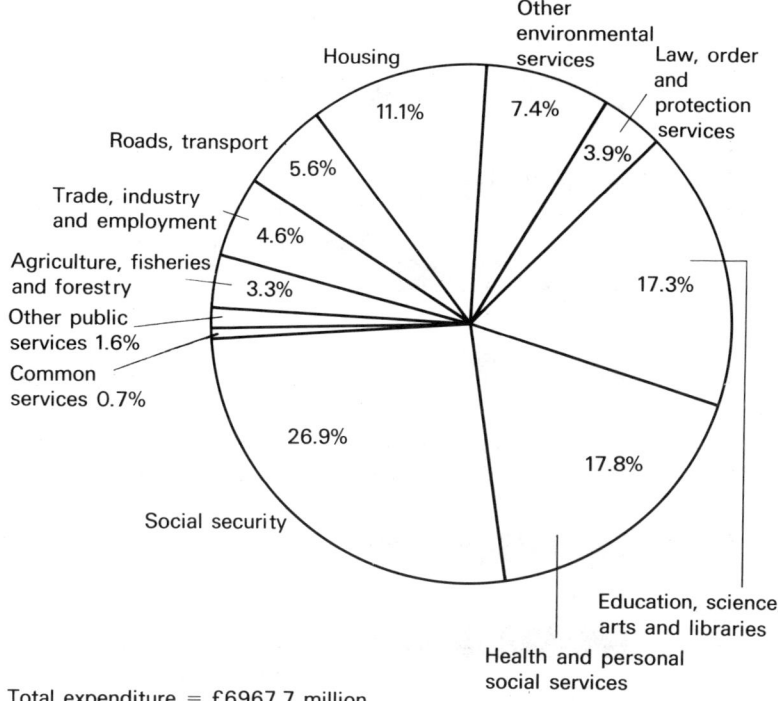

Total expenditure = £6967.7 million

Fig. 15.1   Identifiable public expenditure in Scotland, 1979/80

rammes are relatively small and have almost halved since the mid 1970s.

In 1978 UK public expenditure per head was £1006. However, over the UK regions there is a wide variation around this average (Fig. 15.2). Northern Ireland has the highest public expenditure per head with £1313: the West Midlands the lowest with £826. Scotland lies in the higher end of this range with a per capita expenditure of £1155.

Why are there such regional variations in *per capita* public expenditure? Three main general explanations have been put forward.

(1) Some government expenditure is of a redistributive nature: that is to say, income transfers from the rich to the poor, e.g. social-security payments or grants particularly aimed at low-

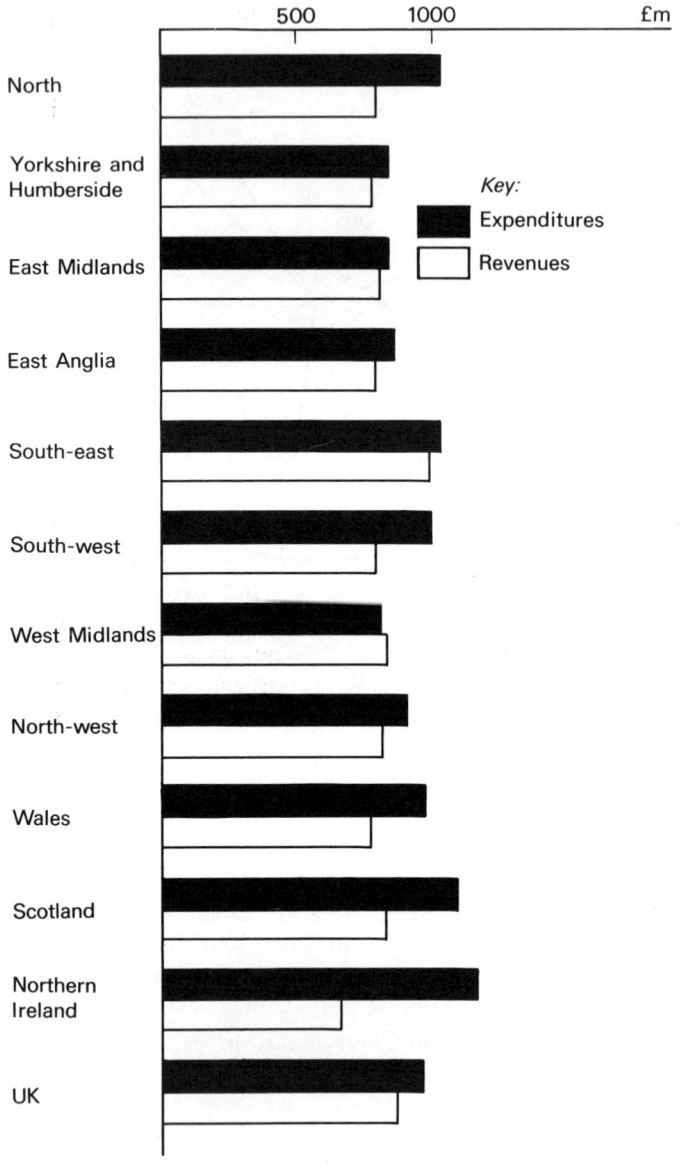

Fig. 15.2   Public expenditure and revenues per head, 1977/78, current prices

income regions as part of regional policy. In so far as average incomes vary between regions, so will expenditures in these particular government programmes.

(2) The government provides many goods and services which are complementary to other privately produced goods. The clearest example here is the provision of roads: there will be the largest demand for roads in those areas where car ownership is highest.

(3) Many services the government provides are directed at, or heavily used by, particular age groups, e.g. education, old-age pensions. Thus, the age composition of a region can affect the level of public expenditure.

Public expenditure in Scotland is relatively high for four more particular reasons. First, Scotland has a very large area for its population: there are, therefore, relatively large subsidies on agriculture and roads. Secondly, Scotland has high unemployment. Therefore, it receives high social-security payments and grants under regional policy. Thirdly, over 50 per cent of houses in Scotland are rented from the local authorities or new towns. This is the largest percentage for any UK region. Finally, demand for state-provided educational and medical services is relatively high in Scotland.

TAXATION

For 1977/8, the average UK *per capita* tax payment was £878 (Fig. 15.2). Again there is a wide range of regional values, though most noticeable is the very large per capita tax payment paid in the South East. Scotland's tax payment per person, £834, is lower than the UK average. In general, the UK tax system is progressive, so that *per capita* tax payments tend to fall as average income in the region falls.

If the figures for expenditures and revenues are considered together, it can be seen that in 1977/78, for the UK as a whole, government expenditure was 15 per cent greater than taxation. This additional expenditure is covered by borrowing, *the Public*

Sector Borrowing Requirement, which amounted to £128 per person. However, again there are wide regional variations. Scotland is a major beneficiary from the government budget: in Scotland expenditure was 38 per cent higher than tax revenues, which amounted to a sum of £321 per person.

MACROECONOMIC IMPLICATIONS

In the traditional *Keynesian* view, the level of government expenditure plays a key role in determining the level of *national income*. Government expenditure, together with private investment and exports, is an *income injection* into the economy. Part of the income generated by these injections is spent on goods and services, creating further income, which leads to further consumption, and so on (see Box 15.1). Therefore any increase in government expenditure will lead to a larger increase in aggregate income. Because of this induced increase in consumption, the effect of the initial injection is multiplied: this is *the multiplier*. The value of the multiplier will be larger, the greater is the *marginal propensity to consume*, i.e. the greater is the proportion of any increase in income which is consumed. On the other hand, an increase in taxation will reduce *aggregate demand* and, therefore, reduce national income. Taxation represents a *withdrawal* of income from the economy, and reduces the proportion of any additional income which will be consumed. Therefore an increase in taxation reduces the multiplier.

The application of the simple Keynesian approach to the UK economy as a whole has been challenged. The alternative view is that any increase in government expenditure not financed by taxation will increase borrowing and interest rates, and therefore *crowd out* private investment. However, this criticism is much less valid when applied to an individual region. If government expenditure is increased in Scotland, any possible offsetting effects (such as reduced private investment) will be spread over the UK economy as a whole and will not necessarily be concentrated in Scotland. Increased government expenditure will generally create a net income injection in the Scottish economy, increasing aggregate demand and output.

Exports to the rest of the UK were the major income injection

TABLE 15.1 *Income injections in the Scottish economy, net of direct imports, 1973 (£ million)*

Government current expenditure	1075.8
Government fixed capital formation	236.9
Other fixed capital formation	690.7
Exports to the rest of the world	1214.2
Exports to the rest of the UK	2502.5

into the Scottish economy in 1973 (Table 15.1). Clearly this is what would be expected, given that the Scottish economy is closely integrated into the UK economy as a whole. Similarly, imports from the rest of the UK are a major source of income withdrawals from the Scottish economy.

After exports to the rest of the UK, combined government expenditure is the next largest income injection. The figures given in Table 15.1 actually understate the importance of the government because they do not include expenditure on income transfers, such as pensions and social-security payments. Government expenditure dwarfs private investment as an income injection.

Government macroeconomic policy is not only concerned with maintaining a high level of aggregate demand. It also attempts to reduce short-run fluctuations in output associated with the *trade cycle*. A traditional view concerning depressed regions is that these are very sensitive cyclically. The conventional argument is that the depressed regions are those which concentrate on the production of investment goods (particularly heavy engineering). The demand for these goods is very unstable, rising rapidly in times of economic recovery but falling markedly during recessions. These wide fluctuations in the region's export industries are transmitted, via the consumption multiplier and supply linkages, to the rest of the regional economy.

This argument does not hold for the Scottish economy in the post-war period because:

(1) fluctuations in economic activity in Scotland have generally not been more marked than fluctuations in the UK economy as a whole;

BOX 15.1   *Scottish local employment multipliers*

Since the early 1960s government regional policy has attempted to attract mobile manufacturing and service plants to Scotland. The local impact of the introduction of these plants is often extensive. Income and employment is not only generated directly in these plants, but also in supplying firms, companies producing local consumption goods and services and in local public services. A number of studies have been carried out to assess the economic effects of particular investment projects in Scotland.

Scottish Pulp and Paper Mills, Fort William

In 1969 this mill employed 850 people. However, the overall impact on employment in the Highlands may have been over twice this amount. First, about 400 additional workers were employed in forestry and transport, supplying the pulp mill with timber and transporting the product. Secondly, an estimated 460 people were employed producing local consumption goods and services which were required by the additional workers. This is the effect of the conventional Keynesian multiplier. Thirdly, the pulp mill increased the population in the Highlands and, therefore, raised demand for local public services such as education, health and local authority services. This is calculated to have increased employment in local public services by 230.

Stirling University

In 1973, the expected impact of the new university on Stirling's local economy was estimated. By 1976 the university was expected to have 3800 students and employ 440 academic and 930 non-academic staff. Continuing construction at the university was expected to generate a further 310 jobs. Although the university would create around 1700 jobs directly, the total additional employment generated in the Stirling economy was estimated to be around 3000. An increase in employment in the local labour market of over 8 per cent was associated with the location of a university at Stirling. Here increased local consumption both from the staff and students at the university plays a more important role in generating additional employment than was the case for the pulp mill.

Massey-Ferguson, Kilmarnock

Government support is often sought when large plants threaten to make redundancies. In 1980 the Massey-Ferguson combined harvester plant employed 1500 workers. Its closure is expected to reduce employment in Kilmarnock in the short run by approximately 1650. Notice that again the initial reduction in employment is magnified by further reductions in other sectors of the local economy. However, the downward employment multiplier operating here is much smaller than the upward multiplier estimated in the two other studies. There are three main reasons for this. First, Massey-Ferguson is a multinational corporation and bought a very small percentage of its inputs locally. Secondly, it is thought that with a major closure there will be some offsetting increase in local public expenditure on social work, education, training etc. Finally, it is argued that, at least in the short run, although local income may be falling, there will be some resistance to making workers unemployed.

---

(2) Scotland's industrial structure is no longer strongly biased towards heavy industry. The decline of traditional industries together with the effects of regional policy in attracting growth industries, means that Scotland now has an industrial structure which is very close to the UK average.

Present thinking on macroeconomic management has tended to move away from very active government intervention to iron out short-term output fluctuations. However, certain elements of government expenditure and taxation have the effect of automatically stabilizing the economy. First, as aggregate income falls, taxation will fall, as many taxes are directly related to either current income or expenditure. Secondly, certain government expenditure programmes increase as income and output fall. In particular, expenditure on unemployment benefit and social-security payments will rise. In 1981 the Manpower Services Commission estimated that each additional worker made unemployed added £3000 to the Public Sector Borrowing Requirement, through a combination of reduced taxation and increased welfare payments. However, whilst these measures cushion the impact of rising unemployment on the local economy, they work in reverse when income and employment are rising. When the Scottish economy moves out of the present recession, taxation will rise and social security expenditure will fall.

We have concentrated here on the direct impact of the government on the Scottish economy. However, it must be emphasized that the performance of the Scottish economy is closely linked with that of the rest of the UK. Government action to stimulate the UK economy as a whole will have a strong effect on Scotland through the increased demand for Scottish exports to the rest of the UK. In the immediate future the best prospects for a healthy Scottish economy would come from a strong UK economy.

16

The Scottish Region and the Regions of Scotland

BRIAN ASHCROFT

NO SIMPLE PROBLEM . . .

Scotland is an administrative region of the UK. Scotland and the other regions of Northern Britain have tended to experience more severe economic problems than the regions of Midland and Southern Britain. The rates of unemployment and emigration have traditionally been above the rates found elsewhere, while the level of Gross Domestic Product (GDP) per head has usually been lower.

However, it would be a mistake to believe that all of Scotland experiences the same regional problem. Until the late 1960s, regional problems within Scotland could be viewed in terms of a simple dichotomy. First, there were the *urban-industrial problems* of West Central Scotland and Tayside (see Box 16.1). Secondly, Scotland suffered from *pre-industrial phase problems* in the rural-agricultural regions and sparsely populated areas of the Borders, Dumfries and Galloway and the Highlands and Islands.

West Central Scotland suffered and still suffers from an unbalanced industrial structure. Declining industries such as ship building, textiles, steel, coal mining and heavy engineering dominate the region. However, the diminishing importance of these industries and the *beneficial* effects of regional policy in diversifying the industrial structure have reduced the *structural dimension* (see Box 16.1) of the area's problems. By the end of the 1960s *locational* difficulties (see Box 16.1) were more in evidence. Indigenous industry had failed to expand. This contrasted with the performance of incoming firms and similar industries elsewhere in the UK. Poor local management and industrial relations are often suggested as the likely causes. The sheer scale of the

BOX 16.1   *Regional problems and regional policy*

A regional problem exists when there are sufficient geographical variations in economic activity and prosperity to be of concern. These can arise at all stages of economic development. It has been suggested that Scotland suffers from all these problems simultaneously. A simple way of categorizing economic development is to divide it into four stages.

The *pre-industrial* phase involves a subsistence economy characterized by agricultural regions exhibiting low per capita income levels, low rates of growth of income, low investment, poor social infrastructure and, in particular, inadequate transport facilities. Accordingly, the regional problems associated with this phase require a policy which emphasizes infrastructure provision.

In the *transitional* phase, the national economy is moving from an economy largely based on agriculture to industrialization. This movement, often produces a dualistic structure which contains a modern centre and a relatively backward periphery. Capital and labour flows from the periphery to the centre serve to increase the disparity. Policies of control and the encouragement of 'spread' effects from centre to periphery are likely to be needed at this stage of economic development.

The regional problems of the subsequent *industrial* phase will be familiar to most people living in modern industrial economies. High unemployment rates, low activity rates, net outmigration and low rates of regional GDP growth. Regional economists often distinguish between the *structural* and *locational* aspects of the problem. The former reflects specialization in industries which have ceased to maintain their national comparative advantage, or industries which have failed to retain their importance because of the growth of new products. In addition, the region might fail to exploit fully its own comparative advantage in certain activities. In the latter, there is a general tendency for industry to perform less well in the region compared with industry in the nation as a whole. Both aspects of the problem often exist simultaneously. The structural aspects of the problem require policies to diversify the industrial base or to change specialization in favour of modern fast-growth industries. The locational side of the problem is more difficult to deal with. The problem can have many causes: managerial inefficiency, labour inefficiency, poor industrial relations, use of obsolete production technologies, finance constraints and poor communications. Many of these influences will be interdependent and will vary in relative importance from region to region.

The *post-industrial* phase produces regional problems which are a consequence of overdevelopment. Over-concentration can occur in particular locations because of market failure. Market forces do not provide a mechanism whereby the economic agent pays the social costs of his/her actions, i.e. the additional costs imposed on others. Development proceeds further than would be expected if each person had to meet directly the full costs of his actions; congestion results. This can be seen in shortages of living, recreational and road space, high levels of noise and air pollution and excess demands for factors of production generally. However, continued concentration of development is likely to raise individuals' and firms' private costs above the private benefits associated with a centralized location. Market forces eventually work to produce a 'flight' of industry and the more mobile sections of the population to the suburbs. The familiar inner-city problem emerges: low-quality, overcrowded housing, a predominance of public-sector housing, low car ownership, a relatively unskilled labour force, a high proportion of large households and a population skewed towards the very poor, the very young and the very old. In recent years in the USA and Western Europe, changes in production and consumption technologies, and in the relative price and availability of transport have served to increase further the relative and absolute decentralization of jobs and population. However, this has been occurring not only from the centres of cities, but also from urban areas as a whole. The main beneficiary is the rural periphery. The current dilemma for policy is whether this spatial movement represents a real and permanent shift in production and consumption possibilities. If so, attempts to 'save' the central areas of major cities might be like trying to resurrect the dodo.

---

problems in this region – an area which contains nearly half of Scotland's population – has been sufficient to ensure that the economic performance of Scotland as a whole lagged behind that of the UK.

The problems of the *pre-industrial phase* were particularly evident in the Highlands and Islands. The demand for labour was low in relation to the supply of labour. Seasonal employment in the tourist trade made the problem worse. Moreover, the supply of labour was and is peculiar. There are many crofters, for example, who are available only for part-time work (see Chapter 7). So, the Highlands and Islands experienced unemployment, under-employment and a history of depopulation. The region comprises about 14 per cent of the land mass of the UK – 14 000 square miles – yet today, contains only 0.45 per cent of the UK population – 250 000 people.

In the 1970s things began to change. In 1973, the development of oil and related activities in the eastern regions of Scotland appeared to be producing a dual economy between east and west Scotland. By 1982 it could be argued that the country's economic hub was being shifted from the west to the east coast. The growth of oil and electronics industries began to exert a gravitational pull on Strathclyde's important servicing sector. Moreover, the problems of the west of Scotland have been made worse by the current recession. Those urban areas with highly specialized and *income-elastic* industrial structures have suffered a greater relative decline in production and employment. An expansion of the national economy will restore the demand for many of these products, but not necessarily in the same areas as before. Many manufacturers have taken advantage of the recession to close plants and move production elsewhere. One effect of these developments can be seen in the high unemployment rates in several parts of Scotland. By September 1982 the Rutherglen area, for example, was experiencing an unemployment rate of 76 per cent for males and 59.3 for males and females taken together.

However, it is not certain that the relative decline of the west of Scotland is due solely to the effects of recession and industrial expansion in the east. Other changes have been occurring. The centres of the major cities throughout Scotland have been losing people and jobs. Indeed, the urban areas in general have been declining while the rural areas have been expanding (see Table 16.1). The urban areas appear to be less suited to modern production methods and less attractive as residential locations. Questions can, therefore, be raised about the suitability for future economic development of many of the old urban areas in both west and east Scotland (see Box 16.1).

TABLE 16.1   *Urban–rural shift or west–east drift? Changes in manufacturing employment in Scotland, 1968–76*

Area	Absolute change	Percentage change	Rank	Type of area
Edinburgh	−19 901	−35.39	1	Urban
Glasgow City	−47 400	−28.38	2	Urban
Dundee	−11 572	−27.11	3	Urban
Borders	−2 993	−18.37	4	Rural
Outer Glasgow	−276 711	−16.93	5	Urban
Scotland	−105 838	−14.93	6	
Aberdeen	−3 918	−14.35	7	Urban
Central	−5 424	−13.05	8	Urban
Outer Strathclyde	−5 041	−5.55	9	Urban/Rural
Outer Tayside	−337	−2.24	10	Rural
Outer Grampian	+497	+3.93	11	Rural
South-west	+596	+5.53	12	Rural
Outer Lothian	+2 163	+8.02	13	Urban
Fife	+8 737	+29.04	14	Urban/Rural
Highlands and Islands	+6 426	+80.87	15	Rural

MEANS NO SIMPLE SOLUTIONS

Until 1976 large parts of the country were designated Special Development Areas (SDAs), Development Areas (DAs) and Intermediate Areas (IAs). By 1970 virtually all of Scotland was a designated DA, and areas of even more severe unemployment were designated SDAs. Regional policy sought to divert growth in the demand for labour from the relatively prosperous and allegedly congested regions of southern Britain to these assisted areas. Financial subsidies were provided for new manufacturing. Factories were built speculatively in advance of demand. In addition, the government imposed restrictions on the expansion of offices and factories in the West Midlands and South-east England using the ODP and IDC controls (see Box 16.2).

The local and regional authorities played a passive role by providing transport, housing and other *infrastructure* to accommodate the population, jobs and investment diverted to their areas by national regional policy. New Towns sprang up on the periphery of large cities for example, East Kilbride near Glasgow and Livingston near Edinburgh, built to ease the strains of population growth within these larger cities. In addition, it was hoped that the New Towns would act as centres of growth by attracting mobile firms, both from abroad and other parts of Britain.

BOX 16.2   *A policy in transition: The recent chronology*

Date   *Policy Change*

The death of national regional policy . . .

December 1976   Regional Employment Premium (REP) abolished. This accounted for 39 per cent of regional assistance to industry in Scotland in 1974/75.

April 1977   Government announces no additional assisted areas to be designated. Some areas downgraded including Aberdeen area.

Summer 1977   Reduction in coverage and intensity of the Office Development Permit (ODP) and Industrial Development Certificate (IDC) control policies. Slow-down in Government's own office dispersal programme to the regions.

July 1979   Government office dispersal programme cut by two-thirds from 30 000 to 10 000 posts. IDC control relaxed further. Size of assisted areas to be reduced in stages from 44 per cent of UK working population to 25 per cent by August 1982. New *non*-assisted areas in Scotland predominantly rural and/or oil development areas. Regional Development Grant (RDG), accounting for 42 per cent of regional industrial assistance in Scotland in 1974/75, reduced from 20 per cent to 15 per cent of eligible investments in DAs from August 1980. The RDG in SDAs remains at 22 per cent of eligible investments. More stringent criteria for the provision of Selective Financial Assistance (SFA) in assisted areas under Section 7 of the 1972 Industry Act.

February 1982   Abolition of IDC control.

. . . and the birth of local urban policy?

July 1975	Powers to grant Selective Financial Assistance handed to the Scottish Secretary of State from Department of Industry.
December 1975	Creation of Scottish Development Agency with powers to further economic development, maintain employment, promote industrial efficiency and improve the environment. Preference eventually to be given to certain spatial priority areas in West of Scotland, Dundee and Leith.
June 1977	White Paper (Cmnd 6845) makes specific proposals for the inner areas of major conurbations. Followed by Inner Urban Areas Act which gives effect to 1977 proposals. Power of local authorities to stimulate economic development especially in inner-city areas. Local authorities and public agencies able to enter into partnership arrangements with government in areas of special need.
April 1980	Government propose Enterprise Zones in certain depressed urban areas. Scottish Zone eventually located on a 570-acre site in Clydebank and a small part of Glasgow District.
September 1981	Proposals for 'winding up' the development corporations of the Scottish New Towns.
April 1982	Strathclyde Regional Council's Employment Grants Scheme. Council pays 30 per cent of the wages of a newly employed unemployed worker for first six months of employment.
July 1982	Government propose that two additional Enterprise Zones be established in Scotland. One zone to be located at Invergordon, the other to be decided after submissions from District Councils.

Finally, special regional problems were handled by special agencies. The creation of the Highlands and Islands Development Board (HIDB) in 1965, is one example. The HIDB was given a wide range of powers to stimulate development in the seven rural and sparsely populated counties of Western and Northern Scotland.

Since the middle-70s *spatial policy* in Britain has begun to change. The focus has shifted, particularly in Scotland, from national regional policy to local urban policy. The responsibility for local economic development has been partially transferred to local government and regional agencies such as the Scottish Development Agency (Box 16.2 outlines the recent chronology – see Chapter 17).

Changes in political and economic circumstances appear to be responsible for this shift:

The national recession implies a low level of demand for goods and services; interest rates have also been high. Firms are less likely to want to invest in new factories in these circumstances, therefore, there is a lower volume of mobile factories which regional policy has traditionally relied upon to provide jobs in depressed areas. These areas must, therefore, rely more on local firms to create the employment opportunities. Local authorities and regional agencies with greater knowledge about local economic conditions than central government have, therefore, been given, or have assumed, a more important role in spatial policy.

Employment in British manufacturing industry has been declining since 1966. This has resulted in a narrowing of the gap between the performance of the fastest- and the slowest-growing industries. Therefore, depressed regions with a preponderance of slow-growing industries have performed relatively better. In addition, those regions that have been prosperous but have in the past relied on the superior performance of one or more industries are now experiencing relatively higher unemployment rates. The West Midlands with its heavy reliance on the car industry is a good example. The traditional contrast between the problem regions of northern Britain and the prosperous Midlands and the South is much less apparent. Scotland, for example, which once had one of the highest unemployment rates in the eleven Standard Regions of Britain, now ranks sixth highest. This relative narrowing in regional imbalance, plus the higher absolute unemployment rates experienced in all regions because of the recession, has led central government to doubt the need for a national regional policy on the same scale as before.

Within Scotland and indeed all British Standard Regions the more rural areas have proved to be more attractive to economic development than urban areas. These changes in the desired location of production have served to reinforce the move away from a national regional policy to policy initiatives directed and controlled at the local level.

Finally, the 1979–83 Conservative Government sought to reduce public expenditures. They have reduced national regional policy expenditures. However, they sought to make the lower level of expenditures more cost-effective by being more selective in the areas chosen to receive assistance. Government sought to channel expenditures only to those areas found to be in greatest need. These changes in policy raise several important issues.

Place Prosperity or People Prosperity?

Unemployment rates have traditionally been used in Britain to identify those areas in need of assistance. Other criteria such as the strength of the economic links within and between areas, e.g. travel-to-work flows, marketing links, worker migration and firm movement patterns, were given little attention. This mattered less when broad areas were scheduled for assistance. However, today the areas receiving assistance are much smaller. These small areas are, therefore, more likely to have strong economic links with other areas close-by. This has two implications for policy. First, the unemployment rate in a small area might not prove to be a reliable indicator of the employment opportunities available to the population resident in the area. Secondly, it may be difficult, if not impossible, to reduce the rate of unemployment in the area. An example might make this clear.

Almost the whole of Glasgow and its surrounding areas is one large labour market. Differences in unemployment rates between localities within the Greater Glasgow area are, over time, likely to be due to differences in the occupational composition of the workforce residing in each locality. Areas with relatively poor-quality, low-price housing attract low-income earners who are more likely to be unemployed, particularly during a recession. The high unemployment rates in Rutherglen, or Clydebank, for example, which in the short run are obviously due to local factory closures or contractions will, over a longer period, reflect the occupational composition of the residential workforce. These areas are part of a larger labour market so their high unemployment rates need not mean that the areas are especially disadvantaged compared with other parts of the Glasgow region.

Moreover, attempts to create jobs in these areas alone, such as the decision to schedule 570 acres of Clydebank as an Enterprise Zone, might be doomed to failure. Any jobs created in the zone might be filled by migrants and commuters from other parts of Glasgow. Alternatively, local Clydebank residents might obtain jobs, but at the expense of other workers whose firms might relocate from other parts of the Glasgow area.

Much of the current urban policies being applied in Scotland may, therefore, be misconceived. If two labour-market areas have similar unemployment rates then, with the present policies, it would appear that the area in which unemployment is more evenly spread is less likely to contain areas eligible for assistance. If unemployment is the problem to be removed, then the labour-market area itself should be the target of policy. When disparities between labour-market areas are low or if it is difficult or costly to identify the boundaries of these areas, then the problems of unemployment and poverty might be more cheaply removed by a national policy. This might lack the drama of an inner-city policy but it might be more effective in helping people rather than areas.

Work to the Workers: a Discredited Strategy?

The names read like a roll of honour: Invergordon, Fort William, Clydebank and Linwood. Are these victims of external control and heartless 'foreign' managements who have little concern for Scotland's future? Perhaps. Yet inward investment is important to the Scottish economy (see Chapter 19). It has been estimated that over the period 1960 to 1976, regional policy was directly responsible for the creation of 76 000 jobs in manufacturing industry. This estimate does not include the additional jobs resulting from *multiplier* effects (see Chapter 15). Two-thirds of the jobs created directly by policy, were provided by mobile firms and plants moving into the Scottish economy. Yet, regional policy incentives were available to both local and non-local manufacturing firms investing in Scotland. Perhaps the problem lies in the failure of local Scottish firms to compete successfully with non-local firms.

The growth in external control, due in part to the effects of regional policy, *can* produce harmful effects. Independent creative management might be stifled and the emigration of Scotland's best managers might result. The absence of Research and Development (R&D) and marketing functions in branch plants, can limit the possibilities of future growth. Increased linkages with other economies reduces the degree of indigenous control over the Scottish economy (see Chapter 19). However, given the absence or slow rate of local development, it is by no means certain that inward investment is a second-best policy. It is often only by access to non-local finance, technical knowledge – as, for example, in the recent influx of electronics firms – and larger markets, that a small open economy is able to grow more quickly than on its internal resources alone. To the extent that market imperfections result in direct foreign investment rather than movements of capital through the international capital market, then some external control is the 'price' that must be paid for potentially higher growth.

*Regional Investment Subsidies: Two Steps Forward,
One Step Back?*

The Regional Development Grant (RDG), a subsidy to capital investment in manufacturing industry, is the main regional policy incentive (see Chapter 17). If the objective of regional policy is job creation, then the RDG might be inefficient because unlike a labour subsidy it will lead to some substitution of capital for labour. However, investment subsidies might be considered by entrepreneurs to be more certain than labour subsidies and therefore might be more likely to be taken up. Conventionally, investment grants are paid in full when the investment is under-

TABLE 16.2 Regional development grants (over £25 000) to districts of Scotland 1975–1980 (£ per head of population at 1975 prices)

Administrative District	Grant paid (£ per head)	Rank	Assisted area status, 1979	Administrative district	Grant paid (£ per head)	Rank	Assisted area status, 1979
Motherwell	270.22	1	SDA	Edinburgh City	21.93	29	SDA/DA
Orkney	209.09	2	DA	Cumbernauld	20.61	30	SDA
Falkirk	185.46	3	DA	Midlothian	19.79	31	SDA
Cunninghame	124.16	4	SDA	East Lothian	18.82	32	SDA
Ross and Cromarty	107.68	5	DA	Dundee City	18.53	33	SDA
Banff and Buchan	81.17	6	SDA	Ettrick	18.24	34	SDA
Monklands	78.90	7	SDA	Kilmarnock	17.53	35	DA
Clackmannan	72.35	8	SDA	Dunfermline	17.44	36	DA/SDA
Annandale and Eskdale	70.56	9	SDA	Nairn	16.94	37	SDA
Kirkcaldy	66.89	10	DA/SDA	Berwickshire	16.06	38	SDA
Angus	57.14	11	SDA	Shetland	15.13	39	SDA

Name				Name			
West Lothian	52.52	12	DA	Lochaber	14.50	40	DA
Nithsdale	45.39	13	SDA	Skye	12.26	41	DA
Inverclyde	43.97	14	SDA	Perth	11.42	42	SDA/DA
Inverness	42.95	15	DA	Stirling	9.93	43	SDA
Dumbarton	41.92	16	SDA	Stewartry	8.50	44	SDA
Western Isles	39.15	17	DA	NE Fife	8.00	45	SDA
Renfrew	37.32	18	SDA	Tweedsdale	7.79	46	SDA
Moray	36.67	19	SDA	Wigtown	7.57	47	DA
Glasgow City	35.34	20	SDA	Gordon	7.49	48	SDA/DA
Aberdeen City	33.95	21	DA	Roxburgh	7.38	49	SDA
Clydebank	32.25	22	SDA	Kincardine	6.17	50	DA/SDA
Argyll	31.13	23	DA	Lanark	3.87	51	SDA
Kyle and Carrick	30.03	24	DA/SDA	Badenock	3.26	52	DA
East Kilbride	28.33	25	SDA	Caithness	2.88	53	DA
Strathkelvin	25.50	26	SDA	Bearsden	1.94	54	SDA
Cumnock and Doon Valley	25.17	27	DA/SDA	Sutherland	1.87	55	DA
Hamilton	22.21	28	SDA	Eastwood	Nil	56	SDA

taken. Labour subsidies are paid not as a lump-sum but on a recurrent basis. Therefore, firms might be less likely to respond to a labour subsidy if they believe that they might not receive the subsidy in full if government changes its policy in the future. Moreover, if each new technology is more capital-intensive than the older technology then investment subsidies might accelerate the introduction of new technologies and so foster long-run development and growth. There is, therefore, no simple case to be made favouring new job subsidies rather than investment subsidies.

However, regional investment subsidies should perhaps be applied more selectively to avoid large-scale capital investments which provide few jobs and which are likely to occur whether subsidies are offered or not. It seems that the distribution of RDG expenditures in Scotland is heavily influenced by the location of existing large capital-intensive firms which regularly undertake substantial investments, e.g. the British Steel Corporation in Motherwell and British Petroleum in Grangemouth. Many SDAs, which are designed to receive more assistance, have actually received less than the Scottish average for all areas of £46.45 per head of population (see Table 16.2). Changes in area designation appear unlikely to solve the problem because many of the areas containing large capital-intensive plants are still areas of high unemployment. Obviously, one cannot necessarily expect areas that are unattractive to investing firms to have high rates of RDG expenditures. Also many of the districts receiving little aid are linked functionally to districts that do receive substantial aid. Nevertheless, it seems likely that many subsidized investments are likely to have gone ahead in the absence of the subsidy. At a time when it is seeking to increase cost-effectiveness it seems strange that government has decided to persist with a general subsidy, provided largely on demand to manufacturing industry.

Regional Equity and National Efficiency: an Inevitable Trade-off?

There is a continuing debate as to whether regional policy is essentially a social or an economic policy. Both views accept that regional policy can, to varying degrees, reduce the imbalance between regions. *The social view* contends that greater interregional equity is bought at the price of *reduced* national economic efficiency. The policy, by intervening in fairly efficient spatial market processes, ensures that firms and workers make sub-optimal location decisions. Output from the available national resources is lower than it would be in the absence of intervention. In contrast, *the economic view* suggests that interregional equity *improves* national economic efficiency. Normally, the adjustment process between spatially separated factor and product markets is imperfect. For example, prosperous regions suffer from conges-tion and 'overheated' labour markets, while depressed regions experience excess labour supply and the under-utilization of many other resources. Regional policy, by reducing this imbal-ance, can raise national employment and increase the nation's productive potential.

After a period of several years, especially in the 1960s, when the British Government appeared to accept the economic case for regional policy, recent events suggest a policy change. Yet, if this interpretation is correct, then the government is perhaps confu-sing the economic case for regional policy with the difficulties of implementing the policy at least cost during a recession. Unem-ployment, due to the recession, in relatively prosperous regions, need not vitiate the economic case for regional policy. Regional policy may, by reducing mismatching between jobs and workers in particular areas, lower the level of structural unemployment in the economy. It follows, that regional policy should be directed towards those regions which still suffer excess labour supply when the demand and supply for labour in the country as a whole is in balance. Using this criterion, most of Scotland would still be an assisted area.

17

Industrial Policy in Scotland

J. K. SWALES

In the third quarter of 1981, unemployment in Scotland was 294 000, 13 per cent of the registered labour force, and industrial output, excluding oil, had fallen almost 14 per cent since 1975. Industrial policy, that is direct government intervention in the private sector of the economy, is intended to improve this performance.

What are the effects of industrial policy on Scottish output and Scottish unemployment? Is present government expenditure on industrial policy in Scotland well directed?

REASONS FOR GOVERNMENT INTERVENTION IN INDUSTRY

We live in a mixed economy. Many goods and services are provided directly by the government and are distributed free or at a nominal charge, e.g. health services, /defence, education (see Chapters 10, 11 and 13). In other industries, output is sold in the market, but production is in public, not private, hands. These are the nationalized industries, e.g. British Steel, the National Coal Board, British Rail. However, even where it is thought desirable for production to be left to private enterprise following market forces, the government still often intervenes. Why?

1. The market mechanism is, in general, only efficient where there is a reasonable degree of competition. However, it is usually in the interest of individual firms to reduce competition. This can be done either by a company forming a restrictive agreement

with the other firms in the same industry or by that company taking over, or forcing out of business, competing firms. The government, therefore, has legislation covering monopolies, mergers and restrictive practices which allows it to investigate and to regulate companies' anti-competitive behaviour (see Box 17.1).

2. The free market is a good means of determining the production and allocation of goods only where the private costs and benefits of using resources correspond to the social costs and benefits. There are a number of situations where this will not occur and government intervention might be required. First, social costs and benefits might diverge from private costs and benefits because of *'externalities'*. This occurs where part of the costs imposed on the community by the manufacturing of a product are not paid by the producers, or where part of the benefits received from the product are not paid by the consumers. A good example of an external cost is pollution. Here, a cost is imposed on the community which does not generally have to be paid for by the polluter. Without appropriate government regulation we would expect too much of the product (and too much pollution) to be produced. An example of an activity with associated external benefits is research and development. Here, resources used by one firm to develop a new technology will benefit not only that firm, but also others who eventually use the same technology and consumers who get a better and/or cheaper product. In this case, if research and development were left simply to the free market, one would expect sub-optimal expenditure.

Second, private costs may differ from social costs because the money price of an input might differ from its *opportunity cost*. For example, the standard argument for regional policy is that there is an excess supply of labour in regions with high unemployment. The product of unemployed labour is zero or, at least, very low. So the cost to society of employing such labour, in terms of lost output, is almost certainly lower than the cost to the potential employer who must pay the going wage. On the basis of this low social cost of labour, output and employment should be expanded in depressed regions but this may require government intervention to make it worthwhile for a private employer.

BOX 17.1   *Competition policy*

In the UK this has three main related strands:

(1)   the removal of restrictive practices and collective agreements between firms;
(2)   the supervision of firms with significant market power;
(3)   the control of mergers.

The Office of Fair Trading (OFT) directs the activities of the two major institutions created to implement policy: the Restrictive Practices Court (RPC) and the Monopolies and Mergers Commission (MMC).

The *Restrictive Practices Court* was set up in 1956 by the Restrictive Trade Practices Act. This Act required the registration of all restrictive trading agreements. These are agreements amongst firms to limit competition by, for example, setting common prices or sharing out the market on a geographical basis. The 1956 Act took such agreements to be against the public interest. If a restrictive agreement were to be retained, the firms had to present a case to the RPC arguing, first, that the agreement conferred a particular benefit and, second, that this particular benefit outweighed any general detriment. Two examples of particular benefits which would be considered by the court are: (i) where serious and persistent unemployment would occur in some regions if the restrictive agreement were removed; (ii) restrictions help maintain a high level of exports in the industry.

The 1956 Act prohibited the collective enforcement of resale price maintenance: the 1964 Resale Prices Act extended this to the individual enforcement of resale prices. In general, firms could no longer specify the price at which retailers must sell their product. Firms wishing to be exempt from this legislation had again to make a case to the RPC arguing that the retention of retail price maintenance in their industry would confer specific advantages which would outweigh any general detriment.

The *Monopolies and Mergers Commission* started life as the Monopolies Commission in 1948. It was renamed in the Monopolies and Mergers Act of 1965. The MMC investigates monopolies referred to it by the Director General of Fair Trading. For the purposes of this legislation, a monopoly is defined as a situation where a single supplier has at least 25 per cent of a particular market. Unlike the position taken over restrictive practices, there is no prior presumption that monopoly generally operates against the public interest. Each particular case referred to the Commission is investigated on its own merits. If the MMC feels that a monopolist has acted against the public interest, it will recommend various actions to be taken by the government. The powers that the government has in these circumstances are very wide and include the ability to break up the monopoly.

The Monopolies and Mergers Act of 1965 extended the power of the MMC to consider mergers and the present procedures on merger control date from 1973. The mergers panel of the OFT scrutinizes all proposed mergers which involve assets of more than £15 million or which would give the merged company more than 25 per cent of the market. The Director-General of Fair Trading then advises the Trade Secretary on which of these should be referred to the MMC. The Trade Secretary does not have to accept this advice, but generally he does. The MMC then has six months in which to investigate the merger and decide whether or not it is in the public interest. The Commission's report then goes to the Trade Secretary, and the Director General of Fair Trading offers his advice on the report. The Trade Secretary can then act on the Commission's conclusions and is able, if required, to stop the merger taking place.

A recent controversial and unusual case was referred to the MMC in June 1982. The MMC was asked to consider a proposed takeover of the mining engineering company Anderson Strathclyde by the Chartered Consolidated mining group. Anderson, based in Motherwell, is the third largest engineering company in Scotland with just under 4000 employees. Provision of supplies and services to Anderson and some sub-contracting accounts for a considerable number of jobs in other firms. In December 1982, the majority on the MMC concluded that there would be adverse effects on management effectiveness and industrial relations and that consequently the merger would have adverse effects on employment, both in Anderson's own works and among suppliers. No compensating advantages were seen to set against these effects. However, the Trade Secretary overturned this recommendation of four members of the Commission in favour of the minority dissenting position of two members. Chartered then proceeded with the takeover bid and achieved control of Anderson Strathclyde in March 1983.

3. In a free enterprise economy, markets allocate present resources between present demands. However, decisions have to be made concerning the future and, in general, future markets do not exist. This means that firms have to invest without knowing for certain what future demand for their product and future input prices will be. It is clear that investment involves much risk for the individual firm and there is no guarantee that the level of investment undertaken in a free market economy would be socially optimal. Generally, governments attempt to increase the level of investment through various forms of subsidy. Also, attempts can be made to reduce the amount of risk by providing firms with more information about probable future trends in their industry and by trying to co-ordinate the investment plans of the major companies within an industry.

These are economic arguments which could be used to support government intervention in private industry. But remember:

(1) we have not talked at all about the bureaucratic costs and difficulties involved in implementing these policies;
(2) industrial policies are, it is sometimes suggested, undertaken for no sound economic reason, but rather for political expediency.

AID TO PRIVATE INDUSTRY IN SCOTLAND

In the financial year 1979/80, government aid to private industry in Scotland totalled £167 million, excluding specific employment subsidies (see Table 17.1). In absolute terms, this seems a great deal of money but it represents only 2.5 per cent of total identifiable government expenditure in Scotland and only 1 per cent of the Scottish Gross Domestic Product. Government expenditure on industry is dwarfed by public spending on sectors such as health, education and housing (see Chapter 15). What is more, government expenditure on industry in Scotland has been falling rapidly in the last few years (see Table 17.2). The drop between 1975 and 1977 is particularly sharp.

TABLE 17.1   *Identifiable public expenditure on industry in Scotland, 1979/80*

	£m
Regional support and regeneration	103.1
Industrial innovation	50.9
General support for industry	12.5
Regulation of domestic trade	0.6
Total	167.1

It seems curious that aid to industry has been falling in this way at a time when the Scottish economy, and particularly manufacturing industry, has been in so much trouble. There are three main reasons for this decline in public expenditure. First, at the beginning of 1977 the government stopped paying a major subsidy, the Regional Employment Premium (REP). This was a subsidy on all employment in manufacturing in Development Areas (see Chapter 16). In the financial year 1975/6, it made up 25 per cent of all industrial aid in Scotland. It is argued that this subsidy was dropped at least partly due to pressure from the EEC who saw REP as a subsidy on the running costs of a major section of British industry and, therefore, as a distortion to trade.

TABLE 17.2   *Industrial policy expenditure (IPE) in Scotland (£million*) as a percentage share of total government expenditure (TGE) in Scotland and Scottish GDP*

	Expenditure	IPE/SGDP	IPE/TGE
1972/3	402.2	3.1	7.1
1973/4	411.5	3.0	6.8
1974/5	439.4	3.3	6.5
1975/6	512.6	3.7	7.2
1976/7	381.2	2.7	5.5
1977/8	212.8	1.5	3.2
1978/9	209.2	1.4	3.2
1979/80	167.1	1.1	2.4

Note: *1979/80 prices.

Second, the amount the government spends on industry is likely to be low when the general level of activity in the economy is low, because the activities which attract most aid – investment, research and development and plant relocation, are likely to be cut back by firms during a recession. Third, attempts to control public expenditure, particularly when social security and unemployment benefit payments are rising, are reducing the amount available to be spent as industrial policy.

We should recognize, however, that there are major elements of policy towards industry which do not directly involve government spending. These include the following.

1.   *Tax relief* on the purchase of new buildings in manufacturing and on investment in machinery or plant used in industry and commerce. It is estimated that in the financial year 1979/80, £660 million was forgone in Scottish taxes as a result of such policy on tax relief. This tax relief is high relative to the expenditure figures in Table 17.1.

2.   *Controls on industrial expansion* in prosperous areas of the UK have also benefited Scottish industry in the past. In the post-war period, firms wishing to expand their activities were required to obtain an Industrial Development Certificate (IDC). This was much easier to obtain in a Development Area than in a non-Development Area. An IDC refusal in a non-Development Area, together with the provision of investment grants in Development Areas, led many firms to relocate part of their production in the Development Areas, including Scotland. However, since the mid-1970s, IDC control has collapsed, and it was abolished in 1982 (see Chapter 16).

3.   *Competition policy*, particularly measures to change the degree of industrial concentration, might have affected the performance of Scottish industry. In 1973, only 41 per cent of Scottish manufacturing employment was in plants owned in Scotland: 39 per cent was in English-owned plants and the remainder in foreign-owned plants. It is sometimes argued that this has adverse consequences for Scotland – that Scotland is caught in the 'branch plant syndrome'. Concern is felt over the loss of high level management functions, the lack of local research and development

and the possibility that branch plants will be closed first in economic recessions (see Chapters 16 and 19). It is also feared that when decisions are made outwith Scotland, Scottish suppliers will be neglected. But on the other hand, branch plants often supply much needed employment, investment and technology to the Scottish economy. It is clear, however, that the level of branch plant operation in Scotland will depend on the degree of industrial concentration in the UK as a whole. Large companies generally have head offices in London and operate a large number of branch plants in other parts of the country. A permissive monopolies and mergers policy will, therefore, tend to encourage the growth of large firms and so the growth of external ownership in peripheral regions such as Scotland.

THE COMPONENTS OF INDUSTRIAL AID IN SCOTLAND

Industry in Scotland is assisted by two national policies – regional and industrial.

Regional Policy

This aims to stimulate production and to increase employment in specific designated areas (see Chapter 16). Over two-thirds of government expenditure on regional policy in Scotland is on assistance given under the Industry Act (1972) (see Table 17.3). This assistance comes in the form of:

(1) *Regional Development Grants* (RDGs), automatic grants on manufacturing investment of 15 per cent in Development Areas and 22 per cent in Special Development Areas. After their election in 1979, the Conservative Government reduced the area within Scotland designated as Development and Special Development Areas (Chapter 16). However, RDGs remain an important source of industrial aid.

(2) *Selective Financial Assistance* (SFA) which consists of discretionary grants or soft loans on investment projects in Development and Special Development Areas. This aid is

TABLE 17.3   *Regional preferential assistance*
(£million)

	1981/2
SDA	58.4
Industry Act 1972	
Selective Financial Assistance	19.0
Regional Development Grant	142.7
HIDB	
Loans	7.0
Grants	6.3
Tourism	2.0
Total	235.4

additional to RDGs. To be eligible, the investment project must be shown both to be economically viable and to increase new employment, or at least safeguard existing employment.

(3)   Most of the remainder of this assistance is channelled through the Highlands and Islands Development Board (HIDB) and the Scottish Development Agency (SDA). These agencies give aid on a more flexible basis to industry in Scotland and also provide factory space. The HIDB operates in the Highland Region, the surrounding islands and parts of Strathclyde Region. It is mainly concerned with assisting rural industries and tourism. The SDA is a much larger organization which operates throughout Scotland (see Box 17.2).

BOX 17.2   *Scottish Development Agency*

Perhaps the most visible aspect of government industrial policy in Scotland, the Scottish Development Agency (SDA), was established in 1975 by the then Labour Government. It has five main objectives:

(1)   the development of Scottish entrepreneurship;
(2)   support for growth sectors;
(3)   the promotion of new technology;

(4) the improvement of industrial efficiency and competitiveness; and
(5) the regeneration of local economies.

The annual expenditure of the SDA has risen from £19.7 million in 1976/7 to £94.8 million in 1980/1. Most SDA expenditure is not directly related to industry, but is on factory and industrial estates and on urban and land renewal (see the table below). Moreover, to a large extent, these expenditures do not represent net additional spending in Scotland, as the SDA took over the responsibilities of two existing public bodies, the Scottish Industrial Estates Corporation and the Scottish Office Derelict Land Unit.

The SDA's expenditure on factory building makes it the largest single provider of industrial space in Scotland: in 1980 it let 730 factories which employed in total 75 000 persons. Initially, the agency could subsidize industry by offering rent free periods to tenants, but the 1980 guidelines, issued by the Conservative Government, directed the SDA to adopt market pricing on the sale or letting of factories. Indeed, the SDA is now only to become involved in factory provision where private provision is clearly inadequate. The SDA has always had a great interest in land renewal and, increasingly, it is becoming involved in specific urban renewal projects. For example, the Glasgow Eastern Area Renewal (GEAR) programme involves planned capital expenditure of £47 million to regenerate the east end of Glasgow physically, socially and economically. The SDA is not only participating in GEAR in its own right through environmental improvement, some social initiatives and factory building, but is also co-ordinating the other agencies participating in this project. The SDA is also involved in other urban initiatives in Glengarnock, Clydebank, Dundee, Leith and Motherwell.

The SDA can intervene directly in industry in a number of ways. It can make grants for craft-training schemes, provide loan capital for buildings, equipment and working capital, and it can purchase equity stock in private companies. At present minor activities are also the provision of venture capital and loan guarantees. At March 1980, the agency had committed £25.4 million investment funds to 42 companies (plus companies funded by the Small Business Division of the Agency). Of the 42 named companies, the majority were small: 27 employed less than 150 workers. It is clear that the agency's role of channelling investment and private industry in Scotland and, thereby, restructuring Scottish industry is a minimal one. The SDA's concentration on small firms might simply reflect the limited funds which the agency has available, though the SDA claim that they have identified a 'gap' in the availability of finance (particularly equity finance) for small and medium sized Scottish firms.

SDA Expenditure for Financial Year 1980–81
(£ million)

Industry, investments and small businesses	6.3
Factories and industrial estates	47.0
Land renewal	22.8
Urban renewal	13.3
Research, promotion information and capital equipment	5.4
Total	94.8

Industrial Policy

1. *Industrial innovation* support is the main element of government spending in Scotland under industrial, rather than regional, policy. These expenditures are made by the Departments of Industry and Energy to develop and promote new industrial technologies. Details of the projects in Scotland on which this money is spent are not known, but in the UK as a whole a large proportion of the Department of Energy's expenditures in this programme was on energy research, both oil and gas and nuclear power. It is likely that Scotland has a significant share of this expenditure.

2. *Enterprise encouragement* was a major aim of the 1979–83 Conservative Government's industrial policy. A number of schemes have been introduced, at the UK level, to encourage entrepreneurs to set up new businesses, to encourage worker profit-sharing schemes and to reduce the tax and administrative burden

on small companies. The most visible aspect of this policy has been the introduction of Enterprise Zones. Within these small, inner city areas, tax and administrative demands have been sharply reduced in an attempt to stimulate industry (see Box 17.3). Of the first nine Enterprise Zones set up in 1980, one was to be located in Scotland at Clydebank. In 1982, the number of Enterprise Zones was increased and Scotland was allocated two more.

BOX 17.3. *Enterprise Zones*

In the 1980 budget, the Chancellor of the Exchequer, Sir Geoffrey Howe, announced a novel policy package designed to halt the decline of certain inner city areas. These areas were designated as Enterprise Zones and each has a maximum size of 500 acres (approximately 1 square mile). Firms within Enterprise Zones benefit from various forms of tax relief and planning and bureaucratic restraints are removed as far as possible. In Enterprise Zones firms are:

(1) exempt from Development Land Tax;
(2) exempt from all rates and property taxes on industrial and commercial property;
(3) eligible for 100 per cent capital allowances (for Corporation and Income Tax purposes) on commercial and industrial buildings.
(4) subject to much simplified planning procedures;
(5) excluded from the scope of the Industrial Training Boards;
(6) exempt from the need for Industrial Development Certificates;
(7) eligible for much faster customs facilities;
(8) required to supply the bare minimum of statistical information to the Government.

These measures apply over and above benefits that firms might receive from other existing policies, such as regional policy, urban development or derelict land policies.

Initially, seven UK central city areas were chosen as Enterprise Zones, of which one, Clydebank, was in Scotland. As is typical, the Clydebank Enterprise Zone is not concentrated in one single unit, but it is split into seven separate sites which include the abandoned Singer and Albion works as well as three sites on the banks of the Clyde. More recently (up to the end of 1982), a further 15 UK Enterprise Zones have been announced, of which 2 have been in Scotland. These are at Invergordon, where the large British Aluminium Company smelter was recently closed, and on Tayside (Dundee and Arbroath).

The philosophy behind setting up Enterprise Zones is that British industry in general, and central city firms in particular, have suffered from too much government intervention and too high levels of taxation. The government hopes that Enterprise Zones will rejuvenate the depressed central cities by stimulating enterprise and private initiative. The scheme has only been going a relatively short time and, as yet, opinion is sharply divided about the effectiveness of Enterprise Zones. The government's critics argue that the zones are too small, that they will distort local labour markets, rather than create new jobs, and that they are likely to be more attractive as warehousing and wholesaling sites than for manufacturing.

Criticisms and Comments

1.   The weakening of industrial and regional policy in Scotland at a time of very high unemployment and dramatic manufacturing decline seems to suggest negligence or indifference. It must first be remembered, however, that there has been increased expenditure by the Manpower Services Commission on temporary employment and training schemes which partly offsets this decline. It was also part of the Conservative Government's view that public expenditure must be cut in order to reduce interest rates, inflation and taxation. Moreover, they regard much assistance to industry in the past as maintaining inefficient plants in inefficient locations. Whether the present industrial recession will leave Scottish industry leaner and fitter or just smaller and weaker is a matter of debate.

2.   Expenditure on RDGs and tax relief on investment are major items in the government's aid to industry. Both are automatic for all investment in manufacturing in Development and Special Development Areas. This means that much aid is given for investments which would have gone ahead anyway. More-

over, capital intensive projects are particularly favoured by these subsidies. In these cases, the government can pay out large amounts in RDGs and tax relief for a handful of jobs. If the government is concerned about reducing its own expenditure, some form of selectivity might be favoured, investment grants might be limited to new, rather than replaceable investment, and a ceiling might be put on the amount of subsidy per job in an assisted investment project.

3. Selectivity might be achieved by channelling more aid through a flexible agency such as the SDA. It would then be the Agency's responsibility to identify marginal investment projects and to give the appropriate aid. The government, perhaps rightly, has not adopted this course. The SDA is only a minor source of aid to Scottish industry and recent guidelines laid down by the 1979–83 Conservative Government emphasized the use of commercial criteria in assessing possible investments in Scottish industry.

4. A weakness of both industrial and regional policy in Scotland is the neglect of service industries: for example, service industries are not eligible for RDGs. In the last decade however, there appears to have been a secular shift in employment in the UK economy in general. Employment in manufacturing has been contracting, whilst service sector employment has risen (see Chapter 2). Perhaps a greater effort should be made to attract mobile service sector jobs to Scotland. A start could be made by the government devolving more civil service jobs to Scotland. Recently, the Overseas Development Administration has moved to East Kilbride and part of the Ministry of Defence is scheduled to move to Anderston Cross in Glasgow in late 1985. But these moves are much smaller than had been planned in the mid-1970s.

5. It is clearly a sound objective to attempt to encourage enterprise, but even if government policy is successful it will only generate significant economic effects in the long run. Most new companies are very small and subject to a very high failure rate. Moreover, the Conservative Government's Enterprise Zones have received a very mixed reception. Although the government

claim that they have been successful, they have been criticized on a number of grounds. It is argued that

(a)   companies within Enterprise Zones will benefit at the expense of other local companies located outwith these zones, and that economic growth within Enterprise Zones will come mainly from plants diverted from other parts of the city;

(b)   Enterprise Zones will be very attractive to large concerns outside manufacturing industry, particularly commercial, retailing and warehousing developments. These activities are land-intensive and generate relatively few new jobs.

(c)   the Enterprise Zones are very small, around one square mile in area. Even if this whole area were fully occupied by businesses, it is estimated that this would only generate 15 000 jobs.

18

Enterprise or Service? Nationalized and State Owned Industries

DAVID LIVINGSTONE

Nationalized industries and other state-owned enterprises provide diverse and important goods and services for both people and firms in Scotland. These include energy in the form of gas, electricity and coal; transportation by air, canal, ferry, road and rail for passengers and freight; postal services and the key industrial input, steel. These activities create a great deal of income and employment within Scotland. For example, the South of Scotland Electricity Board has about 13 000 employees, the North of Scotland Hydro-Electric Board about 4000, the British Gas Corporation about 7000, the Scottish Transport Group about 11 000 and the National Coal Board about 21 000 (see Box 18.1). Through the demand created for intermediate goods and employees' demands for final goods, these industries are of great importance to private-sector firms in Scotland. They have an important indirect impact through *industrial linkages* and *regional Keynesian multiplier effects*.

The development of public ownership in the UK accelerated after 1945. Prior to that Britain was a predominantly *capitalist economy* with the means of production and distribution mainly in the hands of private enterprise. However, several activities had already been transferred to the state. As far back as 1657, the Post Office had become a government monopoly. Fear that the mails might be used for treasonable purposes led Cromwell to appoint one of his officers as Postmaster General with powers to open letters. Although the duties were subsequently altered, the title remained in use until 1969. Other undertakings became publicly owned before 1945 including the Port of London Authority, the BBC, the Central Electricity Board, British Overseas Airways and the North of Scotland Hydro-Electric Board.

BOX 18.1 *Nationalized industries and public corporations in Scotland*

	Numbers employed in Scotland	Main locations	Main activities
Scottish nationalized industries			
North of Scotland Hydro-Electric Board	4000	Highlands and Islands	Generation, transmission and distribution of electricity
South of Scotland Electricity Board	13005	Central and Southern Scotland	Generation, transmission and distribution of electricity
Scottish Transport Group	10755	Country wide	Passenger traffic with some road haulage – the Highlands and Islands
Other nationalized industries in Scotland			
The British National Oil Corporation	2155	North Sea and East Coast	Exploration in North Sea
National Coal Board	21000	Central Scotland	Mining of Coal, and sale to industrial but not domestic users
British Gas Corporation	7000	Towns and cities in Scotland	Distribution of gas, mainly natural gas from North Sea
British Shipbuilders	12261	Upper and Lower Clyde and Aberdeen	Shipbuilding and ship repairing
British Steel Corporation	11000	Ravenscraig, Craigneuk	Steel making (strip and pipes)
The Post Office	14364	Whole country	Postal Service and giro banking
British Telecom	18000	Whole country	Communication by telephone and telex
British Airways	825	Scottish Airports	Internal flights to UK airports mainly from Glasgow and Edinburgh
British Airports Authority	1402	Prestwick, Glasgow, Edinburgh and Aberdeen	Administering airports and cargo terminals
British Railways Board	17200	Whole country	Passenger and heavy freight transport by rail
British Transport Docks Board	Not available	Ayr and Troon	Coal and general cargo; fish exports
British Waterways Board	150	Caledonian, Crinan, Monkland, Forth and Clyde and Union canals	Some commercial and passenger traffic on Caledonian Canal Leisure activities.
Other public corporations			
United Kingdom Atomic Energy Authority	Not available	Dounreay and Thurso	Fast reactor development
British Broadcasting Corporation	1200	Glasgow, Edinburgh, Aberdeen Dundee	Transmission of TV and radio programmes
Independent Broadcasting Authority	50	Glasgow and Aberdeen	Licensing of commercial TV and radio stations
Civil Aviation Authority	1423	National Airports and Aerodromes at Benbecula, Inverness, Islay, Kirkwall, Stornoway, Wick, etc.	Air traffic control safety and miscellaneous services

BOX 18.2 *Definitions*

Nationalized industries – corporations whose assets are publicly owned; whose board members are not civil servants but are appointed by a Secretary of State and which are mainly involved in industrial and trading activities.

Other public corporations – different because they are less engaged in the direct sale of goods and services to customers.

WHY PUBLIC OWNERSHIP?

Unlike defence, which is a *pure public good,* the goods and services produced by nationalized and publicly-owned enterprises could generally be produced by private enterprise. Several inter-related economic, political and social factors account for the development of the *mixed economy.*

Economies of scale. The market mechanism operates through *decentralized, uncoordinated* decisions by individuals. This may result in competing firms setting up relatively small-scale, high-cost plants. Nationalization may permit coordination of investment and, thus, the maximization of scale economies.

Control of monopoly power. Markets for many products have tended to become dominated by a few large, competing firms, i.e. *oligopolists.* Their scale of operations may generate scale economies which may be passed on to consumers in lower prices. However, collusion among oligopolists may allow them to earn monopoly profits by raising prices and reducing output. Other measures such as price controls are available, but the state may react by nationalizing the industry. Prevention of companies' abuse of monopoly power is particularly important where resources such as energy supplies and products such as steel are essential to industrial-growth. Of course, nationalization does not remove monopoly power. Rather, it is to be hoped that state control will deter its use to exploit the customer and society as a whole.

Political ideologies and control of the 'commanding heights'. Differences in governments' political ideologies determine their attitudes to public ownership. Equating ownership with power, the Labour Party has advocated the transfer of ownership of certain activities to the state, especially in the essential sectors of the economy. As an extension of this policy, the Labour Party is currently intending to extend public ownership into the financial sector, through the nationalization of a commercial bank. Differences in ideology between the two dominant political parties in the UK are reflected in alternate periods of nationalization and privatization. In the post-war period the Labour Government nationalized the iron and steel and road transport industries. Subsequently, the Conservative Party which came to power in 1951 denationalized both industries, although certain firms in road transport remained in public hands because they could not be sold back to the private sector at the asking price. The 1964 Labour Government nationalized the iron and steel industry again. The Conservative Government elected in 1979 was firmly committed to reducing state ownership.

Social aspects of state ownership. Certain industries owned by the state provide services, often essential to the maintenance of particular areas, which the market system would not provide or would provide only at greater cost. Postal services in the sparsely-populated and remote areas of the Highlands and Islands, for example, are charged at the same rates as apply throughout the rest of the UK.

Firms and industries have also been supported by the state, again often at heavy losses which private enterprise could not or would not sustain to help secure some regional balance in economic activities. This explains the original siting of the British Aluminium Company smelter plant at Invergordon. This closed in 1982 when the government declined to continue the large subsidy from the nationalized industry which supplied electricity, the major input into the aluminium smelting process. Support has also been given to help overcome problems of economic and social adjustment as certain industries go into decline. Particularly important to Scotland has been the delaying of closures of mines, shipyards and steel plants. For example, in the 1950s and 1960s many Scottish mines were to be closed and many mineworkers migrated from areas heavily dependent on coalmining such as Ayrshire and West Fife to the Yorkshire and Nottingham coalfields. The closure of loss-making mines was delayed to reduce the personal and social trauma of the more efficient, quick closure.

Pragmatic reasons. Governments, both Labour and Conservative, have taken over firms or industries either to avoid the employment and income consequences of closure and/or to prevent the loss of an important service. Such events can be thought to have important potential political consequences. Poor industrial relations, technical inefficiency and inadequate investment had long characterized the railway and coal industries and led to their nationalization. Similar problems led to the public ownership of British Leyland, with a plant at Bathgate, and the shipbuilding industry in the 1970s. Rolls Royce (UK) Ltd, an aeroengine manufacturer, with plants in Hillington, East Kilbride and Glasgow, was taken into public ownership in 1974 when the company suffered severe and costly technological difficulties in the development of the RB211 engine. The problems were resolved with the aid of public finance and the engine is used widely in the jumbo jets of the 1970s and 1980s. The British National Oil Corporation, with headquarters in Glasgow, was established to capture oil revenues directly and to provide governments with first-hand knowledge of North Sea oil operations.

The range of motives accounts for the diversity of activities and also for differences in the nature of state ownership (see Box 18.1). Some industries are wholly state-owned such as coal, electricity and postal services while public ownership in some cases extends to only one company in an industry, for example, British Leyland in vehicle manufacturing and BNOC in the oil industry.

THE SCOTTISH DIMENSION

Nationalized industries are British rather than specifically Scottish, English, Irish or Welsh. Usually there are no separate Scottish data, only those for the UK as a whole. For administrative purposes each industry is divided into areas or regions and a Scottish area may embrace part of England and vice versa.

In Scotland, for example, there are two electricity boards responsible for the generation, transmission and distribution of electricity. In England and Wales on the other hand, these functions are separated. There is a Central Electricity Generating Board responsible for generation and transmission and twelve area boards responsible for distribution. The North of Scotland Hydro-Electric Board (NSHB) was created in 1943 to develop hydroelectric resources. Its territory covers about one-quarter of the land area of the UK but contains only about 2 per cent of the national population and serves only some 454 000 customers. Until the creation of the Highlands and Islands Development Board (HIDB) in 1965 it was also involved in promoting the economic and social welfare of the area and, although that responsibility has largely disappeared, it is still actively engaged in the development of salmon and trout fishing in the Highlands.

The South of Scotland Electricity Board (SSEB) was created in 1947. Its area is relatively compact, covering from the industrial belt of Scotland down to part of the north of England, and contains over 1.605 million customers. The NSHB and SSEB are responsible to the Secretary of State for Scotland, unlike other nationalized industries operating in Scotland which are responsible to the relevant Ministry in Whitehall.

The absence of adequate data and different operating circumstances limit useful comparisons between operations located in Scotland and those in the rest of the UK. From available data for 1980 it appears that:

(1) with just under 10 per cent of all NCB employees, Scottish coal-mines produce about 7 per cent of total UK output, i.e. 7.7 million out of 109.6 million tonnes. Output per man was lower, and costs higher, than the national average;

(2) gas supplied to domestic consumers in Scotland is about 1p per therm more expensive than the national average while supplies to industrial consumers are about 5p per therm more expensive;

(3) the Scottish Transport Group had 2.96 employees per vehicle compared to 5.39 for London Passenger Transport and 3.61 for the National Bus Company.

PUBLIC MONOPOLIES

Certain public enterprises have considerable monopoly power. Poor productivity performance may result in the exercise of this power to raise prices, as with the electricity industry. But having an industry monopoly does not necessarily insulate state enterprises from competition. This competition comes from private enterprises and/or other publicly owned enterprises.

The major public-sector transport undertaking is British Rail, which was nationalized in 1947. The Scottish region of British Rail extends from Carlisle to Kyle of Lochalsh and from Berwick-upon-Tweed to Wick and Thurso. It provides commuter services in the main conurbations and express services to all parts of the UK. Freight services are provided largely for specialized traffic such as coal, steel products, petroleum products and chemicals. Much of the freight is handled through the five Scottish motorail terminals. Both passenger and freight services are operated in markets in which customers often have a choice of methods of transport. The development of motorways has raised average speeds for long-distance road transport and the internal airlines offer competition in the longer-distance passenger markets. Socially, railway commutor services face competition from cars and subsidized bus services. Strathclyde spend £21.3 million in 1982 on subsidizing BR commuter services in the region. This is more than the total subsidy on buses, ferries and the Glasgow Underground. Yet in 1981 the number of rail passengers fell by 14 per cent.

The various state monopolies supplying energy are also, to some degree, competing with one another. Some industrial consumers may choose to run their machinery and equipment and heat their factories using oil-, electric- or coal-driven generating plants. Domestic consumers have similar choices with respect to central-heating systems. However, the ability to change is often limited by the nature of equipment once a commitment has been made to a particular source of energy.

In some industries there is an element of international competition. For example, supplies of coal from abroad, notably from Poland and the USA compete with the output of the

National Coal Board (NCB). Fifteen of the NCB's 211 collieries and 1 of its 6 open-cast mines are in Scotland.

Public Monopoly Prices

The prices nationalized industries charge in Scotland, as in the rest of the UK, do not simply reflect their costs of production.

(1) Natural gas, piped from the North Sea is, in the short run, relatively very cheap to produce. If sold at a price which would earn a normal profit, many customers would be attracted away from other energy suppliers. Great public investment has been made in these other industries. To protect them, the government has ordered the British Gas Corporation to increase prices considerably. In 1981, the industry earned in the UK record profits of £726.4 million.

(2) Rapid developments in communications technology are causing British Telecom to make huge investments in new equipment. Some public monopolies have a reputation for using funds, borrowed to pay for new capital equipment, to finance current spending which is often increased by generous wage settlements in the face of concerted union action and by general administrative inefficiency. British Telecom's borrowing has been severely limited by the government. The high spending on new equipment is being paid for by high monopoly prices for telephone calls and other services. In 1981, British Telecom earned in the UK record profits of £1024.4 million.

(3) The National Coal Board sells coal at a price below production cost to the SSEB and the Central Electricity Generating Board in England. Scottish coal cost £39.60 per tonne to produce in 1981 and was sold to SSEB for £37.53 per tonne, including transport cost. The NCB deficit is covered by a government grant. This grant has recently been increased to cover the loss of coal sales caused by the switch to burning gas condensates from the North Sea oil fields in the Peterhead power station. The continuation of production and employment in the coal industry is, politically, a very sensitive issue.

By their nature, providing social benefits and having been taken over for political reasons, publicly-owned industries cannot be judged on a market criterion of profitability. Reflecting the complexities of the industries' origins and functions, no satisfactory system of assessment has been developed. Attempts to develop criteria to appraise investment plans, for example, have foundered on difficulties of determining; (a) appropriate break-even periods, (b) appropriate target discount rates, (c) the basis for depreciation, and (d) values to be assigned to social functions.

The losses of publicly owned enterprises are met by the state. In 1980 the NCB had a loss of £135 million, of which £29 million was in Scotland; British Shipbuilding had a loss of £41.4 million with £29.3 million being attributable to Scottish yards (only the division building warships, including Yarrow's of Scotstoun, was profitable).

Such losses may be interpreted as arising from the provision of social benefits but may, in contrast, be regarded as the result of; (a) bureaucratic inefficiency and lack of dynamism, perhaps resulting from an awareness that losses will be met by the state, (b) failure to resolve internal problems, such as poor industrial relations and inadequate investment performance, which led to public ownership in the first place, and (c) an inability to change and diversify away from their traditional activities in response to changing market conditions.

PRIVATIZATION

Such critical views have been widely held in the Conservative Party with its adherence to the doctrine of free competition. It was no surprise, therefore, that after the election in 1979 of Mrs Thatcher's administration, there were moves to curb the monopoly powers of the nationalized industries. These moves followed two lines. First, in some cases, such as the National Bus Corporation and the Central Electricity Generating Board and their Scottish equivalents, competition from private enterprise has been allowed, and the British Gas Corporation no longer has the sole right to sell North Sea gas. Secondly, some of the industries have been sold either in whole or in part to the private sector. The National Freight Corporation, for example, became an employee-owned company in January 1982. Shares in British Aerospace and Cable and Wireless Ltd are now partly privately owned. Certain 'up-stream' activities in the oil industry have been transferred from the British National Oil Corporation through the sale to the public of shares in Britoil. The British Railways Board has sold some of its properties including the prestigious Gleneagles Hotel and golf complex to private investors and pressures for further denationalization are to be expected in the future from within the Conservative Party.

Part V

Scotland's External Relations

19

Foreign Firms

KEITH P. D. INGHAM

Foreign firms are very important to Scotland for employment and production. Why do *they* want to come here and why do *we* accept them? Why do Scottish public authorities actively encourage foreign firms to set up in this country?

In 1977, 101 300 workers in Scottish manufacturing industry worked for foreign firms controlled from outside Britain. This is 16.4 per cent of manufacturing employment and is higher than the UK average; the only region with a higher percentage is Northern Ireland where extra efforts have been made to attract employment to an area with its own particular political, social and economic problems. Foreign firms undertook 16.6 per cent of manufacturing investment in Scotland and were 14 per cent more productive (in terms of net output per head) than all Scottish firms in 1977.

Why should so many foreign firms, which are clearly an important part of the Scottish economy, want to set up or buy factories here? Scotland may well seem to them to be remote, with an unfamiliar culture and society, and an easier avenue of investment into Scotland, or Britain generally, would be through the international capital markets, the banks, the Stock Exchange and other associated institutions of the City of London. These institutions exist primarily to distribute savings between competing borrowers who wish to invest directly in productive activities. The foreign investor could select a portfolio of financial assets at an adequate rate of return at acceptable risk and allow investment in real assets to be made by those who borrow these funds.

There are two main reasons why foreign firms such as those in Table 19.1 by-pass these financial institutions and go directly into

TABLE 19.1 *Who are they? The largest foreign firms in Scotland, 1979/1980*

Company	Product	Location	Brand names	Date
Seagram Distillers Ltd (Canada)	Whisky	Paisley	Chivas-Regal, Noilly Prat, Glenlivet	1950
Timex Corporation Ltd	Watches and clocks	Dundee	Timex	1946
General Motors Scotland Ltd	Heavy earth moving equipment	Newhouse	—	1950
Hiram Walker and Sons Ltd	Whisky	Dumbarton	Ballantines, Inverleven	1938
CPC United Kingdom Ltd	Refined corn products, foods	Paisley	Knorr, Brown and Polson, Dextrasol	1935
Uniroyal Ltd	Rubber and rubber products	Newbridge	Royalite, Flexlite	1966
Honeywell Ltd	Electric instruments	Newhouse	Honeywell	1948
Caterpillar Tractor Co Ltd	Tractors	Glasgow	—	1958
Burroughs Machines Ltd	Computing machines	Cumbernauld/ Glenrothes	**Burroughs**	1958/69
IBM United Kingdom Ltd	Electric typewriters and computers	Greenock	IBM	1951
Hoover Ltd	Cleaners and household appliances	Cambuslang	Hoover	1946
Polaroid (UK) Ltd	Photographic products	Alexandria	Polaroid Land	1965
Inverhouse Distillers Ltd	Whisky	Airdrie	Coldstream, Garnheath	1964
Cummins Engine Co Ltd	Diesel engines	Shotts	—	1957

Notes: All US owned except where stated. Ranked by size.

the industrial sector of the host economy. First, direct investment allows them to retain control of, and exploit, assets which cannot be channelled through the City. These are *human capital* or *knowledge* which give the company a *monopolistic* or *oligopolistic advantage* over indigenous firms in the markets of the host economy. There are four main elements to this advantage.

Product differentiation, which may come from a genuinely new product or by the application of marketing and advertising skills to which the indigenous firms do not have access. Polaroid (Table 19.1) with their instant picture process have clearly had a product different from all their competitors until very recently and have chosen to enter the British market from a Scottish assembly plant.

Technological advantages arise from advanced production techniques, which may be protected by patents, or from new managerial skills and organizational forms within the subsidiary or the multinational group of companies. The Timex Corporation established precise and delicate but large-scale assembly of clocks and watches in Dundee in 1946. The competition of electronic watches has shifted the exploitation of this technological production advantage, and incidentally of product differentiation, to the assembly of cameras (the Nimslo 3-dimensional picture camera) and Sinclair home computers and flat-tube pocket televisions.

US firms were the first to develop, and gain the increased efficiency of, the multidivisional form of company structure. Giant corporations, which may suffer diseconomies of scale have been divided into smaller units with formal links between them but with some independence. They are less affected by bureaucracy and can concentrate more easily on making profits. CPS (United Kingdom) Ltd is part of the European division of CPC International – related to divisions for Africa, South America, Asia and two in North America – and one of a total of forty-four principal subsidiary companies which together in 1980 generated net sales of over $4 billion. The Paisley plant, one of three in Britain, manufactures consumers' food products and is separate from the division which makes a vast range of *intermediate products* for many sectors of the economy.

Internal and external economies of scale. Horizontal integration with an indigenous firm – that is, one native to the host economy – by a foreign firm can create internal economies of scale which can reduce production costs and allow a price advantage for the product. *Vertical integration,* often backwards to capture raw material sources, allows the *internalization of external economies.* Whisky distillers such as Seagrams, Hiram Walker and Inver House have, as major alcoholic spirit manufacturers in North America, moved into Scotland to broaden their range to include a product unique to this country (horizontal integration) and have acquired distilleries (e.g. Glenlivet by Seagrams; Ballantines by Hiram Walker, and Kiltarie, Moffat and Bladnoch by Inver House) to control important sources of high-grade raw materials (vertical integration).

Tariffs, erected to protect indigenous firms from import competition, may stimulate multinational corporations (MNCs) to create subsidiaries inside the tariff barrier, to maintain their markets and to enjoy the oligopolistic advantage bestowed by trade protection. It is generally recognized that this was a fairly important stimulus in the late 1960s and early 1970s in anticipation of, and after, Britain's accession to the EEC.

The second reason is an *oligopolistic* response to the threat to export markets made by rival corporations establishing or taking-over factories in the foreign markets in which they compete. An American economist, F. T. Knickerbocker, has shown that most American firms, though they were not thinking of foreign investment initially, copied competitors to avoid the

TABLE 19.2   *Share of direct foreign investment owned by US firms, 1977 percentage of employment*

Textiles, leather and clothing	92.8
Metal manufacture, mechanical and instrument engineering	91.5
Electrical engineering	77.6
Chemicals, coal and petroleum products	59.2
Other manufacturing	50.6
Food, drink and tobacco	36.5
Shipbuilding, vehicles etc.	36.3

risk of being shut out of their foreign markets. Table 19.2 shows a high concentration of US firms in particular industries in Scotland. This clustering together of firms from the same country has also been observed in Ireland and Belgium. Recently, Japanese firms coming to Britain have seemed to concentrate in South Wales and North-east England.

Thus the main advantage of MNCs typically covers product differentiation due to a superior product or technological process allied with entrepreneurial skill arising out of management, administrative and marketing skills.

THE CASE FOR DIRECT FOREIGN INVESTMENT

For MNCs, the advantage of *direct* foreign investment (DFI) is that they retain control of the investment in which financial capital is allied with human capital (embodied in the product, the process and the management) for added return to the corporation as either *quasi-rent, interest* or *profit.* Direct foreign investment is a transference of knowledge as well as capital.

For Scotland, the host economy, the advantage is that new firms are established which are technologically and managerially advanced, which are selling new products in an expanding market. (Tables 19.1 and 19.3 show that foreign firms are mainly in those industries which have these characteristics.) Such firms are likely to be highly profitable, grow quickly, be capital intensive and pay relatively high wages. These features are very helpful especially to an area like Scotland which traditionally

TABLE 19.3 *Foreign firms' share of Scottish industry, 1976 percentage of total employment*

Electrical engineering	43.3
Metal manufacture, mechanical and instrument engineering	28.7
Chemicals, coal and petroleum products	18.5
Shipbuilding, vehicles etc.	10.7
Food, drink and tobacco	9.2
Textiles, leather and clothing	5.6
Other manufacturing	11.8

suffers from high unemployment, relatively low wages and an ageing industrial stock.

But Scotland might not receive these benefits without a great deal of official effort to attract foreign firms here. A survey of US firms in Scotland in 1970, at the time of the acceleration of direct foreign investment (DFI), found that easily the most important reason for choosing Scotland was the various financial inducements offered by the government to firms setting up in Scotland. Also, official agencies like the Scottish Development Agency (SDA), the Highlands and Islands Development Board and the local authorities are continuously involved in attracting firms to their areas.

Twenty new firms and expansions of existing factories were announced by US and Japanese corporations in 1980, including Nippon Electric of Japan in Livingston and the Valve Division of Rockwell International (US) in East Kilbride. These were achieved after extended negotiations involving the Scottish Office, the SDA and the respective New Towns Corporations. The SDA runs a continuous campaign to attract firms from abroad. In 1980 there were seminars in New York and the electronics centres of Boston and Santa Clara and campaigns in Texas and Georgia. There were similar initiatives in Japan and Europe. In future these efforts are to be strengthened by being coordinated in an umbrella organization called 'Locate in Scotland'.

THE CASE AGAINST DIRECT FOREIGN INVESTMENT

Not all the impact of DFI is beneficial to the host economy. A more radical view sees MNCs as the foundation of a world-wide hierarchy of dependence which will create and maintain the economic backwardness in the host countries. There are five strands to this argument.

Economic dominance. Multinational corporations are typically very large corporations. General Motors Inc, of Detroit, Michigan, who in 1979 owned a plant making heavy earth-moving equipment in Newhouse (see Table 19.1), had worldwide net sales of $66.3 billion. The Scottish Gross Domestic Product in 1979 was £14.3 billion. So General Motors controls more than twice as much activity as there is in the whole Scottish economy. The Scottish plant was, therefore, probably more important to Scotland than it was to General Motors.

It is feared that the economic power of MNCs will allow them to dominate their industrial sector in the host economy. This sector will, perhaps because of their presence, have greater potential for growth and technological development. Yet because they are from outside the society and their operation in the host economy is a part, and possibly only a small part, of their total activity, and they have a different perspective, the objectives and goals of MNCs will be different from those of indigenous firms, the host government and the society as a whole.

Technological domination and growth. As the foreign subsidiary achieves market power, so the impetus of technological development is shifted towards the MNC and its own research and development facilities which are typically outside the host economy (see Box 19.1). Technological advance, an important engine of growth, is thus shifted abroad. For some people, this is a major disadvantage of DFI for nationalistic reasons. Perhaps more rationally, new technological processes developed in another economy may be held to be inappropriate for the factor proportions and broader needs of the domestic economy.

BOX 19.1   *The product life cycle and direct foreign investment (DFI)*

New products progress through a *life cycle* with stages like those of a person's life. Three main stages are usually described.

Stage one: New products are typically developed in countries such as the USA where they cater for high-income markets or for a demand for labour-saving devices. Production will be located in the USA because; (a) the development of production process requires close supervision, and (b) the monopolistic new product will have a low price elasticity of demand and so siting of the factory at a relatively high-cost location is not important.

Stage two: With a more standardized production process there are opportunities for economies of scale from mass production. Increasing competition raises price elasticity of demand for the individual firm so opportunities to reduce production costs become important. Demand increases in other advanced countries as income and labour costs rise with growth. Both factors encourage entrepreneurs to produce locally – *to invest directly in these foreign markets* – rather than exporting. Further production developments allow foreign subsidiaries to produce for third markets and even for the original home demands; and for MNC subsidiaries in different countries to specialize and export to each other rather than each manufacture the whole range of the products from MNCs for their individual domestic market.

Stage three: The full standardization may make Less Developed Countries (LDCs) feasible as production locations. Ever-increasing competition makes cost minimization imperative. Some parts of the production process (e.g. simple assembly of sophisticated components manufactured in advanced countries) may be transferred to LDCs to take advantage of cheap labour.

Scotland usually receives DFI at stage two of this cycle. It benefits from the production of new technologically sophisticated products aimed at growing domestic and foreign markets. However, as the cycle continues attention shifts from existing subsidiaries to new investments in other countries.

A foreign-owned firm in Scotland may be marginal to the MNC. This allows it to acquire resources and human capital at the marginal cost to the group rather than, as Scottish companies must, at prevailing market prices. However, as the cycle proceeds, the closure cost of what may be a marginal enterprise is also less. An economy such as Scotland, which is well endowed with foreign subsidiaries but which is part of a relatively depressed market, may be vulnerable to the closure of factories.

Monopolistic power. The monopolistic advantage of MNCs may erode competitive forces enough for them to charge higher prices and acquire high profits while nevertheless being inefficient. This creates resource waste and misallocation. It is not clear, however, that the allocation of resources before the advent of a foreign subsidiary was optimal and that any disturbance by it will inevitably lead to decline. High profits may equally come from savings accruing to efficient operation and that new competition may shake up settled and complacent indigenous oligopolistic firms.

Government-MNC relations. The difference in aims between the MNC and the host authorities is wider than that between domestic firms and their government. Multinational corporations are more powerful because, ultimately, they can leave the country. Their international mobility allows them to play governments off against each other.

Multinational corporations can use several locations in different countries to avoid harsh tax regimes and exploit exchange rate and interest rate variations by controlling the flow of funds between subsidiaries, particularly through adjustments of their internal transfer prices (see Box 19.2).

BOX 19.2　*MNCs and transfer pricing*

In a *market*, transactions involve a two-way flow, generally of goods and services in *exchange* for money. The rate of exchange is the *price*, which is, ideally, determined by the interaction of competitive forces which create a profit- and utility-maximizing exchange and, if repeated throughout the economy, an optimal allocation of resources.

Transfers are transactions in which the flow is in one direction only. There is no mutual market evaluation of one flow in terms of the other, so there is no market price. Familiar examples of transfers are income payments for which there is no direct production in exchange: unemployment benefit, family income supplements, disability allowances, student grants and so on. Gifts and voluntary work are also transfers.

Transfers are also very important in the production sector. Though large corporations, typical of the industrial and market structure in the Scottish economy, must exchange in markets for resources and factors and to sell their product, transactions *within* a corporation are typically transfers. When one branch is supplying another within the same firm it is not necessary for a formal exchange to take place. Ownership is transferred from one part of the company to another and the accounting 'price' is not determined by the competitive forces of the market; though some payment may occur to ease internal company accounting.

These internal transfer prices, not subject either to market forces or external scrutiny, can be set at whatever level is convenient to the corporation. This is usually of little interest to the outsider. However, when transfers are *international*, between subsidiaries of an MNC located in different countries, then the prices can be set to the disadvantage of the host economies.

Multinational corporations aim to make the whole international group of companies as prosperous as possible. Company taxation can be avoided by a subsidiary which 'buys' supplies at very high 'prices' and 'sells' very cheaply in transactions with other subsidiaries abroad. Thus profits earned by a subsidiary can accumulate in another country which has a more favourable tax regime. Such *internal transfer price manipulation* can be to exploit lower tax rates, sound currencies or exchange- and interest-rate fluctuations, and can be achieved through intracorporation capital movements as well as current payments for goods and services.

The host economy suffers because it may lose tax revenue, have its currency undermined and be destabilized by short-term speculative money flows in the international capital markets.

The magnitude of these transfers and their impact is not clear. By their nature they are secret and reliable estimates are difficult to find. It is clear that they do occur and are considered by those who do not favour the presence of MNCs in their economy to be a major contributory disadvantage.

Closures and redundancies. Multinational corporations may close or reduce the size of their subsidiaries more readily than Scottish firms if a subsidiary is marginal or if the MNC can shift production internationally. There have recently been some well-publicized closures of foreign firms: Talbot in Linwood in 1981, Singer and Massey-Ferguson in 1980, Monsanto Textiles and Goodyear Tyres in 1979. However, the share of Scottish manufacturing employment in foreign firms has remained constant since 1976. There have been closures and redundancies in indigenous firms and openings of new foreign-owned enterprises, including Digital Equipment in 1976, Devro in 1977 and Levi Strauss in 1980 and 1981.

Additionally, the marxist view sees DFI contributing to the international conflict which will generate the decline of the capitalist system through its later stages. The marxist historical dynamic sees capitalism spreading capital internationally. The argument is that although the neocolonial MNCs are seen as fulfilling the important and beneficial role of spreading advanced technology internationally, the resulting greater interdependence of national economies will bring acute economic rivalry between the governments of the industrialized capitalist countries. As countries are forced to defend their external activities because of the uncertain economic control created by the greater interdependence, conflict will contribute to the downfall of the capitalist system.

ARE ENGLISH FIRMS FOREIGN?

In 1973 41 per cent of Scottish manufacturing employment was in plants owned in Scotland. Nearly 40 per cent was in plants owned in England. This is perhaps not surprising. The British economy is highly integrated and interdependent with few barriers to the spread of investment between regions. Nevertheless, some people see English control of Scottish industry as bad for the Scottish economy.

Whether English direct investment in Scotland brings the advantages of new, growing industries, with the high exports, profits and wages which are associated with direct foreign investment, is doubtful. On the other hand, the disadvantages of monopolistic inefficiency and technological domination, and the erosion of government authority are also less clear. The countries are highly integrated within the British markets, within British

TABLE 19.4 *Location of ownership and average size of Scottish manufacturing plants, 1973*

		No. of workers
North America		593
Rest of UK		365
Europe		285
Scotland		112
Other		408
All		194

Government tax, exchange rate and general economic policy regimes, and in their scientific and technological infrastructure.

There remains the argument that English firms will dominate Scottish industry by remote control. Table 19.4 shows that English subsidiaries in Scotland, which are part of even larger companies, are bigger than indigenous Scottish firms. Whether English firms should be seen as alien to Scotland and to operate in a different economic environment with goals which are against Scottish interests is probably a matter for an individual's political judgement.

20

North Sea Oil and Gas

IAIN McNICOLL

Probably the most significant economic development in the UK during the 1970s was the discovery and subsequent exploitation of large volumes of *crude oil* and *natural gas reserves* in the UK Continental Shelf (UKCS). *Gas* fields had been in operation in the southern North Sea since the mid 1960s but it was the discovery in October 1970 of the giant Forties field, with recoverable reserves of crude *oil* of 261 million tonnes, which sparked off intensive exploration in more northerly areas of the North Sea. Subsequently, discoveries such as the Brent (225 million tonnes recoverable reserves), and Ninian (143 million tonnes recoverable reserves) fields confirmed that the North Sea was one of the world's major oil provinces. Currently there are sixteen oil fields operating in the North Sea with another ten under development.

The total recoverable oil reserves of these twenty-six fields may be about 2000 million tonnes. As further oil discoveries may be made in future and technological developments may increase the proportion of total reserves which can be exploited, recoverable reserves on the UKCS may be as high as 4000 million tonnes.

Interest in North Sea *oil* has tended to mask the fact that there are substantial reserves of natural *gas* on the UKCS. Indeed, gas production preceded the discovery of oil. It is estimated that UK offshore gas reserves total between 1350 billion cubic metres and 2250 billion cubic metres. Production of natural gas to the end of 1981 totalled 418 billion cubic metres.

There is a time lag between the discovery of an oil or gas field and the production of oil or gas, since the field has to be fully appraised for commercial viability and then offshore production systems and onshore landing facilities have to be installed. Hence,

TABLE 20.1   *UKCS oil and gas production*

to	1975	1976	1977	1978	1979	1980	1981
Oil (million tonnes)	1.1	11.5	37.3	52.8	76.5	78.7	87.6
Gas (billion cubic metres)	163.3	38.4	40.3	38.5	39.2	37.3	37.4

in the case of oil, although significant discoveries were made as early as 1971 large-scale production did not begin until 1976. Subsequently, while gas production remained relatively constant, oil production expanded rapidly (see Table 20.1).

By 1981 the UK was the seventh largest oil producer in the world, behind the USA, the USSR, Saudi Arabia, Venezuela, Mexico and China.

THE IMPACT ON THE UK ECONOMY

Scotland is an integral part of the UK and hence any oil impact on the national economy will affect the Scottish region. The main effects of oil and gas production on the UK economy arise through their value as resources and are directly reflected in the following areas.

Gross Domestic Product (GDP)

In 1981 UKCS oil and gas production contributed £9.8 billion to GNP at market prices, representing 4 per cent of total UK GNP in that year. This was an increase from 1980 when oil and gas contributed £6.5 billion to GDP, around 3 per cent of total.

Balance of Payments

The main effect on the balance of payments has arisen through the dramatic change in the UK's international trading position in crude oil (see Table 20.2). From having net crude *imports* of 54 million tonnes in 1977, the UK had net *exports* of crude in 1981 of 14.8 million tonnes. There remained, however, a significant

TABLE 20.2 *Source and use of crude oil in the UK (thousand tonnes)*

Year	Indige- nous crude pro- duction	UK refinery receipts			Foreign trade		
		Total	Indige- nous	Foreign arrivals	Arrivals	Ship- ments	Net
1977	38265	92260	22611	69649	69649	15611	−54038
1981	89396	76665	40304	36361	36361	51149	+14788

two-way trade in oil. This is because much of UK oil is of a light, high-quality type which commands a premium price in world markets. It therefore makes sense for the UK to exploit this *comparative advantage* and to export oil and import cheaper, heavy crude for use, for example, as fuel from countries such as Nigeria and Algeria.

Central Government Tax Revenues

Through a complicated system of taxation, the government received £6.4 billion from North Sea oil and gas in 1981/82. This compares with a total VAT yield of £12.3 billion and income tax yield of £28.5 billion.

THE IMPACT ON THE SCOTTISH ECONOMY

The national impacts discussed above will obviously have ramifications on the Scottish economy. However, the fact that most of the oil and gas fields have been discovered off the Scottish coast has led to a concentration of industrial activity associated with offshore exploitation being located within Scotland, i.e. the industrial impact of North Sea oil and gas has a much more specifically Scottish dimension.

The development of an oil province in a difficult geographical and climatic area such as the North Sea is a massive industrial undertaking involving sizeable expenditures on materials, equipment and services. Total expenditure by offshore operators on the UKCS in 1981 was £4.3 billion and the cumulative total over the period 1977–81 was £15.6 billion. The proportion of this total which was spent on Scottish goods and services is difficult to estimate, but is probably in the region of 15–20 per cent. This would imply that £640–£860 million was spent by offshore operators in Scotland in 1981.

By creating new demands for Scottish goods, the North Sea industry has also generated employment in Scotland. Indeed, in the present era of high Scottish unemployment, the employment impact of North Sea oil is very important.

North Sea oil employment has expanded in each year since 1973 (see Table 20.3). Employment in wholly related companies has increased nine-fold.

TABLE 20.3 *Employment in wholly related companies* – Scotland, 1973–81*

Year	Employment
1973	5 290
1974	13 470
1975	20 050
1976	27 100
1977	28 630
1978	33 990
1979	41 760
1980	46 340
1981	49 610

* Excluded is employment in partly-involved companies, terminal and yard construction, offshore installation and pipe laying.

The most recent comprehensive North Sea oil employment figures are for 1978 (see Table 20.4) and indicate that some 50 000 Scottish employees were directly involved in offshore oil related work in 1978. Some 36 000 of these were in firms entirely involved in supplying oil markets with the remainder being in firms with significant non-oil markets. About 40 per cent of the jobs were in Scottish manufacturing. Approximately 5600 Scottish residents were employed offshore during that year.

TABLE 20.4 *North Sea oil employment in Scotland, June 1978*

Sector	In wholly involved firms	In partly involved firms	Total
Mining and quarrying	9 900	—	9 900
Manufacturing	11 900	8 150	20 050
Services	14 150	2 400	16 550
Total all industries	35 950	10 550	46 500
Direct oil construction	—	—	3 500
Total			50 000

However the *nature* of the employment has changed significantly over the past few years, with a substantial growth in the number of jobs available offshore. Offshore employment grew from some 9000 in 1978 to approximately 22 000 in 1981. Onshore oil-related employment has been relatively static and may have even started to decline in 1981. An important aspect of oil employment is its concentration in certain Scottish regions (see Table 20.5).

Oil employment has been concentrated in Grampian region and this concentration is increasing since most offshore workers

TABLE 20.5 *Regional distribution of oil-related employment in Scotland*

	Percentage of total oil employment	
	1975	1981
Central/Lothian	1.1	2.0
Fife	6.0	2.2
Grampian	44.7	68.4
Highland	22.2	12.1
Strahtclyde	16.5	6.2
Tayside	5.5	4.0
Islands	1.0	5.1

are registered as employed in Aberdeen. Employment in Highland region, mainly in platform fabrication yards, is also significant. The relative importance of the Islands has increased as the
Sullom Voe (Shetland) and Flotta (Orkney) oil terminals have
come into operation. It is noteworthy that the industrialized
regions of Scotland (Central, Lothian, Strathclyde) have received
relatively few oil jobs, and indeed the numbers involved are
trivial relative to the working populations of these areas. The
inclusion of employees in partly-involved firms would change
the picture in favour of these regions somewhat, but, on the other
hand, the inclusion of employees in constructing yards and terminals would reveal an even greater concentration of oil employment in 'outlying' areas (see Chapter 16).

Ironically, many of the areas most affected by oil were among
those least able to absorb development of this nature and size. In
Shetland in the late 1970s, for example, there were 7000 oil
workers relative to a previous population of only 17 500. This has
put a great strain on existing infrastructure (such as housing,
sewerage and roads) and has had disruptive effects on local labour
markets with indigenous firms losing key workers to oil-related
jobs. On the other hand, oil activities have certainly generated
real economic growth in affected areas and have allowed them to
enjoy lower levels of unemployment than elsewhere in Scotland.
Most of the concern in affected areas is not with *permanent* oil-
related activities, which are on balance seen as beneficial to the
local economies, but rather is with *temporary* activities such as
terminal or platform construction. In such circumstances the
regional economy may adjust to the peak of oil-related requirements only to find subsequently that these requirements are no
longer necessary. This phenomenon has already been experienced
in Kishorn for example.

FUTURE DEVELOPMENTS

The North Sea is now a relatively mature oil province and its
future development can be mapped out with some confidence,
though significant changes in government policies and/or world
oil prices could alter the picture. Furthermore if exploration cur-

rently being undertaken off the *West* coast is successful, a whole new oil province may be developed.

Oil production on UKCS is forecast to rise to 95–130 million tonnes per annum by 1985, falling slowly thereafter. Total expenditure on Scottish goods and services may remain fairly static over the next five years, but its composition will change markedly. Demand for fabrications, capital equipment and manufactures generally will fall while the demand for services such as maintenance and transportation will rise. The onshore manufacturing supplies industry, if it is to maintain production, will therefore have to diversify into new product markets or new geographical markets. The prospects for the latter are promising, since world offshore activity is expected to grow over the next decade and North Sea experience should allow Scottish manufacturers to compete. Indeed Scottish companies are already developing export markets and currently perhaps 25 per cent of oil manufactures are sold to non-UKCS destinations.

In the UK itself, the next few years is likely to see major new developments in 'downstream' (i.e. processing) activities. There is already surplus capacity in oil refining and, hence, little further development can be expected in this area. The prospects for gas are, however, much more interesting. In addition to natural gas (methane) which is, and will continue to be, used primarily as a fuel the North Sea contains substantial volumes of natural gas liquids (propane, butane, ethane) which are important petrochemical feedstocks. Of these, ethane is the most significant since it is used in the production of ethylene, a key petrochemical intermediate product. The total volume of natural gas liquids (NGL) recoverable from the UKCS is in the order of 300–600 billion cubic metres and may prove to be much higher. Actual production of NGL in 1981 was 1.6 million tonnes. The completion of the Sullom Voe gas separation plant will add up to 2 million tonnes per annum to UK production. However, the major boost to UK NGL availability will come when the FLAGS pipeline system becomes operational in the next year or so. Connecting the Brent/Ninian field complex to St Fergus, the FLAGS system will produce 3–4 million tonnes per annum. Facilities for processing this new supply of NGL are already being developed: Shell/Esso are building a separator/ethylene cracker at Moss-Morran; BP are converting their ethylene plant at Grangemouth; Dow Chemicals and Highland Hydrocarbons have expressed strong interest in constructing petrochemical complexes at Nigg Bay; and Occidental may construct a plant at Peterhead.

Though much remains to be clarified, gas in the eighties could have effects on the UK economy similar to those of oil in the 1970s.

POSTSCRIPT

But has all oil's impact been to our benefit? Oil exports in the late 1970s and early 1980s have given Britain a balance of payments surplus, making us just about the only such Western industrialized country. These factors have kept the exchange rate of sterling relatively high which, of course, makes our exports relatively expensive and imports relatively cheap. Thus, British and Scottish firms, especially those in manufacturing, have found it difficult to compete in foreign markets and with cheap imports into the domestic market. Many such firms have, in an era of government-induced deflation, closed or contracted with very large losses of jobs. The oil and oil-related industries, which have expanded greatly, are relatively capital intensive and so have created relatively few jobs in compensation.

Thus, it is arguable that North Sea oil has contributed substantially to the great increase in unemployment in the late 1970s and early 1980s. These are not the circumstances which were generally anticipated when the oil was first discovered.

21

Scotland in the UK Economy

KEITH P. D. INGHAM and JAMES LOVE

Scotland is closely integrated with the rest of the UK (RUK). Membership of the UK economic and monetary union means that there are no restrictions on the movements of capital and labour between Scotland and RUK; there are no tariffs on goods traded with RUK; and there is a common currency. There is no economic strategy for Scotland separate from that for the UK, although UK regional policy is aimed at tackling the sorts of problems Scotland shares with some other UK regions (see Chapter 16). Scotland has an advantage over other UK regions, however, in that the Secretary of State for Scotland represents Scotland's interests directly in Cabinet. In addition, there are, as well as the Scottish Office in Edinburgh which is responsible for much of Scotland's share of central-government spending, specifically Scottish agencies such as the Scottish Development Agency (SDA) and the Highlands and Islands Development Board (HIDB) (see Chapter 17).

The close ties with RUK dominate the Scottish economy in many ways; for example, large British firms (see Chapter 2), the nationalized and publicly owned industries (see Chapter 18) and the UK civil service are among the largest employers in Scotland and the bulk of Scottish trade is with RUK (see Chapter 3). How does Scotland fare compared with other regions of the UK? How can we account for Scotland's relative performance as a region of the UK? What type of adjustment takes place in response to problems faced by Scotland? During the 1960s and 1970s there was a revival of nationalism in Scotland. While it was also based on historical, social and cultural issues, that revival, which now largely abated, concentrated a great deal of attention on these questions.

TABLE 21.1   Income per head and unemployment in UK regions relative to the UK as a whole, 1971–80

	GDP per head at factor cost				Unemployment (at July)			
	1971	1974	1977	1980	1971	1974	1977	1980
North	87	92	96	93	163	172	132	147
Yorkshire and Humberside	93	95	96	93	112	99	93	104
East Midlands	97	96	97	97	85	84	81	86
East Anglia	94	92	95	94	91	76	87	78
South East	114	113	112	115	59	60	76	65
South West	95	93	92	95	95	102	111	91
West Midlands	103	101	97	95	85	79	93	103
North West	96	97	97	95	113	129	118	126
Scotland	93	95	96	96	170	153	130	136
Wales	88	87	90	87	128	139	127	138
Northern Ireland	74	74	75	75	221	217	174	182
UK	100	100	100	100	100	100	100	100

SCOTLAND'S WELL-BEING IN THE UK UNION

At the beginning of the twentieth century Scotland was one of the more thriving areas of the UK. Shipbuilding and the iron, steel and coal industries created considerable prosperity. Glasgow flourished as a major city in the British Empire. This prosperity disappeared, however, in the depression of the 1920s and 1930s. Since then Scotland has been considered one of the regions of the UK with structural economic problems, experiencing, like RUK, the impact of cyclical changes in output and employment but typically having a higher than average rate of unemployment and a lower average income.

Scotland entered the 1970s as a relatively depressed region of the UK. Income per head was below the UK average and of the ten other UK regions exceeded only the levels for Wales, the North and Northern Ireland, a region with its own particular political problems (see Table 12.1). Unemployment in 1971 was also considerably above the UK average and was only less than that for Northern Ireland.

During the 1970s the development of oil-related activities was important to the Scottish economy, particularly in the North-east around Aberdeen (see Chapter 20). These activities meant that Scotland's relative position as a UK region improved in terms of both income per head and unemployment. By 1980 Scotland came third in the regional 'league table' for income per head behind the South-east and East Midlands. However, Scotland's income per head was still below the UK average. Although, as in other UK regions, there were substantial rises in unemployment in the 1970s (see Chapter 6), the unemployment position in Scotland was less severe by 1980 than in Wales, the North and Northern Ireland. Nevertheless, it was still over one-third higher than the UK average, and higher than that for seven other regions.

SCOTLAND'S RELATIVE PERFORMANCE AS A UK REGION

The relatively poor performance of the Scottish economy may be analysed in terms of developments since the 1930s in Scotland's trade and payments with the rest of the world (ROW) and RUK.

This approach permits us to identify certain factors contributing to the depression of output, employment and the general level of economic activity in Scotland.

Falling demand for Scottish exports. Scotland's production and exports to RUK and ROW tended to be heavily concentrated on a fairly narrow range of activities such as shipbuilding, heavy engineering, steel making and coal mining. Employment generated by these activities was located in certain areas. Although some shipbuilding and engineering took place in the East on Tayside and at or near the Forth, these industries were of much greater importance in West-central Scotland. Communities in parts of Ayrshire, Lanarkshire, West Fife and the Lothians depended almost entirely on coal mining. As a result of trade with the Indian subcontinent, the jute industry in Dundee employed considerable numbers.

Technological change, foreign competition and the development of substitutes, however, have caused these traditional activities to decline over a long period of time. This has been true not only for Scotland but also for other parts of the UK including South Wales, Northern Ireland and the North-west and North-east of England. This decline has been only partially offset in Scotland by the emergence of firms in other activities such as typewriters, computers and electronics. These firms, many of them branch plants of American multinationals (see Chapter 19), have been attracted to Scotland, at least in part, by the inducements offered through UK regional policy (see Chapter 16). But certain of the government-promoted schemes have been relatively short lived. Attempts to establish a motor-car industry in Scotland, for example, failed, probably due in part to locational factors (see Chapter 16) and in part to international competition from other European and Japanese producers. The Scotch whisky industry emerged in the post-war period as the major export earner but employs relatively few workers (see Chapter 25). On balance, the growth of other firms has not been sufficient to offset the impact on output, employment and exports of the decline in traditional activities.

Increasing Scottish demand for imports. Changes in the structure of the UK economy have resulted in much 'polarization' of economic activity. The head offices and plants of many large manufacturing companies have been located in the South-east and the Midlands, attracted by, for example, the services available, the well-developed social infrastructure and the large markets offered by major population centres. This has fed through into further expansion of the banking, insurance and advertising services available in the South-east. As far as financial services are concerned, however, Scotland may have fared better than other UK regions since a great deal of financial activity is located in Edinburgh (see Chapter 5). An important factor contributing to polarization has been the rapid expansion of civil service employment based mainly in London.

The growth of employment opportunities in both the public and private sectors particularly in the South-east has been thought to attract much highly-skilled labour out of other regions including Scotland. In terms of inter-regional trade Scotland, like other regions such as the North-east, South Wales and Northern Ireland, has increasingly imported goods and services from the more prosperous South-east. These increases in imports from RUK will have reinforced the general UK tendency to import more from ROW reflected in the penetration of UK markets by foreign suppliers.

Net export of capital. The structure of the UK capital market with a concentration of control in the South-east may have created a net export of private capital from Scotland. This may have been offset to some degree by the retention of control in some institutions in Scotland. But whether Scots are lending to London-based or Edinburgh-based institutions, those institutions will advance funds in response to considerations of relative profitability and creditworthiness. They may, therefore, have favoured firms in more prosperous regions with a resulting net export of capital.

SCOTLAND AND THE ADJUSTMENT PROCESS

Markets are often thought to adjust to changes in demand and supply conditions through spontaneous changes in prices. A decline in demand, for example, for the output of Scottish firms might be expected to lead to reductions in both product prices and the prices of factor inputs including labour. Reductions in factor prices may lead to further falls in product prices. Through such adjustments firms may be able to regain some part of lost market shares. Any decline in output may free resources for use in other firms and industries which themselves could benefit from cost reductions.

Prices, however, are rarely that flexible among regions. Wages, for example, frequently a major component of costs, tend to be rigid as a result of wage bargaining between employers' organizations and trade unions at a national level. Refusal to permit a fall in workers' relative earnings is typically a central feature of unions' claims. In addition, many Scottish manufacturing plants are branches of large multi-regional firms. These plants are likely to be part of a corporate structure with an overall development plan in which they have a specific and well-defined role. A company producing a given product in plants in different regions will generally sell all the output at the same price. A plant's relative cost advantage will show up as an addition to the company's short-term profits and may then lead to an expansion in the plant's planned capacity and output. If production is mobile, the region's problems of adjustment will be eased. However, switching production among regions may lead to problems with trade unions. Moreover, within the company's structure the Scottish plant may be producing intermediate products and the lower those products' shares in total cost, the more price inelastic will be the demand for the plants' output.

Where spontaneous price and cost changes do not take place or are insufficient to maintain levels of output, employment and incomes, government intervention may be necessary to achieve appropriate adjustment. This intervention will be directed at tackling the region's structural problems and/or the locational factors influencing efficiency.

UK central government has attempted to induce relative price and cost changes in depressed areas by means of a variety of regional policy measures (see Chapter 16). Prominent among these measures have been capital subsidies and, less often, subsidies to labour costs. Much of government policy, particularly during the 1960s, was aimed at solving structural problems by directing investment and jobs towards regions such as Scotland

and away from the then relatively prosperous West Midlands and the South-east. Specific locational factors are more difficult to identify and, therefore, to deal with. Government spending to improve the economic infrastructure by reducing costs and increasing industrial efficiency help to resolve both types of problems (see Chapter 16).

To the extent that these policies do not resolve the region's problems, other subsidies and transfers are necessary. These are most usually given to individuals in the form of welfare payments to alleviate the consequences of low incomes and unemployment (see Chapter 15). Such transfers help to maintain the region's income level.

The revival of nationalism in Scotland highlighted the absence of autonomy in institutions and of freedom in economic relationships. Dependence on decisions taken in Whitehall for the UK as a whole was seen as limiting the range of possible solutions to Scotland's difficulties.

A country which is not involved in a full union like that of the UK and which experiences falling exports and rising imports will tend under the present exchange-rate system to experience adjustment brought about by exchange-rate depreciation. Such depreciation raises the domestic prices of imports and reduces the foreign currency prices of exports (see Chapter 3). Demand may then be switched from imported goods to domestically produced substitutes; domestic production may be stimulated; and supplies of exportables increased.

Scotland shares a common sterling exchange rate which varies in response to changes in the circumstances of the UK as a whole. A separate exchange rate which adjusts to reflect the particular conditions in Scotland might have the merits of preventing higher unemployment and of possibly leading to an expansion of output, although higher import prices would have a depressing effect on real incomes. In contrast, regional policy, financed through 'external' aid, may be thought to have left more unemployment but with higher incomes for those employed.

Exchange-rate depreciation would influence, however, all the goods and services which Scotland trades internationally or inter-regionally. Protecting all sectors more or less equally may involve prolonging the lives of weak and inefficient firms and supporting, possibly at the cost of lower real incomes, firms which are already able to compete. In terms of the geographic distribution of industrial activities, the more prosperous North-east, with its development of oil-related activities during the 1970s, and the East, where much of the recent investment in, for example, electronics has been located, probably do not require the same degree of economic aid as areas such as the Clydeside conurbation and West-central Scotland generally which have been heavily dependent on the declining, traditional industries.

Regional policy measures are financed by transfers to the sub-sidized region at the expense of others. Such transfers may involve a misallocation of UK resources which may inhibit UK national economic growth. This possibility is likely to be less relevant with high levels of employment for the UK as a whole when the use of excess capacity in depressed regions may permit the expansion of output. Transfers among regions may also be politically unpopular in the regions providing the resources. In contrast, an exchange rate depreciation does not require such direct payments. Rather it would involve a shift in demand away from the firms in the relatively prosperous regions to Scottish firms in response to changes in relative prices.

UK regional policies have typically been investment-oriented. In the 1960s and 1970s development grants were widely available. More recently, there have been campaigns to attract specific mobile firms, especially those from abroad which are thought to have particularly beneficial characteristics. There are now also concentrated programmes of infrastructural provision as in the Glasgow Eastern Area Renewal (GEAR) project and more com-prehensive 'packages' as in the enterprise zone at Clydebank and those scheduled for Invergordon and Tayside (see Chapter 17). It may be that these more-specific measures will be more effective on balance than the less-selective approach of exchange-rate adjustment.

A separate exchange rate, or for that matter independence in economic policy, may not, of course, lead to appropriate adjust-ment. The UK as a whole, for example, has not been particularly successful in resolving its economic difficulties. But the national-ist case was essentially that Scotland, particularly in the circum-stances of the 1970s, would fare better outside the UK union. Much of the argument rested on the potential impact on the structure and performance of the Scottish economy of having oil and gas revenues accruing to and controlled within Scotland. These revenues, it was argued, would transform any deficit in Scotland's transactions with other countries into a surplus and provide resources to regenerate Scotland's industrial base. Higher levels of employment and income might be generated directly by investment in new manufacturing activities and indirectly through linkage and multiplier effects. Outdated capital stock might be replaced and infrastructural provision improved to raise productivity levels. Improved employment prospects in a more prosperous economy would, it was felt, slow down or stop the emigration of skilled labour and might attract back some earlier emigrants.

Leaving aside legal and political aspects of claims to ownership of oil and gas fields in the North Sea, independence might not automatically resolve Scotland's problems. It may be difficult to identify those activities in which Scotland is likely to have a comparative advantage. But, even if that could be done, a substantial injection of investment demand might exert upward pressures on the prices of factor inputs and products. There might also have to be increased imports of capital and intermediate goods to develop and operate new enterprises and of consumer goods as incomes are increased through multiplier and linkage effects. In addition, even with oil and gas revenues, output and employment in an open economy like Scotland would still probably be very susceptible to changes in the levels of economic activity in major trading partners. Most importantly perhaps, there might be upward pressures on an independent Scottish exchange rate which would be determined mainly by the oil surplus rather than by the economic health of the industrial base. An appreciating exchange rate would adversely affect non-oil Scottish production in the same way as appears to have happened for the UK during the 1970s (see Chapter 20).

It is, of course, difficult to compare the theoretical possibilities of untried options with the outcome of regional policies, some of the shortcomings of which may be due to problems of implementation. Clearly the hypothetical arguments associated with independent control of economic policy, and with its outcomes with respect, for example, to exchange-rate changes, would depend on whether independence were achieved with or without substantial oil and gas revenues and on the particular form of economic strategy. However, the possibilities of separate exchange-rate adjustment and of using oil and gas revenues are not available to Scotland within the UK union. Making them available would require fundamental changes in Scotland's economic relationships with RUK and in the UK political structure. Whether such changes are desirable is probably in large part a matter for an individual's political judgement.

22

Scotland in Europe

NEIL FRASER

The UK joined the European Economic Community (EEC) in 1973 (see Box 22.1). As a region of the UK much of Scotland's relations with the EEC must be seen in a British context but certain aspects of membership have particularly important consequences for Scotland. Between 1974 and 1980, for example, the proportion of Scottish exports going to EEC markets increased from 30.1 per cent to 40.4 per cent (see Table 22.1).

The central economic characteristic of the EEC is the *customs union* which provides the foundation for policies designed to create a common market. The customs union has two basic features.

(1) Members do not impose customs duties or quantitative restrictions on trade with one another. Thus, Scottish goods may be sold in European markets and European goods can be sold here on a common basis.

(2) A common external tariff is applied to imports from countries outside the union. Thus, goods coming from non-member countries are subject to the same tariffs in all EEC countries.

TABLE 22.1 *Destination of Scottish exports*

Year	EEC (%)	North America (%)	Other (%)
1974	30.1	16.7	53.2
1977	38.2	13.6	48.2
1980	40.4	12.4	47.2

BOX 22.1   *The European Economic Community*

The European Economic Community (EEC) was formed by the Treaty of Rome in 1958. Much of the impetus to form the Community arose from the Second World War, with the economic and political integration of Europe being seen as a prerequisite for peace. Initially there were six members – West Germany, France, Italy, Belgium, Netherlands and Luxembourg. In 1973 they were joined by the UK, the Republic of Ireland and Denmark. Greece joined in 1981 and negotiations are currently under way regarding the entry of Spain and Portugal. The economies of these countries vary considerably and certain features are outlined below.

	Population 1979 (million)	Gross Domestic Product 1980 (1975 prices $B)	Unemployment* percentage December 1981
Belgium	10.2	70.0	12.9
Luxembourg	0.4	2.6	1.3
Denmark	5.1	43.2	9.5
France	53.2	397.0	8.9
West Germany	61.4	501.4	6.5
Greece	9.4	25.5	1.8
Ireland	3.4	9.6	11.5
Netherlands	14.0	94.2	9.1
Italy	56.9	232.0	9.6
UK	55.9	249.8	11.3
EEC	269.9	1625.3	9.0

* The unemployment figures are compiled in different ways and are not directly comparable.

The Community engages in a number of other activities outside the economic sphere. Several institutions such as the European Parliament and European Court of Justice now influence our administrative and legal affairs. Early in 1982, for example, the European Court of Justice supported complaints about corporal punishment in schools brought by two Scottish parents. The ten EEC countries are also trying to develop a common approach to various international problem areas like Poland and the Middle East. For some the EEC is seen as an important political counterweight to the USA and Soviet Union.

Others feel the Common Market infringes on our own national sovereignty and political processes.

While the customs union does provide opportunities for enlarged markets and for improved efficiency and competition within Europe, its effects have been criticized. There is some sentimental regret at the shift away from our traditional trading partners in the USA and Commonwealth countries. Moreover, cheaper products from other EEC countries have penetrated some domestic markets previously supplied by British producers and membership of the EEC prevents Britain from unilaterally introducing import controls (see Box 22.2).

Linked to the growth of trade with Europe is the increased attractiveness of Scotland as a location to investors from outside the Community. Regional assistance, low labour costs and lack of customs barriers are strong inducements to firms seeking a base within Europe. This has been an important factor in many foreign firms' decisions to locate in Scotland (see Chapter 19).

BOX 22.2   *Trade creation and trade diversion*

Trade-flows between Scotland and the rest of the customs union have increased since the UK joined the EEC. This is due in part to *trade creation* and in part to *trade diversion*. Trade creation occurs when the members of a common market exploit *economies of scale* and *comparative advantage* in a large market. *Trade diversion* occurs when a country switches its purchases from a country outside the common market to one within. This diversion is induced by imposing tariffs on the goods produced by non-member countries, while allowing the produce of the other members of the common market to be imported duty-free, thus making externally produced goods relatively more expensive.

The overall effect of trade diversion depends on the relative prices of goods produced within the common market and goods produced outside the common market. The impact will affect the consumer and the producer differently. If a good can be produced cheaper outside the Community, the imposition of a common external tariff will; (a) make the good more expensive for the consumer who can no longer buy from the cheapest source, (b) divert production from outside the Community to partner countries, thereby providing jobs and increasing output within the customs union, and (c) raise revenue for the customs union from tariffs imposed on goods still imported from outside the Community.

The net effect on the economic welfare of the Community of trade creation and trade diversion is uncertain. Political considerations of trading relationships will affect the overall desirability of tariffs on goods produced outside the customs union. For example, restricting imports through tariffs or quotas may invite retaliation from the affected countries who may place restrictions on goods produced within the customs union.

THE COMMUNITY BUDGET

The EEC has developed policies on agriculture, industrial and regional support, social matters, energy and research. Consequently, the Community spends large sums of money and must raise the necessary revenue from its members. While it is agreed throughout the EEC that the principle of 'juste retour' (i.e. getting back the same amount as paid in) is inappropriate, Britain and West Germany are the only countries consistently making a net contribution to the budget. The British Government argues that, given the relative weakness of our economy (measured in unemployment, growth, inflation and social conditions), our contribution is disproportionately high. In 1981 the EEC spent £10.6 billion (see Table 22.2). It is estimated that EEC member-

TABLE 22.2   *Composition of EEC expenditure, 1981*

	(%)
Agriculture	67.4
Regional	10.2
Social	3.5
Research, energy, industry, transport	1.6
Refunds and reserves	7.9
Development cooperation and non-member countries	4.0
Administration and miscellaneous	5.4
Total	100

ship cost Britain £127 million net in 1981, a significant reduction from the 1980 figure of £1 billion. This reduction is largely attributable to temporary refunds negotiated in 1979 which have now expired. The controversy over UK payments centres around the very expensive agricultural policy from which the UK derives little benefit.

Similarly it is likely that as part of the UK Scotland makes a net contribution to the EEC budget despite her poor economic performance. It is estimated that in 1978 Scotland paid £34 million more into the budget than was received. Scotland does relatively better, however, than some other regions of the UK as the area is eligible for more forms of regional assistance. Political negotiations are continuing in an attempt to rectify Britain's budget problems but without fundamental reform disproportionate sums will continue to be paid throughout the 1980s.

COMMUNITY SPENDING

The *Common Agriculture Policy* forms the centrepiece of the Community budget and is the cause of much intra-Community argument. Using a system of price supports, it provides stability to food supplies and so is a valuable insurance in an unpredictable world. Critics of the policy argue that; (a) it is excessively bureaucratic and expensive, (b) farmers benefit at the expense of consumers, and (c) price supports have stimulated production above market demand resulting in overproduction and the creation of 'lakes' and 'mountains' of certain products (see Chapter 7).

The reduction of regional inequalities is an important aim of the EEC but the task is difficult given the diversity of economic activities, peoples and climate in the regions of Europe. Within Scotland the Central Region displays a decline in traditional industrial activity, while the Highlands and Islands display underemployment in agriculture and high outward migration (some oil-affected areas excepted – see Chapter 16). While the principal responsibility for regional problems rests with individual countries, the Community has developed a number of policies and acted to coordinate the various national schemes. Scotland has received several allocations since Britain joined the Community (see Table 22.3).

TABLE 22.3   *Identified financial allocations from EEC sources in respect of projects in Scotland (£ million)*

	European Regional Development Loans[2] Fund	European Agriculture Guidance and Guarantee Fund (FEOGA)	European Social Fund[1]	European Investment Bank
1973	—	1.910	5.4	—
1974	—	2.233	5.4	24.8
1975	9.852	2.964	8.5	96.9
1976	14.607	8.285	8.5	66.2
1977	13.928	7.821	15.1	103.0
1978	24.826	9.250	14.85	63.4
1979	37.133	5.759	29.0	62.8
1980	26.687	5.581	5.35	86.7
1981 (to Nov)	58.210	2.54	1.22	25.0

Notes: 1. The figures given are estimates of the Scottish share of UK payments. 2. Figures refer to specific Scottish projects. There have also been a number of loans for UK projects where the share of expenditure in Scotland cannot be identified with any precision.

The *European Regional Development Fund* (ERDF), set up in 1975, is the principal instrument of regional policy within the Community. The Fund provides grants to industrial and infra-structural projects. Amongst Scottish projects to have benefited are Levi Strauss Ltd who make jeans, various whisky distillers, Grampian Region to help construct dual carriageways in Aberdeen, the Western Isles Council to build roll-on/roll-off ferry terminals, improvements at Ayr Docks and the provision of additional sewers in Dundee. The industrial grants are paid to projects which are economically sound, already receive state regional aid schemes and either help to create or preserve at least ten jobs. Infrastructural investment such as roads, sewerage and harbours can attract a grant of up to 30 per cent of the total outlay. This is paid on projects carried out by public authorities, in particular the Regional and District Councils. These expenditures are not a net addition to the package of UK government regional incentives. The EDRF payments are made to the Treasury who then, in a practice common throughout the Community, pass them on to industry and local authorities but reduce grants funded by British regional policy.

The *European Social Fund* (ESF) is mainly intended to assist the operation of the labour market through training schemes and by assisting mobility. Scotland has benefited through particular projects and also through the general assistance given by the fund to bodies such as the Manpower Services Commission which operates throughout the UK. Most recently the Social fund has allocated £1 million to Strathclyde Regional Council to pay subsidies to firms to take-on unemployed people. The European Coal and Steel Community (ECSC) gives grants and loans mainly to schemes involving these industries. Since both of these industries have a substantial presence in Scotland we have received a relatively large share of the assistance available.

The *European Investment Bank* (EIB) finances up to 50 per cent of the cost of investment at preferential rates of interest, i.e. rates of interest below that which would be paid on the market, on a wide range of projects, the loans normally maturing at between 7 and 12 years. Large schemes such as the Hunterston terminal and the Meggat reservoir have benefited from these loans. Finally, the *European Agricultural Guidance and Guarantee Fund* (FEOGA) provides grants, through a number of different schemes, to Scottish agriculture. These range from special assistance for hillfarmers to financial inducements to reduce milk production.

COMMUNITY INCOME

(1) Agricultural Levies – these are raised from 'third country' agricultural exports to the Community, e.g. New Zealand lamb or American wheat. The sums raised in this manner are unpredictable. The amount depends on the common threshold prices, world market prices and currency fluctuations.

(2) Customs Duties – all of these are payable to the Community and are dependent on the structure of tariffs and the real and nominal growth in imports.

(3) VAT Contributions – up to 1 per cent of each country's VAT revenues are paid to the EEC. This is the most flexible source of finance as the rate can be adjusted to compensate for shortfalls in revenue from duties and levies.

There are continuing discussions as to how the growing EEC budget should be financed, particularly as the VAT contributions are close to the 1 per cent limit. Radical changes are unlikely given the difficulties surrounding negotiations between ten countries with separate interests.

FISHING AND THE EEC

The Community had, for a number of years, been trying to develop a *Common Fisheries Policy* (CFP). Agreement was finally reached on 25 January 1983, when Denmark finally accepted the policy agreed upon by the other member states on 1 July 1982. The negotiations had proved contentious and many fishermen held back investment in boats and equipment because of uncertainty surrounding the future permissible level of catches.

The fishing industry in Scotland employs around 17 000 people and its influence dominates certain communities and regions. This influence is both direct through catching and indirect through activities like processing, retailing and boat building. Scotland relies heavily on fishing and accounted for 51 per cent of UK landings by value in 1980. The fishing industry has, however, contracted in recent years for two reasons. First, the loss of access to fishing grounds, particularly Icelandic and Faroese. Secondly, there was overfishing of species such as herring and sprat. It is now hoped that the new CFP will provide a stable environment in which both fishermen and processers can plan for the future. If so the industry will stop contracting and may even enjoy a limited amount of growth.

The foundation for a CFP was laid in 1970 when a regulation was passed requiring equal access to all fishing grounds under the jurisdiction of the member countries. On entering the Community the UK was given special conditions within all waters within a 6-mile limit and some within a 12-mile limit exclusive to British fishermen. On 1 January 1977 the EEC created the European Economic Zone which set 200-mile fishing limits in the North Sea and North Atlantic. This regulation restricted other countries but did not affect the rights of vessels from other EEC countries to fish in UK waters.

The special conditions negotiated by Britain expired at the end of 1982 necessitating a speeding up in the search for a settlement. The agreement finally reached on 25 January 1983 has a number of key elements:

(1) Britain is to get 37.3 per cent of the seven main edible species (mackerel, cod, haddock, whiting, saithe, redfish and plaice).

(2) Six-mile exclusive zone round all of Britain. This is extended to 12 miles for all of Scotland except for areas off the Butt of Lewis, North Rona, around Fair Isle, and from the West of Barra Head to the Mull of Kintyre where some German, French and Dutch boats will be allowed in up to 6 miles. Danish boats have been guaranteed access to catch mackerel off the West of Scotland whenever North Sea stocks provide insufficient for their needs.

(3) An EEC financed package of £150 million over 3 years to modernize boats, scrap others and encourage fish farming and fishing in new waters.

(2) A price-support structure and other measures to help freeze and process fish.

THE EUROPEAN MONETARY SYSTEM (EMS)

The movement towards a full customs union and the growing importance of the Community budget have initiated moves towards a monetary union. In its most extreme form monetary union would result in a single European currency with centralized economic decision-making. Such a possibility is unlikely in the foreseeable future with each member keen to retain its own currency. However, given the interdependence of the Community, a system has developed in an attempt to harmonize financial and monetary activities.

This European Monetary System (EMS) is designed to reduce exchange fluctuations between Community members. The EMS is an exchange rate mechanism where each currency must trade within fixed but adjustable rates. If any country has problems remaining within the agreed bands, support will be given by the Central Banks of the other participants. It is felt that this reduces uncertainty in trade and payments within the Community and provides a framework for closer economic policy coordination. However Britain is not yet a member of the system despite the fact that all other countries have participated since its inception in

March 1979. The official reason for this has been that member-ship of the system is incompatible with the government's domes-tic monetary policy and that when domestic problems are brought under control, it will be possible to join the system.

23

Scotland and the Third World

ANTHONY CLUNIES ROSS

Scotland's involvement with the Third World has taken the form of imports, exports, investment, enterprise, management, aid, training and manpower. There has been a mixture of influences in both directions that has gone with the sojourns of missionaries, traders, administrators and technicians on the one hand and of students on the other.

In 1979, about 10 per cent by value of UK *merchandize* exports going to the world outside Europe and North America left through Scottish ports but only about 4 per cent of imports from those areas entered through Scottish ports. It is known that such figures for the trade of Scottish ports understate total overseas trade to and from Scotland. This is because much more Scottish trade passes through English ports than the reverse. However, the figures do suggest that Scotland's merchandize export trade is biased toward, and its import trade against, those parts of the world by comparison with Scotland's total export and import trade in goods and services with all overseas countries. (A study for 1973 shows Scotland, with about 10 per cent of the UK's population, as providing 7.2 per cent of the UK's total exports of goods and services overseas and receiving 6.4 per cent of the UK's imports.)

Scotland's overseas trade and investment, however, are hard to disentangle from those of the UK as a whole. For many purposes we have to resort to UK figures for actual quantities and to assume that Scotland represents something like a tenth, more or less, of the total. So Tables 23.1 and 23.2 show the size and composition of UK trade in *goods* with the Third World. Trade in *services* with the rest of the world at large adds a further 25–30 per cent to UK exports of goods and 10–15 per cent to UK imports

TABLE 23.1 UK Merchandize imports from less-developed countries* by category, 1972, 1980 (Values: £ million in constant 1980 (UK) prices)

	1972		1980		Percentage rise (+) or fall (−) 1972 to 1980
	Value	Percentage of total UK imports of category	Value	Percentage of total UK imports of category	
Food, drink, tobacco	1673	23.0	1454	23.6	−13.1
Crude materials and vegetable oils, etc.	920	22.6	783	20.4	−14.9
Fuels	2903	75.8	3972	57.6	+36.8
Chemicals	107	5.3	91	2.9	−15.0
Machinery, transport equipment	233	3.4	544	4.2	+133.5
Textiles, clothing	566	31.2	956	34.5	+68.9
Footwear	54	28.2	88	24.8	+63.0
Other manufactures	706	9.0	1146	8.3	+59.0
Other	51	13.3	86	13.5	+68.6
Total imports to UK from LDCs	7213	21.0	9120	18.0	+26.4

* All non-OECD countries expect members of Comecon and South Africa; includes the rich Mid-eastern oil exporters.

of goods, but it is not easy to say how much of this trade in services is with less developed countries, except in the case of 'travel' (tourism), for which about half the UK surplus of receipts over payments is earned from countries roughly corresponding to the Third World.

During the period of British imperial expansion Scotland is generally reckoned to have had more than its fair share of overseas traders and adventurers. In the eighteenth century Glasgow was a centre for the import of sugar and tobacco from the Americas; from the nineteenth century or earlier, Scottish firms have sold their wares in the Third World, grown and processed tropical crops, and managed trading, manufacturing and service businesses there. The 'managing agencies', which controlled and supervized much of India's industry and commerce in the colonial period, were very largely Scottish enterprises.

J. and P. Coats of Paisley and James Finlay of Glasgow are examples of the changing role that Scottish businesses have adopted. Coats in the last century exported cotton thread across the world. Latterly it has set up subsidiaries, or jointly-owned companies, in a number of developing countries, mainly to make its traditional products, and turned much of its attention in Scotland to new lines such as office-equipment systems, medical measuring devices and fish farming. Finlay's was for long a producer and trader of tropical crops and became a major manufacturer of cotton textiles within India. Most of its Indian and Sri Lankan concerns have now been sold to, or are jointly owned with, local interests in those countries, and it too has largely shifted to other activities, such as merchant banking, oil extraction in the USA and oil servicing at home.

Scotland provided some of the most colourful of the pioneer missionaries, such as David Livingstone in Central Africa, James Chalmers in New Guinea and John Paton in the New Hebrides, and has been an important source of cultural influence. Scottish Presbyterianism is still visibly dominant in Malawi, where the long-serving President Banda is a Presbyterian elder and the largest town bears the name of the Lanarkshire village of Blantyre, and it is a persisting force in a number of other countries. The equally long-serving President of Tanzania, Julius Nyerere, is a graduate of the University of Edinburgh.

The proportion of people from overseas among full-time stu-

TABLE 23.2   UK Merchandize exports to less-developed countries by category, 1972, 1980 (Values: £ million in constant (UK) 1980 prices)

	1972		1980		Percentage rise (+) or fall (−) 1972 to 1980
	Value	Percentage of total UK imports of category	Value	Percentage of total UK imports of category	
Food, drink, tobacco	471	23.2	399	12.2	− 15.3
of which alcoholic drinks	(161)	(19.8)	(255)	(25.6)	(− 39.8)
Crude materials and vegetable oils, etc.	64	6.4	75	5.2	+ 17.2
Fuels	55	7.5	314	4.9	+ 470.9
Chemicals	703	23.8	1317	24.9	+ 87.3
Machinery, transport equipment	3420	27.7	5030	29.6	+ 47.1
Textiles, clothing	296	16.3	388	17.9	+ 31.1
Other manufactures	1619	19.8	2307	18.6	+ 42.5
Other	39	4.7	407	38.5	+ 917.9
Total imports to UK from LDCs	6683	22.3	10270	20.9	+ 53.7

dents at Scottish universities rose until 1978/79, when it stood at 9.7 per cent (4194) slightly less than the UK proportion of 12.4 per cent. Most of the overseas students have come from the Third World. For the UK, and probably for Scotland as well, there were also rather more overseas students in Polytechnics and Further Education Colleges than in universities. Apart from support by studentships in some cases there was for long a substantial subsidy to students in publicly-supported institutions because fees charged were below average cost. From 1980, however, the then government aimed to remove what was left of that subsidy by reducing its grant in proportion to the numbers of non-EEC students in universities and pressing the universities to raise the fees that such students had to pay.

WHAT IS THE THIRD WORLD?

'Third World' is one of the terms used to cover the 'poor' nations, those with yearly incomes per head of population below a line somewhere between £1250 and £2500 in 1982 prices. Most have at some time been parts of European empires.

The countries of the Third World are extremely diverse, far more so than those of the industrialized 'First World'. China has nearly a billion people; the Solomon Islands has less than 200 000, that is less than Dundee or Aberdeen. Bangladesh has over 600 inhabitants per square kilometre, which makes it three times as densely populated as the UK and nine times as densely as Scotland; Chad has less than four per square kilometre, and Botswana less than two. Poor countries generally derive only a small proportion of their output from manufacturing industry, yet China, Brazil, Mexico and India are among the world's twenty largest industrial-producing countries; and a small number of Third World members (India, Pakistan, Vietnam, South Korea, Taiwan, Hong Kong, Singapore) gain more than half of their export earnings from manufacturers.

Those countries that contain the bulk of the Third World's people are densely populated, predominantly peasant, societies, the heirs of ancient civilizations such as those of China, India, Java and Egypt, which have had their towns and courts, literature, armies and officials, for hundreds or thousands of years. Others are composed largely of 'primitive' peoples, living in small villages or nomadic groups, which are sparsely scattered in forest, savannah or desert, and were only in the last century or so brought into close contact with the wider world. Such are Zambia, Botswana, Papua New Guinea, and many of the outlying peoples of Indonesia and the Philippines. Between these extremes there are many intermediate types: peoples who before European contact formed large 'tribes' with powerful chiefs or kings; who had townships and specialized craftsmen such as those of parts of West Africa; or who produced goods of export value such as spices, ivory, indigo or slaves, for which there was a world market; or who centuries ago adopted one of the major world religions and hence have long had links with major centres of civilization. Tropical America is different again, where European settlers have been established for over four centuries, where they crushed the earlier civilizations in their first onslaught, merged as a dominant class with some of the native peoples or with African slaves, and kept up a continuing traffic in goods and ideas with Europe.

Despite these vast differences in background and origins, all Third World countries now possess town-dwelling segments of their populations who have taken on many of the trappings of the modern state and the modern industrialized economy, with government departments, airlines, banks and universities.

Some countries of the Third World are the sites of major mines or oilfields which now provide a large part of their national incomes. Such are Venezuela, Zambia, Gabon and Botswana. In extreme cases, such as Kuwait and Libya, desert states that were among the world's poorest fifty years ago, have joined the ranks of the rich by virtue of oil alone. Other countries or regions have become specialized producers of export crops in either plantations or smallholdings. Such is the case of parts of Malaysia and Indonesia with rubber; Sri Lanka and parts of India with tea; the Philippines and Sri Lanka with coconuts; Ghana and the Ivory Coast with cocoa; Brazil, Colombia and many others with coffee; the Philippines, Swaziland, Cuba, Fiji, Mauritius and a number of other island states with sugar. Some sell timber or fish.

LIFE AND WORK IN THE THIRD WORLD

Until the Industrial Revolution of the last two centuries most households in any part of the world were principally occupied in producing food. The enormous technical progress since then in those areas that have industrialized has made it possible not only to grow far more food per acre than before but also to grow it with a small fraction of the workforce, so that one farm worker can produce enough to feed fifty or more families. Since people as they grow richer show only a limited increase in their demand for food, rich countries employ only a small proportion of their workforces in agriculture: 13 per cent in Japan in 1979, 9 per cent in France, 6 per cent in Australia, 2 per cent in the US and UK.

Third World countries, on the other hand, apart from some of the richest among them and a few very fast developers, have not gone far with this great transformation that draws most workers off the land while increasing many times the productivity of those that remain. On the whole, the poorer a country is, the bigger the proportion of its workers engaged in agriculture. For the percentage of the workforce in agriculture (including forestry, hunting and fishing), industry (covering mining, manufacturing, construction, electricity, water and gas) and services (the rest) in a selection of countries from very poor to affluent see Table 23.3.

TABLE 23.3   *Distribution of workforce, 1979*

Country	GNP per head (US dollars)	Percentage of Workforce in Agriculture	Industry	Services
Ethiopia	130	80	7	13
India	190	71	11	18
China	260	71	17	12
Philippines	600	47	17	36
Brazil	1780	40	22	38
Greece	3960	38	28	34
Ireland	4210	19	37	44
UK	6320	2	42	56

Farm families in the poorest countries are generally producing food mainly for their own use. Thus the workforce in such countries is far less *specialized* than it is in industrialized parts of the world. In some of the more 'primitive' areas (usually those that are sparsely populated) each family makes most of the essentials of life for itself with very little reliance on goods bought from outside. Primitive people often have to be the most versatile. Most households in New Guinea and the Solomon Islands build their own houses, many without purchase of any materials or equipment for doing so, and some still make their own clothes from bush materials. In industrialized countries, by contrast, almost all of the workforce are specialists doing particular limited jobs, often tiny parts of highly complex production processes; and their own families do not enjoy, or even see, the product of their labour.

Thus, beside the people who live in the great cities of Third World countries (Mexico City and Shanghai are now probably the largest in the world), there are hundreds of millions of people living an older-style, and in varying degree more self-sufficient, life. In Third World cities, workers are specialized, as in the cities of Europe, though there is generally more petty trading, and living conditions for most people are far more crowded and very much poorer. Away from the cities, you enter a different world, the world of the small community in which people know each other's business; the world of extended-family loyalties and intense personal feuds; a quieter world, generally neglected by governments, in which there may be a landlord, a councillor or a headman, but there is often no large employer; in which people have only their own health and energy and ingenuity, supported by the help of relatives, to keep them from destitution. Here people's standard of living depends largely on how much land they can use and at what rent . . . or else, in those parts where land is still abundant, it may depend on their capacity to mobilize wives, relatives and associates or to assemble cattle, pigs, horses or camels. Where crop land is abundant, people have plenty to eat most of the time. But in much of the South and East Asian mainland, and in Java, Luzon, Egypt, Ethiopia and elsewhere – in fact, where the majority of the world's people live – land is scarce, and most people have much less ground than they could usefully work, even by primitive methods. Worst off are the landless, whose life is not only poor but highly precarious, and in South Asia a large minority of rural families have no land.

Yet almost everywhere there is some truck with the cash economy. In even the most primitive areas, families may need salt, which they can not readily collect for themselves, or paraffin for lamps, or matches, or steel implements. These are objects that people once did without, or went long journeys to acquire, or for which they found inferior substitutes (such as firesticks and stone tools); but such commodities prove so useful that villagers will market some of their food, or devote part of their land to export crops, in order to buy them. Cash may also be needed for taxes or school fees, for religious offerings, for bride-prices or dowries, for marriage and funeral feasts: all unavoidable incidents of social life.

SIGNS OF HOPE

Three promising changes have begun in the Third World since 1975:

(1) A slight fall, evident by about 1975 over the world taken together, in the explosive rates of population growth that have become typical of poor countries.

(2) The development and propagation, from the mid 1960s, of new strains of rice, wheat and maize, which have made possible much larger yields per acre with small-scale cultivation under tropical conditions.

(3) The rapid development of manufacturing for export in a small number of Third World countries. This has enabled the favoured ones to raise their average living standards at a considerable rate, and in some the benefits seem to have spread widely to the poorest classes. The star examples of these 'newly industrializing countries' are South Korea, Singapore, Taiwan and Hong Kong, but Spain, Israel, Greece, Brazil, Mexico and Colombia might also qualify (see Table 23.4). This third change has depended largely on the capacity of the peoples concerned to sell their manufactured goods in rich-country markets such as that of Britain, and this in turn depends on whether rich-country governments allow these goods to be imported freely.

TABLE 23.4 *Basic indicators for selected semi-industrialized countries*

	GNP per head, 1977 (US$)	Average annual percentage growth 1960–77		Percentage of labour force in agriculture		Percentage of manufactures in merchandize exports	
		GNP per head	GNP	1960	1977	1960	1976
Brazil	1360	4.9	8.0	52	42	3	25
Taiwan	1170	6.2	9.1	56	34		85
Greece	2810	6.2	6.7	56	40	10	49
Israel	2850	4.8	8.0	14	8	61	78
S. Korea	820	7.4	10.0	65	44	14	88
Philippines	450	2.5	5.5	61	51	4	24
Spain	3190	5.2	6.4	42	19	22	69
Turkey	1100	4.1	6.4	78	62	3	24

CHANGING RELATIONSHIPS

Capital

Since the early 1950s the British Government, like those of other rich countries, has provided 'economic aid' (grants and cheap loans) to a number of Third World countries, either directly or through 'multilateral' institutions (mainly UN agencies and the World Bank group). Twenty years ago aid in this sense provided about two-thirds of the net flows of capital from rich to poor countries. Now it forms only a third or less, with most of the rest provided by private transactions conducted on business terms: some of it *direct investment* by multinational companies, but the bulk of it *loans* from banks and other private institutions. Bank lending to the Third World (especially to middle-income countries such as Mexico, Brazil and Turkey) increased enormously in the 1970s. The UK figures show these trends, with government aid ('official development assistance') only about a seventh of the total in 1980 (see Table 23.5).

United Nations bodies have set a target for aid from rich countries of 0.7 per cent of their respective gross national products (GNPs). Like most of the others (the main exceptions being France, Sweden, Norway and Holland) the UK has never reached this target, and its aid has fallen, even in cash terms, since 1979; yet 2–3 per cent of the country's GNP may move as private invetment and loans to the Third World. More than a quarter of the value of British Government aid in 1980 was for 'technical cooperation': the provision of experts and volunteers and of studentships and training. A small part covered the forgiveness of debts and an even smaller part free food. Much of the rest was for investments in 'infrastructure', a term covering facilities for transport, water and power. Nearly 30 per cent went through multilateral agencies.

Trade

Britain's trade with the Third World has gone through various phases over the last two centuries. Shortly before the Industrial Revolution its imports from Asia and America consisted mainly

TABLE 23.5 UK Flow of finance to less developed countries and multilateral agencies (Net disbursements. Values: £ million in constant 1980 (UK) prices)

	1970–72 average		1979		1980	
	Amount	Percentage of UK GNP	Amount	Percentage of UK GNP	Amount	Percentage of UK GNP
Official development assistance ('aid')	806.3	0.42	1170.2	0.51	765.6	0.34
of which:						
Grants	(408.5)		(862.3)		(742.1)	
Loans	(397.5)		(307.7)		(23.8)	
Multilateral	(189.0)		(523.8)		(226.0)	
Bilateral	(617.3)		(646.4)		(539.6)	
Other government	174.1		78.7		−70.3	
Grants by private voluntary agencies	58.6		59.9		45.0	
Private flows on market terms:						
Direct investment	435.3		572.1		450.0	
Other	436.4		5720.3		4310.0	
Total	1910.8	1.00	7601.1	3.33	5500.2	2.43

of a few foodstuffs and materials of a luxurious character (sugar, tea, coffee, tobacco, spices, indigo, precious stones) and some high-quality handcrafts (fine cotton goods, china, silks, lacquer-work). Long-distance trade was costly and dangerous and the goods exchanged correspondingly valuable. Britons probably paid for these goods largely out of the rewards of shipping, trade, West Indian plantations, and the beginnings of Indian adminis-tration, with a balance covered by movement of precious metals. Manufactures flowed from Asia to Europe rather than the reverse.

This pattern changed decisively in the early nineteenth century when Britain led the world in the mechanized production of textiles and followed this with revolutionary improvements in iron and steel production and in the development of rail and steam transport. Central Scotland, with its swift streams, its coal, its deep-water ports and its enterprising tradesmen, became one of the main centres of the Industrial Revolution. Cheap British cloth came to be sold wherever traders found it worthwhile to penetrate, and as the century wore on rails and rolling stock, metal goods and machinery, steel ships and pottery, found their way across the world. In return Britain, with its growing popu-lation and living standards, demanded more of the tea, sugar and tobacco, which changed from luxuries to necessities; and also coffee and cocoa; grain; and the industrial raw materials: cotton, jute, wool, copra, and at the end of the century petroleum and rubber. Metals and petroleum came from wherever they could be found. Grain and wool came largely from temperate countries. The rest came from the tropics, and thus mainly from what we now call the Third World.

Yet techniques of production can spread. Not only Europe and North America but by the 1850s India, and by the 1870s Japan, had begun mechanized textile production. India was exporting cotton piece-goods to world markets at about the beginning of this century and Japan soon after. Both India and Japan began modern steel production shortly after 1900.

World export markets for most kinds of manufactures have continued to grow, generally faster than world income. Britain's proportional share in them has fallen, though the real value of its exports has continued to rise. And, while trade between industrial countries has grown, there have also, since the mid 1960s, been rapid increases of trade in manufactures from certain Third World countries to the industrial heartlands.

Typically the exports from the Third World that have won large overseas markets are textiles, clothing, footwear, and certain other classes of light consumer goods. These goods are relatively large direct users of labour, requiring skills that are easily learnt. Consequently they are goods in which low-wage countries often have a *comparative advantage* so that they can outsell producers in high-wage countries (see Chapter 3). For other classes of goods as well, *multinational companies* have frequently shifted to poor countries those stages in production that make much use of unskilled or semi-skilled labour (see Chapter 19).

Where a country has a commercial tradition and low labour costs, where it also provides a favourable environment for foreign as well as domestic enterprise, and encourages, rather than obstructs, international trade, the result has often been the explosive growth of manufacturing (see Table 23.4).

Japan was the pioneer of rapid and prolonged industrial growth impinging on a very poor peasant economy, in large part through the medium of manufactured exports. Now it appears that the pattern of trade in manufacturers is continuing to alter as one low-wage country after another begins to tread the same path to affluence.

The changes associated with the growth of industry overseas have required drastic adaptation in Central Scotland and Northern England, the heartlands of the first Industrial Revolution. The cotton and woollen textile industries, clothing and shipbuilding, have all declined over more or less the last sixty years. Jute manufacture has disappeared.

Yet the rise in income in the newly industrializing countries also means a rise in their spending and a rise in their demand for those goods in which British industry has a continuing relative advantage. The recent concentration of new electronics production in Scotland is one sign of which those goods may be. From 1972 to 1980, the UK's exports of merchandize to Third World countries rose much faster than its imports from them, and this is still true even if fuels are excluded (49 per cent for exports as against 19 per cent for imports – see Tables 23.1 and 23.2).

Ensuring that *enough* goods can be sold overseas to keep the

British workforce productively employed is a matter of seeing that actual cash prices are low enough and quality high enough: something in which government (with its influence on wages, exchange-rates and interest-rates) has a role to play.

The pattern of the UK's trade with the Third World has changed, with these countries as a whole becoming relatively, as well as absolutely, more important as a *source* of textiles and clothing and of machinery, and also as a *market* for the same categories of goods from the UK, as well as for chemicals and shoes (see Tables 23.4 and 23.5).

Such changes are not the same for all countries within the Third World. Import and export trade with India and Pakistan–Bangladesh, which have generally followed highly protective policies, has fallen, and both imports and exports with South Korea, Taiwan and Hong Kong, three countries whose policies have been highly trade-oriented, have shown a very great rise (see Table 23.6).

An international trade treaty known as the Multifibre Agreement, first concluded in 1973, has allowed industrialized countries to use quotas in order to keep their imports of each class of textile and garment originating in each Third World country from rising at a rate of more than 6 per cent a year. This rule is designed to allow the rich countries' industries time to adapt while not closing off avenues for growth in poor countries. But the individual rich countries, including the UK as part of the EEC, have imposed separate, much more restrictive rules of their own, which at present seem likely to halt the growth of textile and clothing exports from precisely those poor countries that have been most successful in promoting them.

Quite probably the present newly industrializing countries will meet these checks by moving 'up-market' to less labour-intensive exports. South Korea, like India and Brazil, already exports steel, and, like Brazil, already exports ships.

A VITAL QUESTION

Will possible changes of policies of Third World governments, especially toward export-promotion among the giant countries (such as China, India, Indonesia, Bangladesh and Egypt), set them also on the path of rapid growth? If that happens, Scottish industry will be faced with further drastic problems of adjustment, but it will also be presented with great opportunities as those countries' markets expand.

TABLE 23.6   *Value of UK trade with selected less-developed countries, 1956–80 (Values: £ million in constant 1980 (UK) prices)*

	UK Imports from		UK Exports to	
	Value	*Percentage of total UK imports*	*Value*	*Percentage of total UK exports*
South Korea				
1956	0.7	0.0	20.1	0.1
1964	2.2	0.0	4.6	0.0
1972	10.1	0.1	77.5	0.3
1980	243.3	0.5	96.9	0.2
Hong Kong				
1956	117.3	0.5	192.9	1.0
1964	369.3	1.4	262.6	1.3
1972	568.9	1.7	311.0	1.0
1980	747.6	1.5	530.0	1.1
Taiwan				
1956	7.9	0.0	5.9	0.0
1964	9.2	0.0	5.0	0.0
1972	73.0	0.2	33.8	0.1
1980	232.8	0.5	90.9	0.2
India				
1956	822.7	3.6	988.1	5.1
1964	664.1	2.6	605.7	2.9
1972	345.4	1.0	433.9	1.4
1980	306.5	0.6	433.7	0.9
Pakistan and Bangladesh				
1956	132.6	0.6	191.0	1.0
1964	126.3	0.5	211.0	1.0
1972	107.3	0.3	109.5	0.4
1980	77.3	0.2	188.5	0.4

Part VI

Economics in the Real World (Economic Data)

24

What do Indicators Indicate?

DAVID BELL

At the end of 1981, industrial production in Scotland was 89.3 per cent of the 1975 level. Of the 1.88 million people employed, 817 000 were women. There were 304 000 people unemployed, an unemployment rate of 13.6 per cent. The numbers employed in special schemes were 54 200 of which 30 000 were in the Youth Opportunities Programme. There were 13 600 unfilled job vacancies. Average weekly earnings for all males were, in October 1981, £140 and for women £87. In the first half of the year, 120 000 working days were lost due to industrial stoppages. North Sea oil production for the year was 87.6 million tonnes. Companies wholly related to North Sea oil production employed 55 260 workers.

These figures give us a simple snapshot of the Scottish economy in one time period. More data of this kind, and built up over a period, are very useful to the economist. They make it possible to understand the relationships between economic phenomena, to test hypotheses derived from theories and to make predictions of how the economy will behave in the future. All these are very important. However, the certainty with which the features of the Scottish economy can be measured is limited.

The problems of measurement facing the economist are different from, and are in certain respects more difficult than, those facing other scientists.

MEASURING ECONOMIC ACTIVITY

For the physical scientist, the problem of measurement appears relatively straightforward. He knows what to measure, how to measure it and how accurate the results are likely to be. The economist, however, is frequently unsure of what he is measuring, does not know how best to measure it and is uncertain how precise his observations are. Further, the economist must realize that economic relations are much more volatile. The law of gravity stays constant through time and space, but the relationship between changes in the money supply and the rate of inflation can, and does, alter frequently.

GENERAL DIFFICULTIES

There are several general difficulties facing the economist:

Difficulties of experiments. A major difference between measurement in physical science and in economics is the extent to which a natural scientist can control the environment which he is observing. He sets up an experiment in such a way as to exclude all those factors which he considers irrelevant. Economists might wish to work with such a controlled environment: in reality they cannot. Their only 'experiment' is the real world which is subject to all manner of unexpected disturbances. These add greatly to the economists' measurement problems.

Collection and use. A further difficulty is that economists rarely make measurements directly. Instead they normally rely on government to collect statistics for them: most economists use 'second-hand' information. They make pronouncements on government policy, forecasts of economic activity and judgements on recent trends all on the basis of statistics which they have played no part in collecting. This division between the collector and the use of economic measurement is fraught with danger. Government statisticians do not always have the economists' interest in mind when they collect figures: economists often do not understand or gloss over the problems which the statisticians must contend with.

Legal legislative constraints. The legislation which surrounds the process of data collection adds further complications. The Statistics of Trade Act was designed to prevent users of government statistics from gaining any information on individual firms or enterprises. While this safeguards firms' confidential business information it certainly makes life difficult for economists. Studying economic structure without detailed knowledge of firm behaviour is like studying nuclear physics without knowing anything about atoms.

DIFFICULTIES WITH SCOTTISH DATA

Almost all Scottish economic statistics are collected by the government. The only major exception to this rule is the Industrial Trends Survey which is carried out quarterly by the Confederation of British Industry. As far as the London-based Central Statistical Office (CSO) is concerned, Scotland is one of the eleven standard regions which comprise the UK and deserves no special treatment. Thus, Scotland receives exactly the same set of statistics as does East Anglia or the South-west.

The Edinburgh-based Scottish Economic Planning Department (SEPD) in the Scottish Office takes a slightly different view. It attempts to supplement the meagre diet provided by the CSO with some additional figures. In particular, SEPD produces an index of industrial production for Scotland and keeps records of the number of manufacturing establishments in operation. Even with these additions, the provision of economic statistics in Scotland is fairly poor and compares badly with the range provided in, say, the American states.

Scottish economic statistics suffer from a number of deficiencies: the major ones are as follows:

Accuracy. There are two forms of inaccuracy in economic measurement. The first of these concerns the correspondence between what you want to measure and what you actually do measure. Economists think of the level of unemployment, for example, as measuring the number of people who could work, but do not. Yet the published unemployment figures show the number of persons who obtain unemployment benefit. Those who are ineligible to receive unemployment benefit are excluded from the monthly totals.

The second form of inaccuracy occurs when the economist

correctly identifies what he wants to quantify, but is not very successful in actually making his measurement. A good example here is earnings. To discover what total earnings in the economy are, the logical approach would seem to be to add together the declared earnings of all employees. But it would be very costly to identify the earnings of each Scot who is employed. Some form of sample must be taken: an estimate of average earnings in the employed population can then be made from the results. Total earnings are estimated by grossing up (multiplying) this average by the size of the employed population. For maximum accuracy, the sample must be representative of the population as a whole. A biased sample will lead to biased results.

Biases can arise in many ways. In the earnings example, for instance, they can result from the fact that there is a large group of workers who will go to great pains to ensure that their earnings are not recorded in any official statistics. Tax evasion is now widespread throughout the Scottish economy. The 'black economy' operates exclusively in terms of direct cash payments. Such earnings will not enter any sample survey. Consequently, the sample will be biased and the government's estimate of total earnings will be inaccurate.

Lateness. Frequently there is a considerable lag between events and the publication of the statistics which describe them. Several groups are interested in economic statistics. Journalists and reporters use these figures to inform the public and to comment on the progress of the economy. Politicians make use of statistics in formulating policy. Researchers construct forecasts and analyse trends by reviewing economic statistics. To carry out their tasks effectively, these individuals must have access to the most recent figures. There is no point in making policy decisions on the basis of figures which are outdated.

Informed discussion of the Scottish economy is greatly hampered by the time it takes government statisticians to produce figures. For example, the information in the first paragraph of this brief, about the end of 1981, was first published in the summer of 1982. At that time, the most recent estimate of Gross Domestic Product was for 1980. The most up-to-date figures for household expenditure were for 1979/80 and for net capital expenditure in manufacturing industries as a whole and overseas enterprises in particular were for 1979. The most recent statistics were for unemployment and vacancies in early 1982.

Probably the major reason for this slowness in compiling Scottish statistics is the lack of political pressure for the production of information on the regions of the UK. Economic policy in the UK is determined almost exclusively at the national level, with the regions having very little economic autonomy. Thus, there is no immediate need for regional statistics for policy-making purposes and their production proceeds at a more leisurely pace.

Revisions. While the late production of statistics is inconvenient, there is little to be gained from more rapid compilation if the statistics need subsequently to be heavily revised. With few exceptions, unemployment and vacancies being the most notable, Scottish economic statistics are typically subject to substantial revision following their initial publication. Consider, for example, the Scottish Index of Industrial Production from which we obtain the indices for construction, manufacturing and mining and quarrying (see Table 24.1). The indices for each sector are estimates for a *single* period, second quarter of 1979. The time periods given relate to the time at which the estimates *were published.*

Clearly your view of the behaviour of the economy in the second quarter of 1979 is heavily dependent on the time at which you examined the statistics. Later estimates tend to give a more rosy view of output in mining and quarrying in the second quarter of 1979. Optimism regarding manufacturing output would have peaked in Spring 1981 and then receded.

TABLE 24.1   *Estimates of Index of Industrial Production, quarter 2, 1979*

Publication date	Construction	Manufacturing	Mining and quarrying
Spring 1980	91	102.5	95
Summer 1980	94	103.2	95
Spring 1981	92	103.6	96
Summer 1981	92	103.5	96
Spring 1982	91	103.0	98

Given that Scottish output rarely fluctuates by more than 1 per cent between quarters, the size of the revisions to the statistics could overshadow the real changes which are taking place. This fact is not well-appreciated by the media. Commentators are prepared to speculate on the implications of the latest figures even though these may subsequently be drastically revised in the light of new information.

Omissions. UK regional statistics only give a very vague picture of the economy which they describe. There are many areas of interest to economists which are almost completely ignored. For example, we do not know precisely how prices behave in the different parts of the UK. One may have a feeling that Scottish prices are higher than in the Midlands, but lower than in the South East. Yet there is no firm evidence to support this feeling.

There is a similar lack of data about investment. The speed at which regions develop is very much dependent on the amount of plant and machinery at the disposal of each worker. However, the only data available relate to the manufacturing sector, which normally accounts for less than one-third of total employment, and these are three years out of date.

Perhaps the major omission, however, is trade. The Scottish economy is very *open*: a high proportion of the goods which we produce are exported and a high proportion of the goods consumed are imported. There is, however, virtually no regular information on Scotland's external trade. In particular, there is almost complete ignorance regarding Scottish trade with the rest of the UK. Thus, it is almost impossible to tell which areas within the UK trade extensively with Scotland and what types of good make up this trade (see Chapter 3).

It is then difficult to build up a precise picture of the Scottish economy from statistical sources. Most observers, however, are only interested in a particular part of the scene. And in some of these parts considerable detail can be filled in. For example, there is a large amount of information available on the labour market (see Chapter 6). And in some industries which are particularly important to Scotland, government statistics can be supplemented by trade associations. A good example is the whisky industry (see Chapter 25).

Measuring economic activity requires considerable human

resources and is fraught with difficulties. There is no substitute for hard facts when it comes to addressing the numerous economic and social problems we face.

SOURCES

The best source for up-to-date Scottish economic statistics is the *Scottish Economic Bulletin* which is published bi-annually by SEPD. It contains tables of the major annual and quarterly economic indicators which are available for Scotland and is available from HMSO. The *Scottish Abstract of Statistics,* also available from HMSO, contains mostly the same information, though these are supplemented by social and demographic statistics which help place the economy within a wider context.

Some Scottish economic statistics are only available through UK publications. The *Department of Employment Gazette* is an invaluable source of information on the labour market. And *British Business*, a publication of the Department of Industry, contains some of the most recent indicators for the Scottish economy. Again, both these publications are available through HMSO.

SOME IMPORTANT STATISTICS

The Index of Industrial Production

The Scottish *Index of Industrial Production* attempts to measure the level of *net output* in the *Index of Production Industries*. The Index of Production Industries covers those industries which produce some tangible output including mining and quarrying, manufacturing, the utilities (gas, electricity and water) and construction. The *net* output of an industry is the value of all the goods which it produces *less* the cost of all the materials which are used in the production process. Thus, the net output of the shipbuilding industry is the value of the ships produced, less the cost of, for example, steel and wood used in their production.

Understandably, economists and others often want a simple measure of the *quantity* of some groups of goods; these goods may be bought by consumers or produced by industry. However, there are particular problems to be overcome and the usual solution is the creation of an *index number*. Suppose, for example, that we wished to measure the output of the clothing industry in a particular year. Let us imagine that clothing production consisted only of socks, jerseys and coats. How are we to add these together to measure the *quantity* of clothing output? Do we say five jerseys equals one coat and forty socks equals one jersey? How might we determine such ratios? The answer is to let the price system do the determination for us. If socks cost 50p a pair and jerseys £10 and coats £40, then these prices should reflect the cost of the labour and materials which have gone into their production and can be used as a base for comparison between the various goods. In other words, we use the *value* of the goods to assist in finding a simple measure of *quantity*.

These values can be used to set up an index for the *base year*. Whatever the value of the output, it is artificially set equal to 100 for that year. For the Scottish Index of Industrial Production the base year is 1975 (see Fig. 24.1). However, in the following years the value of the output can change, for two reasons: either because the quantities of output have changed, or because the prices of the goods have changed. To derive an index for differ-

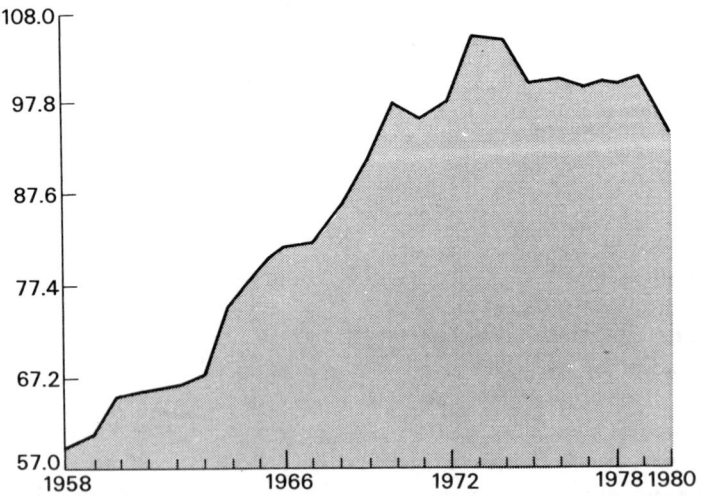

Fig. 24.1   *Scottish Manufacturing Index of Production (1975 = 100)*

ent years, the procedure is to take the ratios of output quantities in the various years to that in the base year. Thus if steel output in some year is 1100 tonnes compared with 1000 tonnes in the base year, the index of production for that industry will increase to 110.'

A sequence of figures can be constructed, one for each year or quarter. This series indicates how the volume of output has fluctuated relative to the base year. For example, the index for Scottish manufacturing output over the period 1958–80 shows how the output increased during the 1960s and early 1970s but has tended to decline since then.

Employees in Employment

The Department of Employment is responsible for the collection of employment statistics. It does this in two ways.

(1) Periodic censuses are conducted to enumerate *all* employees. These are classified by area, sex and industry. The basic collection unit is the *local employment office area*. There are employment offices throughout the country; these have responsibility for a well-defined area. Employment returns from within this area are allocated to the local office. Since Strathclyde region alone contains fifty-six such offices, it is obvious that very detailed employment information is available. Unfortunately, the most detailed published information is at the level of the local authority region. Thus, the published information contains no details on the distribution of employment within Strathclyde.

(2) Information is collected by sample survey. Only a proportion of establishments are surveyed: no attempt is made to enumerate each employee. These have become more common in recent years because of their lower cost. Indeed the censuses of employment for 1979 and 1980 were abandoned and replaced by such surveys. Much less detail is available from this approach and there are no longer published estimates of employment within Scotland, even at the regional level. Government statisticians obviously feel that the uncertainty which accompanies their survey-based estimates is too great to justify the publication of detailed figures.

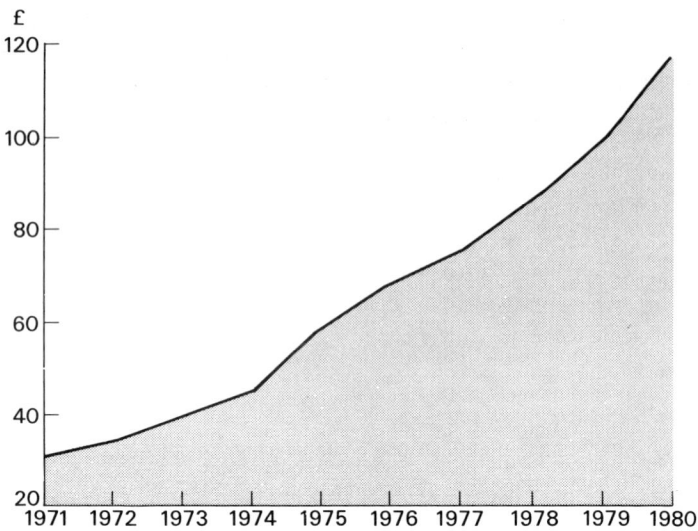

Fig. 24.2   *Full-time male manual weekly earnings in manufacturing
industry in Scotland*

Earnings

The Department of employment is also responsible for compiling
wages and earnings statistics. This information is invariably collected by sample survey. The most important of these surveys is
known as the New Earnings Survey which is conducted in April
of each year. This survey is based on a 1 per cent random sample
of employees and is selected in an impersonal way so that every
employee has an equal chance of being included. The names of
the individuals involved, however, are kept strictly confidential.

The information obtained relates to a single pay period during
April. Data is collected on all payments by the employer to the
selected employee during that period. These will comprise standard wages, but may also include items such as overtime pay,
bonuses and sick pay. Further information is collected on hours of
work, age, sex and area of employment.

The results are published in five volumes each year. Data on
average weekly earnings for Scottish male manufacturing
workers over the period 1971–81 show a rapid increase in earnings from the mid-1970s (see Fig. 24.2). These increases relate, of

course, to money or *nominal* earnings. Employees *real* earnings (the amount of goods and services which their wages could buy) increased much more slowly because prices were growing almost as rapidly over the same period.

25

The Case of Whisky: Use of Data

ROBIN L. W. ALPINE

Microeconomic theory considers specific markets, for example the market for a single factor of production or for a given product, and involves the construction of models to help us understand the behaviour of households and of firms within a particular industry. At the level of economic theorizing the industry does not require to be given a particular name: it is described instead in terms of other characteristics, such as the number and size of the firms it contains or whether the output produced is part of final demand or is used in further production. When an industry is apparently named the product is usually something which can be readily visualized, like the 'motor-car' industry or the Scotch-whisky industry.

The testing of economic theory requires the collection of 'real-life' data. The industry to which the model refers must therefore have a real-world counterpart for which observations about actual behaviour relating, for example, to output and prices, will be available. But how easy is it to describe a specific industry such as the Scotch-whisky industry? What is whisky? How is whisky produced? How is the whisky industry recorded in official statistics? Who makes Scotch? How can we interpret data on important items such as value-added, labour, stocks and fixed capital?

THE SCOTCH WHISKY INDUSTRY

What is Whisky?

Scotch whisky has a history which goes back several hundred years. Traditionally it was a spirit distilled from malted barley, the other major ingredients being peat and water. Peat is used to dry the barley, which has been soaked in tanks for two to three days, and convert it into malt; water is then required to turn the malt into a liquid which ferments, with the aid of yeast, into a beer-like substance. After that comes the distillation process in which the fermented liquid is turned into vapour and then condensed back into a liquid (spirit): distillation takes place in a pear-shaped copper still called a pot still, a piece of equipment perfected in the Highlands of Scotland during the eighteenth century.

Malt whisky is the original type of whisky produced in Scotland and for much of its history its consumption was concentrated in the Highlands. Production usually took place in small illegal stills. For more than a century now, however, production has been more tightly controlled. The spirit produced in pot stills today requires several years of maturing, preferably in oak casks. Little malt whisky is sold for direct consumption below five years of age; much is aged for at least eight years in cask.

In the 1820s another type of still, the patent or Coffey still, was introduced into whisky making. This differs in several important ways from the pot still: in particular it is a continuous process whereas the pot still is a batch process. The patent still produces whisky more quickly and in far greater quantity so that the unit cost of production is lower. The type of whisky differs also; it is based on a mixture of cereals, principally maize with a little malted barley. The barley is not dried over peat fires, however, and grain whisky (as it is called) is a relatively neutral spirit unlike the often peaty flavoured malt whisky.'

Over 90 per cent of whisky sold for consumption in the UK at present is blended whisky, i.e. a mixture of both grain and malt whisky. The more expensive blends contain a higher proportion of malt whisky, often too of greater average age. The minimum period of ageing, even for grain whisky, before the spirit can legally be called whisky in the UK is three years.

How is Whisky Production Organized?

The production of whisky involves three major stages.

Distilling. Those distilleries producing spirit from malt alone are small-scale units; average annual production is less than 10 per cent of the normal annual production of the average grain distillery. At this stage the spirit is termed 'plain cereal spirit'.

Maturation. Ageing takes place in oak casks which are stored in 'bonded' warehouses under the watchful eye of an official of HM Customs and Excise.

Blending and bottling. Whiskies are blended together and bottled once the mixture has had a short time to settle down. Many blended whiskies will contain between 50–60 per cent grain whisky; the remainder of the blend may well comprise forty or even more different malts depending on the blending formula being used.

Not all firms involved in the whisky industry, however, are involved at each stage. Some firms do not operate any distilleries or even directly hold maturing stocks of whisky. They concentrate instead on buying casks of matured whiskies from other firms which they then blend to their own 'recipes' and later bottle for sale under their own names. Other firms operate one or more distilleries but sell their output to others to bottle or use in blending. Finally, there are a number of firms which are involved in all three stages of production, bottling some of their own production of malt whisky as well as buying and selling malt and grain whiskies for blending purposes.

How is the Whisky Industry Recorded in Official Statistics?

The real-life counterpart of the economist's concept of an industry is the minimum list heading (MLH). Each firm in the economy is assigned to a particular MLH according to its major economic activity. Under this system MLH 239 covers alcohol for human consumption other than beer (MLH 231). For some purposes MLH 239 is subdivided, into 239.1 (spirit distilling and compounding) and 239.2 (British wines, cider and perry). The activities covered by 239.1 relates principally to the UK production of whisky, gin and vodka, by means of either distillation (whisky) or rectification (gin and vodka). The latter spirits do not change materially with ageing and do not, therefore, have to remain in bond for several years before being consumed.

The firms covered by MLH 239.1 thus include all those who own one or more whisky distillery. This MLH will of course also include firms engaged in the production of gin and vodka, and exclude firms engaged only in the latter stages of whisky making (maturation and blending/bottling). These latter firms are treated as part of the distribution sector of the economy, for which much less detailed information is available.

Some of the data for MLH 239.1 is broken down by product: sales information is available for whisky separately from other British spirits. However, other information, for example, on value added, employment and investment, is not subdivided. But where it is shown on a regional basis it is reasonable to equate data for Scotland with 'the whisky industry'.

Another important data source for whisky is HM Customs and Excise, on account of the high rate of duty (excise tax) which is levied on spirits sold for UK consumption. Statistics on foreign trade are published on an entirely different basis, *viz* by commodity instead of by MLH or industry. It is therefore possible to obtain information on whisky exports directly. A very useful secondary source of information relating to Scotch whisky is the annual Statistical Report published by the Scotch Whisky Association (SWA): this report brings together data relating to production, consumption, exports and stocks held in bonded warehouses.

WHO MAKES SCOTCH?

The distilleries are the basic production plants of the 'whisky industry' and the SWA publishes a map listing them and showing their locations. A count of the number of distilleries, however, will not reveal how many firms there are in the industry, since several distilleries may be owned by the same firm. Since the firm has an important role to play in economic theory, an interesting feature of any industry is the number of firms it comprises.

Counting the number of firms involved in a 'real life' industry is often not a simple matter. For example, in many cases a distillery is registered as being owned by a particular company, which in turn is owned by another company. Indeed one 'higher-level' company may own several 'lower-level' companies, and the SWA list shows only the names of the 'lower-level' companies.

The relationship between the levels can be of considerable importance. Certainly it is customary for the day-to-day decisions to be taken by the 'lower-level' firm. Indeed, even though several 'lower-level' firms are owned by the same 'higher-level' company, they will usually compete against each other for sales. But longer-term decisions, relating in particular to investment or disinvestment, will normally be taken at the higher level. For this reason a count of the number of truly independent companies is important.

Information on ownership appears both in directories relating to the wine and spirit trade and in books concerned with the history of whisky production. Using these sources enables the following pattern of ownership to be revealed for 132 distilleries named on the fourth edition of the SWA map (January 1977), plus a malt distillery at Brora, which were in existence in mid 1978 (see Table 25.1).

TABLE 25.1   *Ownership of distilleries in mid 1978*

Number of distilleries per company	1	2	3	4	5	6	7	8	9	10	50
Number of companies	12	7	2	3	0	1	2	0	1	1	1

The pattern of distillery ownership is highly concentrated: only one company, Distillers Company Limited (DCL), owned more than ten distilleries. That company owned fifty distilleries in mid 1978, including five of the fourteen grain distilleries. The two largest companies after DCL in terms of distillery ownership were both Canadian (Hiram Walker and Seagrams), and one of the next two (Long John International) had US connections. The North American influence is not surprising, given the geographical distribution of Scotch whisky sales. The total number of 'higher level' companies in 1978 was thirty. The skewness of the distribution, however, suggests that market power is highly concentrated, so that the industry resembles the textbook classification of 'oligopoly'.

Some Uses of Census of Production Data

A most important source of information regarding the economic activity of firms involved in the manufacturing sector of the economy is the annual *Report on the Census of Production* (produced by the Business Statistics Office of the Department of Industry). The census forms are collated so that published data relate to individual MLHs and not to particular firms. These data relate to; (a) output and costs (in value terms), (b) labour and capital services, and (c) capital expenditure.

Output and costs. The value of a firm's output by itself does not tell us much about that firm's own contribution: for example, the firm might merely assemble expensive components purchased from other firms. The *Census of Production* thus distinguishes between the *value of gross output* on the one hand and *gross value added* on the other. The word 'gross' here means that no deduction has been made for the wearing out of capital. Gross value added measures the contribution made by the factors of production (labour and capital) employed directly within the industry: it essentially represents the difference between the value of total output and the cost of bought-in materials and services. In some cases, however, including MLH 239.1 the value of output includes excise taxes levied by the government on producers (as distinct from VAT which is a sales tax levied essentially at the final stage): in these cases the value of excise payments must also be deducted to arrive at value added.

For MLH 239.1 as a whole around 80 per cent of value added and 85 per cent of employment were attributable to Scotland. Thus, these data may be taken to be broadly representative of what is happening to the 'whisky industry' subgroup of this MLH. Value added, for example, is around 30 per cent of the value of gross output; and in 1973 and 1976 was less than the value of excise taxes (see Table 25.2).

Labour and capital services. The *Census of Production* definition of employment for any given year is average employment over that year and covers working proprietors as well as operatives (manual workers) and other employees (administrative, technical and clerical – ATC – staff). Employment in MLH 239.1 rose

TABLE 25.2   *Output and costs in MLH 239.1 (£ thousand)*

	1973		1976		1979	
Total sales	731		1229		1802	
Increase in stocks[1]	40		64	1293	155	1957
Gross output		771				
Materials[2]	253		412		646	
Services	35		75		161	
Excise payments	252	540	437	924	561	1368
Gross value added		231		369		589

Notes: 1. Stocks of finished goods and work in progress. 2. Purchases of materials less increase in stocks of materials.

steadily from 1973 to 1979, increasing by around 2 per cent per annum over this period (see Table 25.3). The time series for gross value added (GVA) per head is measured in terms of the prices current in each year and is thus rendered meaningless by itself because of the impact of inflation. However we can compare each year's figure with the corresponding figure for all manufacturing industry. This reveals that GVA per head is much higher in MLH 239.1 than for manufacturing industry as a whole, although the ratio of the two did fall slightly over the period.

But the relatively high figure for GVA per head does not mean that workers in MLH 239.1 enjoy relatively high remuneration. Labour costs (wages and salaries plus employment overheads, paid by employers, including national insurance and pension contributions) are a much smaller proportion of GVA in MLH 239.1 than in all manufacturing industry (see Table 25.4). Thus the average salary level for ATC staff in MLH 239.1 has remained just above that for manufacturing as a whole while the

TABLE 25.3   *Employment and gross value added per head in MLH 239.1*

		Gross value added per head (£)		MLH 239.1/ all manufactures
Year	Employment	MLH 239.1	All manufactures	
1973	24 100	9569	3116	3.07
1976	25 400	14542	5316	2.74
1979	27 200	21684	8154	2.66

TABLE 25.4   Labour costs in MLH 239.1

	Labour costs/GVA (%)		Wage per head (£)		Salary per head (£)	
	MLH 239.1	All manufactures	MLH 239.1	All manufactures	MLH 239.1	All manufactures
1973	22	60	1740	1575	2209	2075
1976	24	63	2730	2753	3604	3537
1979	24	63	3977	4062	5742	5327
1973–79 (percentage per annum)			14.8	17.1	17.3	17.0

TABLE 25.5 *Percentage of total stocks held in different forms*

	End year stocks/Sales %		Materials/total stocks %		Work in progress/total stocks %		Finished goods/total stocks %	
	MLH 239.1	All manufactures	MLH 239.1	All manufactures	MLH 239.1	All manufactures	MLH 239.1	All manufactures
1973	60	21	18	37	72	41	10	22
1976	57	23	32	37	58	37	10	26
1979	68	23	31	35	57	37	12	28

average wage level for operatives started off 10 per cent above the all manufacturing industry figure in 1973 but then fell below the latter. Most of GVA is paid for capital services. The stocks which firms hold are classified into three groups. Materials held in reserve for future production and finished goods represent two obvious categories. The third category comprises stocks of semi-finished goods named 'work in progress'. Since grain whisky requires at least three years maturation whilst much malt whisky is given eight or more years in cask, we would expect work in progress in the whisky industry to be of greater than average importance.

The stocks to sales ratio in MLH 239.1 is almost three times as high as that for all manufacturing industry (see Table 25.5). Furthermore, work in progress is much more important in this industry, even allowing for sizeable year-to-year fluctuations in its share. Thus, since factors of production require payment before the goods are finally sold, a relatively larger proportion of GVA is required in MLH 239.1 to pay for 'working capital'.

In addition, a large element of the final selling price of spirits in the UK market is excise duty paid initially by whisky firms shortly after the bottles leave bonded warehouses at the start of the distribution chain. These payments are relatively large, being approximately the same size as all bought-in materials (see Table 25.2). Interest payments have therefore to be made to providers of working capital for this purpose also.

Capital expenditure. The *Census of Production* provides data on investment spending but not on the value of capital employed within different industries. Accounting conventions regarding depreciation and the problem of dividing the capital value of firms which operate in more than one industry into the constitu-

TABLE 25.6   *Net capital expenditure as a percentage of gross value added*

	MLH 239.1	All manufactures
1973	10.6	9.6
1976	7.6	10.0
1979	8.1	12.3

ent parts makes analysis of capital input a very time consuming task, even when the relevant data can be obtained. Generally, however, it appears that investment spending in MLH 239.1 as a share of GVA has fallen in comparison with that in other manufacturing industry (see Table 25.6). This is related to some important recent changes in the industry.

RECENT CHANGES IN THE WHISKY INDUSTRY

Total sales are dominated by exports (see Table 25.7). During the 1970s the UK market accounted for less than 20 per cent of total sales compared with 25 per cent in 1960. There has, however, been a slow-down in growth and then decline in sales in both the UK and export markets in the last five years. This has clear adverse implications for production and investment.

The behaviour of total sales reflects mainly changes in exports to the major market, the USA (see Table 25.8). There has been some diversification of markets to compensate partially for the reduced importance of the US market but only two other countries, Japan and France, account for more than 5 per cent each of total sales.

Market diversification has been accompanied by considerable changes in the nature of whisky exports which also have implications for production in Scotland.

TABLE 25.7 *Sales of Scotch whisky in million proof gallons*

	Sales		
Year	UK	Exports	Total
1970	10.7	62.6	73.3
1971	11.2	70.8	82.0
1972	12.7	69.4	82.2
1973	15.5	79.3	94.8
1974	17.6	88.0	105.6
1975	16.5	90.7	107.2
1976	18.8	92.0	110.8
1977	15.7	94.0	109.7
1978	20.0	105.8	124.8
1979	20.5	101.3	121.8
1980	19.6	96.4	115.9

TABLE 25.8 *Major export markets for Scotch whisky*

Market	Percentage of total exports in selected years				
	1960	*1965*	*1970*	*1975*	*1980*
USA	54	52	54	38	30
Japan	1	1	2	9	11
EEC*	8	14	14	16	19

* Original six countries only

(1) Before the 1970s less than 4 per cent of exports were of malt whisky. Apart from small amounts of immature spirit and pure grain whisky – less than 1 per cent of the total – whisky had traditionally been exported already blended. About 75 per cent of this was bottled in Scotland, the remainder exported in cask to be reduced to the required alcoholic strength (by the addition of water) in the country of sale. The latter form of trade was developed in connection with exports to certain countries (such as the USA and Australia) where customs duty was levied on the basis of weight rather than alcoholic strength. Such a form of tax clearly makes a substantial difference to the selling price of Scotch whisky, since the water is being taxed at the same rate as the spirit. Exporting in bulk enables the whisky to be sold at a lower price than whisky bottled in Scotland. The drawback is that sales of bulk whisky generate no employment in Scotland at the bottling stage, one of the more labour-intensive parts of the production process. Exporting bulk whisky is likely to generate additional demand for Scotch, but it may also lead to a substitution of cheaper whisky bottled abroad for dearer whisky bottled in Scotland. There is, therefore, likely to be a trade-off between additional output for distilleries and reduced employment at bottling plants.

(2) A growing proportion of exports has been of malt whisky. Some of this has been in bottle from individual distilleries (the Scottish equivalent of wine from a particular vineyard). This is a prestige market, but although fast growing is still very small in overall terms. The major change has been the export of malt whisky in bulk to countries where local grain whisky can be

added, thus producing an alternative to 100 per cent Scotch whisky. Sales of blended whisky in bottle account for a fairly constant proportion of total exports (around 70 per cent): the rise in exports of bulk malt whisky has largely been at the expense of a fall in bulk blended whisky, brought about by the decline in the importance of the US market.

By far the biggest importer of malt whisky in bulk has been Japan. The arguments for and against this form of trade are rather similar to those given above relating to the exportation of blended whisky in bulk. Total sales may increase since the practice enables some whisky to be marketed at a price which attracts customers who could not afford 100 per cent Scotch whisky, but who might be induced later to move 'up market'. But the existence of a cheap substitute may lead to a switch in buying habits by customers who would otherwise have bought Scotch whisky: this argument suggests that it may not be in the long-run interests of the Scotch whisky producers to export malt whisky.

A complicating factor in the debate about bulk malt exportation has been the relatively high proportion of malt distilleries which are under foreign control. The official statistics do not throw light on the identities of the companies who export bulk malt. Those who support such sales can point to the fact that the proportion of whisky exports to Japan in the form of bulk malt has remained fairly close to 60 per cent throughout the 1970s. Given that total sales to Japan have increased by over 400 per cent during this time, it is clear that exports to Japan of blended whisky in bottle have also risen substantially. Nevertheless the combined effects of the world recession, the comparatively greater drop in sales to the biggest market, the USA (due probably to a change in consumer tastes) and the increased international competition from the Japanese (making a similar product) have forced DCL to make a major cutback in current production. In February 1983 it was announced that eleven of DCL's malt distilleries would be closed, plus one grain distillery and a plant producing malt from barley. Other recent closures include blending and bottling facilities and three other malt distilleries, as the industry painfully attempts to adjust production capacity to anticipated sales several years ahead.

Conclusion—The Future:
An Open Question

KEITH P. D. INGHAM and JAMES LOVE

By mid-1983, Scotland, like many other countries, was experiencing considerable depression of real income and employment and faces a future of great uncertainty. Many of the problems of the Scottish economy are associated with the process of adjustment to the decline in traditional activities. These problems have been made worse in recent years, first, by the relatively depressed levels of economic activity and demand in the major industrial economies throughout the world and, second, by a relatively strong pound sterling in the foreign exchange market.

The impact over several decades of the decline of industries such as shipbuilding, mining and steel-making have been reinforced in the last few years as the world recession has led to the closure of many firms. These have included several well-known closures with very severe consequences for some local communities such as Clydebank, Paisley, Invergordon and Fort William. In contrast, there have been two developments which have tended to improve income and employment. First, during the 1970s, North Sea Oil developments did much for the prosperity of the North East and East of Scotland. However, these oil production and oil-related activities, although important for certain local labour markets, created few jobs relative to the size of the Scottish labour force and, in particular, had little impact on West Central Scotland, the area which has suffered most from the decline of traditional activities. Second, Scotland has fared well in UK and European terms in the growth of largely foreign-owned, high-technology firms specializing in electronics and micro-chip systems. Recently, for example, there have been investments by WANG in Stirling and ACT in Glenrothes. But, on balance, Scotland still has a higher unemployment rate and a lower level of income per head than the averages for the UK as a whole.

Scotland does have policies on certain important matters, such as education and housing, which are different from those affecting other parts of the UK. The high degree of openness of the economy means, however, that many of the factors which might ease or help resolve Scotland's problems are outside direct control. Easily the largest element of demand for Scottish output is for export. An increase in demand for Scottish products will most obviously come from a recovery in world markets. This depends greatly on the performance of the major industrial countries, particularly the USA, Germany and Japan. Higher US income, for example, might stimulate Scotland's exports directly and also indirectly through its impact on growth in other countries. The prospects of world market recovery might be improved by actions by governments to create expansion through fiscal and monetary policies, or by other factors such as improved business optimism or possible cost reductions through lower oil prices.

In the late 1970s and early 1980s, Britain's position as a politically and socially stable industrialized economy with large oil revenues and a balance of payments surplus, kept the sterling exchange rate relatively high. This made UK, and, therefore, Scottish, manufactured exports less price-competitive in foreign markets and has probably helped foreign suppliers to penetrate UK markets. Oil price rises in the 1970s, contraction in the major industrial countries, and energy and oil conservation and substitution – increasing the price elasticity of demand for oil – have, however, resulted in reduced demand for oil. In early 1983 the OPEC cartel showed signs of failing to keep the price of oil at its previously high level. Downward pressures on oil prices and lower oil revenues for the UK are likely to keep sterling's international value below the levels of the past few years. This may stimulate industry within the UK; both in producing for export and for the home market. Against that, a weaker pound may induce capital outflows and produce pressures for higher domestic interest rates.

It is not clear to what extent Scotland would be in a position to benefit from any increased demand for UK goods. The high exchange rate, recent tight domestic monetary and fiscal policies and the world-wide depression have caused many firms to close down. Whether the elimination of less efficient Scottish and Scottish-based plants has left Scottish industry 'leaner and fitter' or 'smaller and weaker' is a question that will only be answered in time. UK regional and industrial policy may help overcome certain of Scotland's structural and locational problems but new investment may still be attracted to the South East and not to the regions like Scotland. It remains to be seen whether schemes such as the Enterprise Zones will generate a net increase in investment and employment.

As well as the influence which UK macroeconomic policies might have on the level of domestic demand, central government policies towards enterprises in the public sector are important to Scotland. The public sector, which includes much of what remains of traditional activities, is a major employer in Scotland. There are, however, considerable doubts about the future of, for example, the Ravenscraig steel plant and parts of the Scottish coalfield. Closure of Ravenscraig would have serious consequences for the local economy in the Motherwell area and loss of steel-making might make Scotland a less attractive location to potential investors. Decisions on closure are likely to be determined on the largely political grounds of whether market forces should be allowed to determine the viability of such enterprises.

Fundamentally, the Scottish economy is wide open to pressures and changes in the world economy. More than anything else it is what happens abroad in the growth of demand in the USA, Europe and Japan, changes in world oil prices and the international value of sterling, that will determine the future prosperity of Scotland. Whether the improvements in the structure and efficiency of the Scottish economy lead to a favourable response to expansion, these changes will be of only limited value if such expansion does not come.

References and Further Reading

CHAPTER 1

Bell, D. N. F. *et al.* 'The Development of a Medium Term Model for Scotland. I: Projections to 1984', *Fraser of Allander Research Monograph*, No. 10, 1982.

Bulmer-Thomas, V. 'The Regional Accounting Framework', *Fraser of Allander Research Monograph*, No. 5, 1978.

Central Statistical Office, *Regional Studies* (Annual).

Fraser of Allander Research Institute, *Quarterly Economic Commentary.*

Fraser of Allander Institute *et al. Input–Output Tables for Scotland 1973*, Scottish Academic Press, Edinburgh, 1978.

Lythe, C. and Majmudar, M. *The Renaissance of the Scottish Economy?* George Allen and Unwin, London, 1982.

Mackay, D. (Ed.) *Scotland 1980*, Q. Press, Edinburgh, 1977.

Scottish Office, *Scottish Economic Bulletin* (Quarterly).

Scottish Office, *Scottish Abstract of Statistics*, HMSO, Edinburgh (Annual).

CHAPTER 2

Beckerman, W. *Slow Growth in Britain*, Oxford University Press, Oxford, 1979.

Firn, J. R. 'External Control and Regional Policy', *Environment and Planning*, Vol. 7, 1975.

Galbraith, J. K. *The New Industrial State*, Penguin, Harmondsworth, 1967.

Scott, J. and Hughes, M. 'Ownership and Control in a Satellite Economy', *Sociology*, Vol. 10, 1976.

Scottish Abstract of Statistics, op cit.

CHAPTER 3

Findlay, R. *Trade and Specialisation*, Penguin, Harmondsworth, 1970.
Fraser of Allander Institute, *et al. Input–Output Tables for Scotland 1973*, Scottish Academic Press, Edinburgh, 1978.
Scammell, W. M. *International Trade and Payments*, Macmillan, London, 1974.
Scottish Council Research Institute, *Scotland's Manufactured Exports 1974–77*, Edinburgh, 1978.
Scottish Council Research Institute, *Scotland's Manufactured Exports 1978–80*, Edinburgh, 1981.
Thirlwall, A. P. *Balance of Payments Theory and the United Kingdom Experience*, 2nd ed. Macmillan, London, 1980.

CHAPTER 4

Fay, C. R. *Adam Smith and the Scotland of his day*, Cambridge University Press, Cambridge, 1956.
Macfie, A. L. *The Individual in Society: Papers on Adam Smith*, George Allen and Unwin, London, 1967.
Rae, J. *Life of Adam Smith*, (1895), reprinted with an introduction by Jacob Viner, Kelley, New York, 1965.
Scott, W. R. *Adam Smith as Student and Professor*, Jackson, Glasgow, 1937.
Skinner, A. S. and Wilson, T. (eds), *Essays on Adam Smith*, Clarendon Press, Oxford, 1975.
Smith, A. *An Inquiry into the Nature and Causes of the Wealth of Nations.* The definitive modern edition is that of Campbell, R. H., Skinner, A. S. and Todd, W. B., Clarendon Press, Oxford, 1976. Less expensive editions are published by J. M. Dent, London (Everyman's Library) and by the University of Chicago Press. (It should be pointed out that Penguin Books' edition unfortunately omits substantial sections of Smith's text.)
Wilson, T. and Skinner, A. S. (eds), *The Market and the State*, Clarendon Press, Oxford, 1976.

Short but authoritative articles on Adam Smith will be found in the *International Encyclopedia of the Social Sciences* (1968), the *Encyclopaedia Britannica* (15th ed. 1974) and in *Chambers's Encyclopaedia* (1973).

CHAPTER 5

Bain, A. D. '*The Economics of the Financial System*', Martin Robertson, Oxford, 1981.
Bain, A. D. and Reid, R. D. G. 'The Finance Sector', in N. Hood and S. Young, (eds), *Industrial Policy and the Scottish Economy*, Edinburgh University Press (forthcoming).
Bank of England, *Quarterly Bulletin*.
Bank and Insurance Companies' Annual Reports.
Building Societies Association, *Bulletin*, April 1982.
Investment Trusts, *Yearbook 1981*.
Monopolies and Mergers Commission, '*The Hongkong and Shanghai Banking Corporation, Standard Chartered Bank Limited, The Royal Bank of Scotland Group Limited: A Report on the Proposed Mergers*', Cmnd 8472, HMSO, London, 1982.
Trustee Savings Bank Yearbooks.

CHAPTER 6

Creedy, J. (ed.), *Unemployment in Britain*, Butterworths, London, 1981.
Department of Employment, *Employment Gazette*, HMSO, London.
Rees, A. *The Economics of Work and Pay*, Harper and Row, London, 1973.
Scottish Abstract of Statistics, op cit.
Scottish Economic Bulletin, op cit.

CHAPTER 7

Bryden, J. and Houston, G. *Agrarian Change in the Scottish Highlands*, Martin Robertson, Oxford, 1976.
Commission of the European Communities, *The Common Agricultural Policy*, 1977.
Coppock, J. T. *An Agricultural Atlas of Scotland*, John Donald Publishers, Edinburgh, 1976.
Department of Agriculture and Fisheries for Scotland, *Scottish Agricultural Economics*, Vol. XXX, 1980.
Department of Agriculture and Fisheries for Scotland, *Agricultural Statistics 1978 Scotland*, HMSO, 1980.
Department of Agriculture and Fisheries for Scotland, *Economic Report on Scottish Agriculture 1980*, HMSO, 1981.
Metcalf, D. *The Economics of Agriculture*, Penguin, Harmondsworth, 1969.
The Crofters Commission Annual Report HMSO.

CHAPTER 8

Boster, J. *The economic impact of visitors to Scotland* Scottish Council Research Institute, Edinburgh, 1976.
Brownrigg, M. and Greig, M. A. 'Differential Multipliers for Tourism' *Scottish Journal of Political Economy*, Nov. 1975.
Brownrigg, M. and Greig, M. A. 'Tourism and Regional Development', *Fraser of Allander Speculative Paper* No. 5, 1976.
Henderson, R. A. 'Recent Trends in Tourism and the economic impact of Tourists in Scotland', S.E.P.D., *Economics and Statistics Unit Discussion Paper* No. 15, May 1982.
International Tourism Quarterly.

CHAPTER 9

Clayre, A. (ed.), *The Political Economy of Cooperation and Participation*, Oxford University Press, Oxford, 1980.
Highlands and Islands Development Board, *North 7*, Fort William.
Scottish Cooperatives Development Committee, *News*, Glasgow.
Stephen, F. H. (ed.), *The Performance of Labour-Managed Firms*, Macmillan, London, 1982.
Stephen, F. H. *The Economic Analysis of Producers' Cooperatives*, Macmillan, London, 1983.

CHAPTER 10

Central Statistical Office, *Annual Abstract of Statistics*, HMSO.
Central Statistical Office, *Regional Trends*, HMSO.
Drummond, M. F. *Principles of Economic Appraisal in Health Care*, Oxford University Press, Oxford, 1980.
Gray, A. M. and Mooney, G. H. 'Health in Scotland', in Cuthbert, M. (ed.), *Government Spending in Scotland*, Paul Harris Publishing, Edinburgh, 1982.
Mooney, G. H., Russell, Elizabeth M. and Weir, R. D. *Choices for Health Care*, Macmillan, London, 1980.
Scottish Health Statistics, HMSO (Annual).
Scottish Home and Health Department, *Health in Scotland 1980*, 1981.

CHAPTER 11

Hartley, K. *NATO Army Cooperation: a Study in Economics and Politics*, London, 1983.

International Institute for Strategic Studies, *The Military Balance*, London.

Kennedy, G. *The Economics of Defence*, London, 1975.

Kennedy, G. *Defence Economics*, London, 1983.

Ministry of Defence, *Statement on the Defence Estimates*, London.

CHAPTER 12

Building Societies Association, *Bulletin*.

Employment Gazette, op cit.

Hallett, G. *Housing and Land Policies in West Germany and Britain*, Macmillan, London, 1977.

Niven, D. *The Development of Housing in Scotland*, Croom Helm, London, 1979.

Scottish Development Department, *Scottish Housing Statistics*, HMSO.

Scottish Housing: A Consultative Document, Cmnd. 6825, HMSO, 1977.

CHAPTER 13

Annual Abstract of Statistics, op cit.

Bell, D., Fraser, N., Kirwan, F. and Tait, E. *Youth Unemployment: Some Key Questions*. Scottish Centre for Political Economy.

Blaug, M. *An Introduction to the Economics of Education*, Penguin, Harmondsworth,

Committee on Scottish Affairs, *Youth Unemployment and Training*, House of Commons, Session 1981–82.

Glasgow Herald, 'Exam results map boundaries of apartheid in education', 4 January, 1983.

HMSO, *Public Schools Commission*, Second Report, Volume III: Scotland, 1970.

Kahan, A. 'Russian Scholars and Statesmen on Education as an Investment', in C. A. Anderson and M. J. Bowman (eds), *Education and Economic Development*, Aldine Publishing Company, Chicago, 1963.

Scottish Abstract of Statistics, op cit.

Scottish Educational Department, *Statistical Bulletin*.

The Scotsman, 'School results show wide gaps in standards', 4 January, 1983.

Williams, G. 'The economic value of education: current debates and prospects', *British Journal of Educational Studies*, Volume XXX, No. 1. February 1980.

CHAPTER 14

Atkinson, A. B. '*The Economics of Inequality*', Oxford University Press, Oxford, 1975.
Department of Employment *Family Expenditure Survey*, HMSO. Royal Commission on the Distribution of Income and Wealth, Chairman Lord Diamond, Reports and Background Papers, HMSO, 1978.
Pen, J. '*Income Distribution*', Pelican, London, 1974.

CHAPTER 15

Armstrong, H. and Taylor, J. 'Regional Policy Options: Macro-Policy Instruments', chapter 8 in *Regional Economic Policy and its Analysis*, Philip Allan, Deddington, 1978.
Brownrigg, M. 'The Economic Impact of a New University', *Scottish Journal of Political Economy*, Vol. 20, pp. 123–39, 1973.
Brownrigg, M. 'Industrial Contraction and the Regional Multiplier Effect: An Application in Scotland' *Town Planning Review*, Vol. 51, pp. 195–210, 1980.
Cuthbert, M. 'Public Expenditure and the Scottish Economy' in M. Cuthbert (ed.), *Government Spending in Scotland*, Paul Harris Publishing, Edinburgh, 1982.
Fraser of Allander Institute, *et al. Input–Output Tables for Scotland, 1973* Scottish Academic Press, Edinburgh, 1978.
Greig, M. A. 'The Regional Income and Employment Effects of a Pulp and Paper Mill', *Scottish Journal of Political Economy*, Vol. 18, pp. 31–48.
Scottish Economic Bulletin, op cit.
Short, J. *Public Expenditure and Taxation in the U.K. Regions*, Gower, Farnborough, 1981.

CHAPTER 16

Armstrong, H. and Taylor, J. *Regional Economic Policy and its Analysis* Philip Allan, Deddington, 1978.
Ashcroft, B. 'Spatial Policy in Scotland', chapter 4 in M. Cuthbert (ed.) *Government Spending in Scotland* Paul Harris, Edinburgh, 1982.
Departments of Industry and Trade, *Trade and Industry/British Business*, HMSO.
Fothergill, S. and Gudgin, G. *Unequal Growth, Urban and Regional Employment Change in Britain*, Heinemann, London, 1982.

CHAPTER 17

Boyle, R. M. and Wannop, U. A. 'Area Initiatives and the SDA: the Rise of the Urban Project', *The Fraser of Allander Institute, Quarterly Economic Commentary*, Vol. 8, No. 1, pp. 45–57, 1982.

Devine, P. J., Jones, R. M., Lee, N. and Tyson, W. J., *An Introduction to Industrial Economics*, chapter 9, 'State Intervention in the Private Sector', George Allen and Unwin, London, 1979.

Devine, P. J. and Lee, N. *An Introduction to Industrial Economics*, chapter 9,

Firn, J. R. 'External control and regional development: the case of Scotland', *Environment and Planning A*, Vol. 7, pp. 393–414, 1975.

McNicoll, I. and Swales, J. K. 'Public Expenditure on Industry in Scotland' in M. Cuthbert (ed.) *Government Spending in Scotland*, Paul Harris Publishing, Edinburgh, 1982.

Scottish Abstract of Statistics, op cit.

Scottish Development Agency Reports, Glasgow.

Scottish Economic Bulletin, op cit.

CHAPTER 18

Allan, K. and Harris, D. J. *The Nationalized Transport Industries*, Heinemann, London, 1973.

Annual Reports and Accounts of the individual nationalized industries.

Kelf-Cohen, R. *Twenty Years of Nationalisation* Macmillan 1969

Reid, G. L. *The Nationalized Fuel Industries*, Heinemann, London, 1973.

Thompson, A. W. J. and Hunter, L. C. *Nationalization*, A. H. Hanson (ed.), George Allen and Unwin, London, 1963.

Wood, G. A. 'Nationalised Industries' in *Government Spending in Scotland*, (ed.) M. Cuthbert, Paul Harris Publishing, 1982.

CHAPTER 19

Firn, J. R. 1975, 'External Control and Regional Development: the case of Scotland', *Environment and Planning A*, Vol. 7, pp. 393–414.

Hood, N. and Young, S. *The Economics of Multinational Enterprise*, Longman, London, 1979.

Rugman, A. M. (ed.) *New Theories of the Multinational Enterprise*, Croom-Helm, London, 1982.

Scottish Abstract of Statistics, op cit.

Scottish Economic Bulletin, op cit.

Tugendhat, C. *The Multinationals*, Penguin, Harmondsworth, 1977.

CHAPTER 20

Department of Energy, *Development of the Oil and Gas Resources of the United Kingdom*, 1982, HMSO, London, (Annual).
Department of Energy, *Energy Trends* (Monthly).
Gaskin, M. (ed.) *The Economic Impact of North Sea Oil on Scotland*, HMSO, Edinburgh, 1978.
Lewis, T. M. and McNicoll, I. H. *North Sea Oil and Scotland's Economic Prospects* Croom Helm, London, 1978.
Mackay, D. I. and Makay, A. G. *The Political Economy of North Sea Oil*, Martin Robertson, Oxford, 1975.
Robinson, C. and Morgan, J. *North Sea Oil in the Future*, Macmillan, London, 1978.
Scottish Economic Bulletin, op cit.
Scottish Economic Planning Department, *North Sea Oil Information Sheet*, (Monthly).

CHAPTER 21

Lythe, C. and Majmuder, M. *The Renaissance of the Scottish Economy?* George Allen and Unwin, London, 1982.
Mackay, D. *Scotland 1980: the Economics of Self Government*, Q. Press, Edinburgh, 1977.
Morgan, E. V. 'Regional Problems and Common Currencies', *Lloyds Bank Review*, Oct. 1973.
Regional Trends.

CHAPTER 22

Bell, D. and Fraser, N. 'Scotland and the EEC', *The Scotsman*, 27, 28, 29, November, 1979.
Donges, J. B. 'What is wrong with the European Communities? *Occasional Paper*, 59, Institute of Economic Affairs, 1981.
EEC, *The Community and its Regions*, European Documentation, 1/80.
EEC, *The Customs Union*, European Documentation, 4/80.
Mackay, G. A. 'The UK Fishing Industry and EEC Policy', *The Three Banks Review*, December, 1981.
Scottish Council Research Institute, *Scotlands Manufactured Exports 1974–77*, Edinburgh, 1978.
Scottish Council Research Institute, *Scotlands Manufactured Exports 1978–80*, Edinburgh, 1981.
Scottish Economic Bulletin, 'EEC Regional Policy and the Scottish Economy', Vol. 18, 1979.

CHAPTER 23

Bhagwati, J. *The Economics of Underdeveloped Countries*, Hutchinson, London, 1967.

European Communities, *Balance of Payments Yearbook.*

H.M. Customs and Excise, *Statistics of Trade through United Kingdom Ports.*

HMSO, *Annual Statement of Trade of the United Kingdom.*

HMSO, Universities, Further Education. *Statistics of Education*, 1978.

Little, I., Scitovsky, T. and Scott, M. *Industry and Trade in Some Developing Countries*, Oxford University Press, Oxford, 1970.

Meier, G. M. (ed.) *Leading Issues in Economic Development*, 3rd ed. Oxford University Press, Oxford, 1976.

Morton, K. and Tulloch, P. *Trade and Developing Countries*, Croom Helm, London, 1977.

OECD Development Assistance Committee, *Development Co-operation*, 1981 Review.

OECD, *Statistics of Foreign Trade.*

Overseas Development Administration, *British Aid Statistics.*

World Bank, *World Development Reports*, annually from 1978.

CHAPTER 24

Central Statistical Office, *Economic Trends*, HMSO.

Scottish Abstract of Statistics, op cit.

Scottish Economic Bulletin, op cit.

CHAPTER 25

Daiches, D. *Scotch Whisky: its Past and Present*, Fontana/Collins paperback, Glasgow, 1976.

Department of Industry, Business Statistics Office 'Report on the Census of Production', *Business Monitor* PA (Annual) series 239.1 (up to 1979), 424 (1980 onwards).

Moss, M. S. and Hume, J. R. *The Making of Scotch Whisky*, James and James, Edinburgh, 1981.

Report of the Commissioners of Her Majesty's Customs and Excise, (Annual) Command Paper, HMSO.

Scotch Whisky Association *Statistical Report* (Annual), SWA, Edinburgh.

Index